0010427

D1346230

MURDEROUS INNOCENTS

Also by Frank Jones

Murderous Women: True Tales of Women Who Killed
White-collar Killers: True Stories of Unexpected Murderers

MURDEROUS INNOCENTS

True Stories of Children Who Kill

Frank Jones

HEADLINE

The right of Frank Jones to be identified as the author
of the work has been asserted by him in accordance with the
Copyright, Designs and Patents Act 1988

First published in 1994
by HEADLINE BOOK PUBLISHING

10 9 8 7 6 5 4 3 2 1

British Library Cataloguing in Publication Data
Jones, Frank
  Murderous Innocents: True Stories of
  Children Who Kill
  I. Title
  364.1

  ISBN 0–7472–0876–X

Typeset by Keyboard Services, Luton

Printed and bound in Great Britain by
Mackays of Chatham PLC, Chatham, Kent

HEADLINE BOOK PUBLISHING
A division of Hodder Headline PLC
Headline House
79 Great Titchfield Street
London W1P 7FN

To Ayesha
My Partner in Crime

CONTENTS

INTRODUCTION: THE CRIME THAT SHOCKED THE WORLD

Life at the Strand shopping centre in Bootle, the Liverpool suburb, had pretty much returned to normal when I visited it a few weeks after Jamie Bulger's abduction and murder. Frank Sinatra's voice singing 'Three Coins in the Fountain' emerged in an ethereal whisper from the PA system; at the Mothercare shop where, in the wake of the murder there'd been a run on toddler security reins, parents were again buying stretchy baby sleepers. In A. R. Tyms, 'the high-class quality butcher', where Denise Bulger felt her first moment of terror, mums were buying their Sunday joints while keeping no more than a normal wary eye on their small children. Somewhere a child was crying, but no one paid any attention.

And why should they? Because the whole point of the modern shopping centre is that it makes us feel safe. Safe from inclement weather, safe from traffic hazards and fumes, safe from bad characters and street crime.

That was one of the reasons why Jamie's abduction and murder shocked people around the world. Because, with its Jolly Jack Tar nautical theme, its warmth and bright lights, its trailing plastic ferns and security guards, it was

1

the kind of setting familiar to people from Perth, Australia, to Pasadena, California. Bad things are simply not supposed to happen in shopping centres.

The second reason for the universal shock was the video images of the abduction recorded by overhead security cameras. It was all over in five minutes, yet those images are something people will never forget – because they made us all helpless witnesses to the crime.

They show two lads emerging from a toy shop and ambling along the shopping precinct; the time and date at the bottom of the film frame: 3.37 p.m., 12 February 1993. We see Denise Bulger, a young mother out doing the Friday shopping with her only child, two-year-old Jamie, in tow, walking towards Tyms, the butcher's.

While his mother is busy at the counter, Jamie wanders out of the shop and joins the other two boys standing in front of a shop window; time: 3.39.

Something is wrong. We see Denise rush out of the butcher's looking up and down; time: 3.40. By now Jamie, in his blue coat, white trousers and silver running shoes, is climbing the steps on sturdy little legs to the floor above. On the upper floor of the shopping centre we see him following the other two, one boy beckoning him on; time: 3.41.

And then, the image that would flash around the world: Jamie is walking along trustingly holding the hand of one of the older boys; glowing overhead is a shop sign, Mothercare; time: 3.42.

Less than a minute later the three of them disappear through the doors leading to Stanley Road.

Shown the videos at the police station, Denise identifies little Jamie. She is relieved that it's only youngsters who have taken him away. The policewoman with her says nothing.

After two days in which Liverpool is scoured by police looking for Jamie, some boys playing near the freight railway line leading to the docks at Bootle see what they think is a doll lying between the tracks. As they approach, they realize it isn't a doll at all. The police are called. The autopsy will show that Jamie Bulger was beaten to death before his body was placed on the track. That may be some small consolation. Because a train has cut his body in half.

Horrifying though Jamie Bulger's death was, and disturbing as the videos were, showing how a child could be stolen away from a supposedly safe setting in just a few minutes, what hit people hardest was the age of those suspected of the crime. When computer-enhanced images from the original fuzzy videos were telecast on the BBC's *Crimewatch UK*, the ages of the two suspects were given as eleven and thirteen. By then the Liverpool police were already questioning Robert Thompson and Jon Venables who would ultimately be convicted of his murder. Their ages: ten.

Every year in Britain about twenty-four juveniles are convicted of homicide. In Canada the figure is twice that, and in the US in 1991 241 murders were committed by children aged fourteen and under, and 4,099 were carried out by youngsters aged between fifteen and nineteen. Most of these crimes are passed over with a paragraph or two in the newspaper. Even though Thompson and Venables were finally convicted of murdering Jamie Bulger, whatever the outcome of the trial had been, one thing would not have changed: because of the special circumstances of this case, people everywhere would be forced to confront as

3

never before their own fears and the conflicting emotions surrounding children who kill.

How, for instance, can we reconcile notions of childhood innocence with children who, as we hear nearly every day, shoot, stab, bludgeon, choke and burn – sometimes their parents, sometimes strangers, sometimes other children?

When children kill, it seems the final, irrefutable evidence of a society that has failed. If children of nine, or thirteen, or fifteen, who you'd expect to see playing Nintendo with their friends, kicking a ball in the park, or indulging in make-believe with their dolls, can snuff out the lives of other human beings, what hope is there?

And who should we blame? The parents? Schools? Society as a whole? Or simply a new race of barbaric children?

The whole gamut of confused emotions was on display in Liverpool in those stark February days following Jamie's murder.

Sympathy first for the parents. A grassy bank close to where the body was found was soon mounded high with flowers, drawings and touching messages of sympathy, many of them from children. 'Rest in peace, little one', said one typical message. 'You didn't deserve to die the way you did. Please God, look after him and cuddle him.'

Blame. Among the letters of sympathy that came from all over the world for Denise, twenty-five, and her husband, Ralph, twenty-six, the police kept back many that criticized Denise for not taking better care of her child.

Anger. 'Hang the bastards!' some in a mob of 250 screamed at the two police vans carrying the boys away after their first court appearance. 'Kill them!' others cried, pelting the vans with bricks and eggs. Earlier, a family whose twelve-year-old son had been questioned by police and then released had to flee their home after being attacked by a mob.

Bigotry. 'A horrible cow' was how the *Sun* newspaper described the mother of one of the accused boys, quoting a neighbour. Not waiting for the formality of a trial, the newspaper described one of the boys as 'a bullying nuisance', and, still quoting neighbours, 'a right pain in the backside'. Prime Minister John Major and other political leaders were scarcely more rational, calling immediately for a crackdown on juvenile offenders without a thought to social conditions or the particular circumstances of this murder.

And, finally, sorrow. Jamie's death 'has touched the world', Father Michael O'Connell told weeping mourners at the funeral. And at a Liverpool-Ipswich football game, the fans stood for a heartaching minute of silence for Jamie.

Then, inevitably, people began asking, why?

It's the question asked wherever children are accused of murder, and there is no shortage of answers. Some experts were quick to blame Liverpool's urban decay, its eighteen per cent unemployment rate, the increasing number of single mothers, the drug culture and something called 'individualism' – meaning the death of community values. Other experts, examining these difficult cases, blame violent videos, family break-up, or the fact that most mothers today go out to work. There are experts who say that nearly all children who kill have been sexually abused, and the inexact term 'psychopathic' – meaning devoid of normal feelings – is commonly applied to many child killers.

Evidence about the sort of children who kill is fragmentary, anecdotal. Charles Patrick Ewing, a law professor and psychologist who is America's most widely quoted expert on children who kill, tells me that among the many juvenile killers he has examined, three traits crop up time and again: bed-wetting, fire-setting, and cruelty to animals.

Dr Clive Chamberlain, a Canadian psychiatrist who has examined sixty juvenile killers over the last twenty years, told me he was surprised to discover how many of them – about half – were abnormally well behaved. 'They are the children who are too good, too anxious to please, too overcontrolled,' he said. Even if he'd talked to some of them the day before they committed their crime, he said, he was sure he would not have been able to predict it.

A few generalizations are possible. Usually boys make up ninety per cent of those convicted. In Britain and Canada, the rate of juvenile killings is fairly static. Only in the United States, with the greater access to guns and the emergence of gangs and drug warfare in the ghettoes, is the juvenile homicide rate climbing alarmingly. Between 1965 and 1990 that rate jumped a dramatic 332 per cent, with blacks outnumbering whites nearly two to one. In three-quarters of juvenile murder cases in the US a gun is the murder weapon.

But when you've said all that, you've said very little. After studying hundreds of cases from several centuries and from many parts of the world, the one sure thing I've discovered is that children who kill are just as varied in their motives, their methods and their victims as adult killers. One child you will read about here came from a background of mental illness; some, like Shirley Wolf and

Cindy Collier, were sexually abused from early childhood; some, like Harold Jones and Steven Truscott, both
of whom killed young girls, murder in the course of sexual
experimentation, while others, like Juliet Hulme and
Pauline Rieper, murder out of emotional obsession.
Strangest of all are the perfectly normal young people like
Sean Pica and David Muir who committed murder simply
because someone asked them to.

And when you've extracted all the truths you can from
these terrible events, you're left always with the anguish.
The anguish of the victims' families, the anguish of the
child's parents and, occasionally, the anguish of the young
perpetrator. These are crimes that don't go away.

The route that Jamie Bulger's abductors followed after
stealing him away has become a sort of modern stations of
the cross for many. It's a surprisingly long journey that
leads from the familiar and the reassuring to one of those
darker, sordid corners you'll find in any large city.

Emerging from the Strand on to the busy street outside,
there is no sense of danger at all as buses swarm by and a
man tries to interest the passing throng in novelty tea
towels. Bootle itself looks substantial and Victorian as
you walk by the Merton, a pub in the grand Greek temple
style. Little Jamie would have been tiring already by the
time they passed the Bootle library and the legal advice
centre, but he had a long way to go.

They crossed busy traffic roundabouts, and at Hawthorne
Road another security camera picked up the two boys
dragging Jamie along between them. Near the Breeze Hill
reservoir, an older woman stopped the trio and asked
what was the matter with the little boy, who was crying
and seemed to have hurt his head. He'd fallen down, they

7

told her. They were taking him home.

A little further on they left the main road and plunged into streets of small Victorian terrace houses leading to the Church of St Mary's, Walton – no sanctuary this, but a grimy old building stuck amidst vandalized gravestones and sooty trees with old heroin needles and empty glue tubes littering the ground. Near here one of the boys asked the assistant in a flower shop for directions to the Walton police station. And near here they left any eyes that might see, and turned into an alley foul with dog dirt and litter, a high fence on one side separating it from the railway track.

It was Jamie's last chance. At the bottom of the alley you turn right and come to the Walton police station a few yards up the road. Instead, they turned left. One of the two boys arrested lived in a terrace house at the next corner. By then, regardless of what lay ahead, I knew the journey to this point had been an almost unimaginable ordeal for little Jamie. The distance is two and a half miles. It's a substantial walk even for a fit adult. For a little boy, scarcely more than a toddler, crying, dragged along, not knowing what was happening, fearing what would happen, it was torture pure and simple.

On Cherry Lane, opposite the embankment where people had stacked their flowers in Jamie's memory, another funeral was under way in a little gospel hall. Outside, the ushers in their black coats waited beside the hearse for the service to end. It was a far tidier and more antiseptic version of death than the one that had been played out in that urban no-man's land across the road beside the railway tracks.

There, among the concrete slabs and broken bricks, the rusty tins and the blowing rubbish, Jamie Bulger had died. It was a wasteland not so different from the one in Newcastle that the children used to call the Tin Lizzie and where another little boy, named Brian Howe, who was three, was killed twenty-five years earlier.

It was that case that people kept remembering when they talked about Jamie Bulger. Only it wasn't Brian's name they remembered. It was a little girl, an astonishingly pretty eleven-year-old girl, whose name was Mary Bell.

MURDER ISN'T
SO BAD

Every now and then you'll see her arriving at Newcastle's main station, a tall, attractive woman in her thirties with a frank, open expression and the most striking blue eyes. Apart for the odd appraising male glance, she attracts little attention as she hurries across the pedestrian bridge towards the exit. And she gives no sign of the queasy feeling she gets in the pit of her stomach every time she returns to this tough city on England's north-east coast where she grew up.

It's not simply curiosity – or brazenness – that brings her here. She has calls to make on the handful of people she describes as 'my lifelines' – people from her past who will be there for her if things turn rough again. But she never ever goes up to the house on Whitehouse Road in the rough Scotswood neighbourhood half a mile away where she used to live. Wouldn't be much point really: it's boarded up and derelict and, the woman next door told me, 'It's something terrible the way the kids get in there and rip stuff out and burn it.'

The woman arriving at the station lives somewhere in the north of England. And on the train to Newcastle upon Tyne she can't help thinking how it's all turned out. Not

11

the strange nightmare that was her childhood – that's been dealt with and almost forgotten. But her life since she regained her freedom: her marriage that didn't last; her daughter who is nine now and so pretty – just the way she used to be at that age – that sometimes, looking at her, a shiver of apprehension goes through her.

She thinks of the men who have come and gone in her life, men who maybe left when they sensed they could never really get close to her, who always felt she was holding back. Well, she had to, didn't she? Doesn't matter how crazy she is about a fellow, there's one thing she can't tell him – her real name. After Myra Hindley, the Moors Murderer, it's the most notorious name in the lexicon of female crime in Britain. If it got out, if her carefully constructed cover was blown, the circus would start all over again. It's not even for herself she worries most. Being Mary Bell is bad enough – she's learned to deal with that. But being Mary Bell's daughter would be worse. What did the poor kid ever do to deserve that?

Scotswood today is a grim place. Even in the middle of the day and accompanied by Steve Bell (no relation), a cab driver who grew up in the district, I felt the menace of the boarded-up houses, the deserted streets blocked with bollards in a futile effort to frustrate the teenage joyriders who race up and down at night in stolen cars. Murder is not uncommon. 'If anyone wants to come here after dark,' said Steve, 'I tell them I'll drop them on the main road and they can walk.' Just before Christmas, he said, the owner of the fanciest pub in the district, the Sporting Arms, had simply given up after louts put out all the windows.

Even in 1968 Scotswood, which looks from its hilltop

perch across at the giant Vickers plant where high-tech Challenger II tanks are built, was not exactly a desirable neighbourhood. Where drugs and teenage violence control the streets today, booze was the problem then, with local hospitals girding up on Saturday night for the weekly quota of broken noses and cracked skulls.

But if you were a kid living here in 1968, as Mary was, Scotswood in some ways was a paradise. It was one big adventure playground with derelict houses even then that they could explore, and the Tin Lizzie, a wasteland of weeds and discarded concrete slabs where kids could hide, play forts or gangsters or houses or whatever took their fancy. It might have been poor, it might have witnessed more than its share of domestic violence, but, with many of the council tenants here related to each other, there was, for the children, an enormous sense of security, and parents left even little children free to wander.

If we follow Martin Brown, a chunky little boy, tall for his four years, on his travels on a particular Saturday, 25 May 1968, you'll understand what I mean. Up at around six thirty in the little two-bedroom house at 140 St Margaret's Road, he tiptoed down to the kitchen, careful not to wake his parents, June and George, who were sleeping in. Back in his room, he gave his baby sister, Linda, a piece of bread in her cot and a glass of milk.

By nine o'clock, Martin, after finishing his breakfast cereal and pulling on his blue anorak, was shouting, 'Ta-ra, I'm away, Mam,' and joining the other children already at play. Around eleven o'clock his Aunt Rita – 'Fita', he called her – who lived a few doors away and who looked after him during the week when his mother was at work, blew her top when Martin woke her from her

Saturday morning lie-in, leaning over her, asking her when she was getting up.

'Get out of here!' she yelled. But a few minutes later she relented, and made him egg on toast for his lunch. As Martin set off again on his rambles, two neighbourhood girls, Norma Bell, aged thirteen, and Mary Bell, who would be eleven the following day, not related, but living next door to each other, came by and offered to babysit Rita's little boy, three-year-old John, while she went to call on her mother.

Martin later called at home to get a few pennies from his dad for a lollipop, and just after three o'clock he was in the line of children waiting for Dixon's little convenience shop, just a few yards from the Tin Lizzie, to open.

'Your hands are filthy, Martin!' Wilson Dixon, the son of the store's owner, said, seeing Martin with his mud-smeared fingers in his mouth. 'You better go home and wash them.'

'You can go and wash them at my house,' his Aunt Rita, returned now from her mother's, told him. Martin, whose day seemed to revolve around snacks, managed a piece of bread and margarine at Rita's house before ambling away. It would have been about three fifteen.

Scarcely a quarter of an hour later three boys, aged sixteen, thirteen and eight, climbed through the back fence of a derelict house across the road from Rita Finlay's, got in through the secret entrance only local kids knew about, and went upstairs in search of wood for a pigeon loft they were building. In the back bedroom they saw a little boy lying on his back on the floor, blood trickling from his mouth.

Two Newcastle Electricity Board men working outside

recognized the lad immediately when the frightened youths called them to see. One of the electricians, John Hall, had earlier given the little boy some biscuits from his lunch. As they waited for the ambulance, Hall tried in vain to puff life into the inert little body. Sickened, one of the teenagers, Walter Long, went to the front room and hung his head out of the window for air.

He saw, coming along the street, two girls he knew, Norma Bell and Mary Bell. 'Shall we go up?' he heard Mary say when they were immediately beneath him. 'Okay, let's,' agreed Norma.

They climbed through the window of the derelict house next door, went out the back and a few moments later Long met them on the stairs. 'Get away down,' he told them.

'It's okay, the police know I'm here,' said Mary. With the way barred, the two girls left reluctantly.

'One of your bairns has had an accident,' Mary was telling Rita a few minutes later. 'There's blood all over.'

Rita thought the girls had to be playing a trick on her. Martin had only left a few minutes earlier, it seemed to Rita. But John! She hadn't seen John in a while. She saw someone waving to her in the street, and ran. She didn't know how she got up the stairs of the old house, and then she saw a man in overalls holding Martin in his arms. 'He's asleep,' she screamed. 'That's all, he's asleep.'

And that's what she told June when the boy's mother arrived a few minutes later. 'He's asleep!' But June knew right away that someone had brought her boy up here and harmed him. Because only a while before, he'd fallen down the stairs at home and hurt himself. He was scared of stairs now. He would never have come up here on his own.

15

But perhaps sleep wasn't such a bad word for it. Because, apart from a small haemorrhage in the brain, the pathologist could find nothing to indicate the reason for Martin Brown's death. He hadn't been hit, there were no marks from strangulation, and the dust on the floor of the room showed no signs of a struggle having taken place. His death, the police would conclude, was an accident. And no one connected the peculiar behaviour of Norma and Mary in the following days, or even the break-in at the nursery school, with his death.

'Would you like us to take John out?' Mary was asking at Rita's door the day after Martin died. Rita thought it was really considerate of Mary and Norma – they even brushed his hair and got him ready. They seemed to be there every day after that, asking funny questions, like, 'Do you miss Martin?' or 'Does his mam cry for him?' What made Rita feel funny was that they were always grinning when they asked. After a while she asked them not to come again.

The same Sunday, her birthday, Mary, in the park with Susan, Norma's eleven-year-old sister, asked, 'Did you send me a birthday card?' 'Yes, I did,' replied Susan. 'I don't believe you,' said Mary, and chased Susan to her front door. She had her hands around Susan's neck when Susan's parents, hearing her scream, ran out and pulled her away from Mary. After that, they didn't let Susan play with Mary.

One of the few bright spots in Scotswood's squalor at that time was the nursery school, where a cheerful and involved staff cared for the children of working mums in an old converted house. So on the Monday morning after Martin's death, the teachers were shocked to find that their building had been broken into through the slate roof and that art and cleaning materials had been scattered around indiscriminately. 'Lousy teenagers, I expect,' they said to each other, shaking their heads.

The only odd feature in an otherwise conventional act of vandalism was a series of four scrawled notes found among the debris by a policeman. The text, a jumble of ill-spelled slang and swear words, included this:

'We did murder Martain brown Fuckof you Bastard.' And: 'I murder SO THAT I may come back.'

'Some sort of kids' poetry, I s'pose,' said the officer, handing it in at the station to his sergeant. 'Don't know what to make of it.' The sergeant put it in a drawer for safekeeping. On Friday that week a burglar alarm, installed after the weekend break-in, went off. Police arriving at the nursery found Mary Bell and Norma Bell. No, they insisted, they'd never broken in before. They were booked and given a date to appear in juvenile court. Much would happen before their court date.

The Wednesday after Martin died, his mother, June Brown, answered the door to find Mary standing there, a group of girls hanging back by the garden gate. 'Can I see Martin?' she asked.

'No, love,' said June sadly. 'Martin's dead.'

'I know that,' she replied cheekily. 'I just wanted to see him in his coffin.' June gasped and shut the door without another word. Bloody kids!

Mary Bell seemed to be everywhere, her behaviour often outrageous – as if the death of Martin Brown had excited some strain of wildness in her. 'I am a murderer,' she yelled one day, jumping on Norma and scratching her face. 'And that,' she said, pointing to the derelict house, 'is where I killed Martin Brown.' No one paid her any attention.

17

Scotswood parents, following Martin's death, experienced no wave of panic and fear as Liverpool parents would in 1993 at the death of two-year-old James Bulger. Instead, they saw his death as another proof of municipal neglect, and marched to the civic centre to demand better housing. Front and centre in a photograph of the demonstrators that appeared in a local newspaper next day was a pretty little girl with wide-set eyes, a happy grin on her face. Mary Bell seemed to be enjoying herself.

The children of Scotswood wandered unhampered as before – and why not? Martin's death had been simply an accident. So in no way was Pat Howe, aged fourteen, panicking as, two months later, on 31 July, she scanned the Tin Lizzie for her stepbrother, three-year-old Brian, who no one had seen for a couple of hours. 'Little booger, wait till I catch him!'

'He might be playing behind the blocks,' suggested Mary Bell, who, along with Norma, was helping in the search.

'Oh no,' said Norma quickly. 'He never goes there.'

Brian, like Martin a stocky boy with fair hair, seemed older than his three years, a streetwise youngster you could really hold a conversation with. He had never known his mother – she left when he was eighteen months old, and it was Pat, who had left school early, and her father who looked after Brian and his brother, seven-year-old Norman.

Rita Finlay and Pat, in fact, took it in turns to take Brian and Rita's boy, John, to the nursery every morning. That afternoon Rita had lost her temper and smacked the two boys on their hands when she'd found them hanging around one of the derelict houses that, perhaps thanks to the demonstration, was being torn down.

'Don't you know something could fall on you!' she yelled at them. She put her own boy to bed and sent Brian home with a handful of biscuits. 'Tell Pat I caught you playing at the old buildings, but I've already smacked you for it,' she said. It obviously wasn't a message Brian fancied delivering, because he didn't go home: later he was seen playing with his brother and two little girls on the street.

It was the ubiquitous Mary and Norma who knocked on Rita's door later that afternoon. 'Where's my little boyfriend, then?' asked Norma. 'Can we take him for a walk?'

'John's in bed,' explained Rita, and off they went. A few minutes later, they found Brian playing in the street and took him for a walk instead of John. Lucky John.

Around four o'clock, Pat's oldest brother, Albert, twenty-three, told her to go and look for the little boy because he hadn't come home. One of the first people she met was Mary, sitting on a step. 'Are you looking for your Brian?' she asked.

'Yes, I haven't seen him for a long time. Are you coming to help look for him?' Mary and Norma, who arrived a moment later, joined the search. It really didn't seem worth checking the Tin Lizzie. As Norma said, he never went there. So they went searching in Hodgkin Park instead. When he still hadn't been found at seven o'clock, the police were informed.

It was, in fact, at the Tin Lizzie that, at eleven o'clock, Brian's body was found. He was lying between the concrete blocks, one arm outstretched, his lips blue and frothy and with grass and purple weeds strewn on him as if in a feeble attempt at a funeral rite. This time there was no doubt: scratches and pressure marks on the sides of his neck suggested he'd been choked. His nose too had been scratched and there were puncture marks in his legs. Nearby in the grass a broken pair of scissors was found with one blade bent, the other broken off.

An urgent examination of the body by Dr Bernard Tomlinson, a pathologist, produced an alarming finding: the pressure exerted to strangle Brian had been feather-light, while the stab wounds in his legs also showed a light touch. 'You're looking for a child,' he told Detective Chief Inspector James Dobson, who had been roused from bed after midnight to take charge of the investigation. 'And a very dangerous one.'

In a half-square-mile teeming with children it was exactly the news a copper didn't want to hear. Dobson, who had already made the connection in his mind with Martin Brown's death, responded brilliantly. By eight o'clock the following morning, a murder room had been set up, a hundred officers had been assigned to the case and children between the ages of three and fifteen were being asked, with the help of their parents, to fill in a hastily devised questionnaire about their movements on the day of the killing. In the first twenty-four hours, with no one certain where the young killer might strike again, some 1,200 questionnaires were filled in. Results came in with dramatic speed.

It wasn't simply what children put down that police were looking at: it was how they answered. When an officer ventured into the happy bedlam of Norma Bell's home – she had ten brothers and sisters – he immediately tagged Norma as odd. She seemed not to hear his questions; she was smiling all the time. Yes, she eventually told him, she had last seen Brian playing on the street with his brother and two girls at about 12.45 p.m.

When he called next door at Mary's house, the atmosphere was completely different. Mary's big Alsatian, an unfriendly dog that was her frequent companion, barked threateningly, and the man who answered the door, Billy Bell, denied he was her father. 'I'm her uncle.' Where was her mother? 'Away.'

Uncle, nothing. Billy was Mary's dad. He just claimed to be an uncle so that his wife, Betty, could claim benefits as a single mum. And Betty's absence? That was nothing unusual: she was always going away for stretches and never telling anyone where she went.

Answering the questions, Mary seemed wary and uncertain, looking at Billy each time before replying. Both Mary and Norma were immediately listed with the dozen or so children whose answers, officers felt, needed further probing.

A return visit to Norma produced more detail, but nothing dramatic. The call-back at Mary's home produced gold – or, rather, silver. She told the detective-sergeant she'd remembered something else. Brian was always playing with a certain eight-year-old boy. She'd seen the boy hit Brian. The afternoon Brian died, she'd seen the boy with grass and purple flowers on him, and she'd also seen him playing with a pair of silvery scissors, broken ones. The same scissors she'd seen the boy using trying to cut off a cat's tail.

No mention had been made in the newspapers of the scissors found near the body. When the police checked on the boy's whereabouts at the time of the murder, they found he'd been with his family at Newcastle airport, eight miles away. At that point suspicion turned on his accuser, Mary Bell. But when an officer called, Mary didn't want to talk. 'My uncle's not here,' she said. When he got home from the pub, Billy Bell was equally hostile.

Norma, who always seemed on the verge of tears, was more forthcoming. After insisting her dad leave the room she told an officer, 'Mary took me to see Brian.' It was time, the policeman decided, for her to meet Chief Inspector Dobson.

Dobson, a tall, humorous man, had an easy way with children. What was it, he asked Norma that evening, that she knew about the death of Brian Howe and hadn't told?

'I went with Mary Bell down to the blocks the day that Brian was lost,' she said without hesitation, 'and I tripped over his head.'

'Tripped over his head?'

'Yes, when I went into the blocks I tripped over something. I looked down and saw it was Brian's head. He was covered in grass but I could see all of his face. He was dead.'

'And then?'

'Mary told me, "I squeezed his neck and pushed up his lungs, that's how you kill them. Keep your nose dry and don't tell anybody."'

'How do you know he was dead?'

'His lips was purple. Mary ran her fingers along his lips. She said she had enjoyed it.'

Brian's eyes had been open, Norma told Dobson, and he had a funny mark on his nose. Mary had showed her a razor blade which she'd used to cut his belly. And she'd pulled up his red patterned jersey to show her the minute cuts she'd made. After that she'd hidden the blade under a block and told Norma not to tell her father or she'd get in trouble.

'Can you show me where the blade is hidden?' asked Dobson.

It was still light and children's shouts could be heard as, fifteen minutes later, a police car drew up near the now-trampled grass and weeds of the Tin Lizzie. 'It's under there,' Norma said, pointing to a concrete block. Dobson pulled away the grass to reveal a gleam of blue – a Gillette razor blade. 'Is this it?' She nodded. And where was the body when she saw it? She pointed to the spot where Brian had been found.

It was a lot to ask. He didn't want to overly upset her. But Dobson decided it was worth the gamble. 'Can you show me how he was lying, love?' he asked.

She lay down on her back on the grass, one arm extended, her head bent to one side – exactly as Brian had been found.

Back at the police station, after again asking that her father leave, Norma talked for more than an hour, giving more detail in a statement she afterwards signed. Mary – or May, as her friends called her – had asked her if she wanted to come with her while she took her dog for a walk. When she'd tripped on Brian's head, Mary had said, 'Keep your nose dry. He's dead.' Norma claimed, 'She got hold of my neck under the chin and said that was how she had done it,' adding that Mary had threatened, 'Don't tell your dad or I'll get wrong.' Mary had then told her, 'I'm not frightened of dead bodies. I've seen a few.' They'd left the death scene quickly after hearing a man shouting at some children and coming in their direction.

It was after midnight the same night when Dobson, accompanied by two constables, knocked on Billy Bell's door. 'She's in bed,' Bell said gruffly in reply to Dobson's question. And no, he wouldn't wake her up. If he

23

wouldn't, they'd have to, said Dobson. When Mary emerged shortly afterwards, her Aunt Audrey, from across the street, accompanied her, putting a protective arm around her shoulders as they climbed into the police car.

Dobson, seeing Mary for the first time, thought that this jumpy child, who sometimes took so long to answer his questions he thought she hadn't heard them, was mentally deficient, a nut-case. 'I'm going home!' she told him, getting up when the questions got too hot.

'You can't go yet,' the inspector insisted.

'I'll phone for some solicitors,' was her knowing reply. 'They'll get me out. This is being brainwashed.'

At another point, when the phone in Dobson's office rang, she asked, 'Is this place bugged?'

Mary had picked up her knowledge of police procedures from watching television. Asked later how she knew strangling would kill someone, she'd say she'd seen it on *The Saint*, a detective programme.

Dobson had got her wrong. Mary's intelligence was quick, her answers canny. She'd never been near the concrete blocks, she insisted, and she never played with Brian. But, according to Norma, they'd been at the blocks when a man had shouted nearby. He'd be sure to recognize her.

'He'd have to have good eyesight,' she said.

'Why?' asked Dobson.

'Because . . .' she hesitated, scenting the trap, 'because he was clever to see me – when I wasn't there!'

What about the thing Norma said was hidden under the blocks?

'What was it? I'll kill her,' said Mary.

Did she want to make a statement?

'I am making no statements. I've made lots of statements. It's always me you come for. Norma's a liar. She
always tries to get me in trouble.'

At 3.30 a.m., Dobson reluctantly allowed Mary to go
home. There was no doubt who had won. For a girl barely
eleven years old it had been a remarkable performance.
Dobson had to admit to himself that he was left
wondering whether, after all, Norma was lying.

If so, she was about to embroider her fantastic story
beyond his imagining. That afternoon, after returning
once again to the murder site and showing Dobson again
how she had seen Brian, Norma told him she wanted to
add something to her earlier statement. She had, in fact,
been to the spot three times on the day of the murder.

'I want to tell you all the truth now,' her statement
began. She was playing with Mary at about three o'clock
when they'd seen Brian playing on the street with his
brother and 'two little lassies on bikes'. Brian's brother
had given him the broken scissors. In a scene that would
be echoed twenty-five years later in the Liverpool
abduction of James Bulger, Mary asked Brian to come
with them, and they'd led him down Crosshill Road,
through the hole in the fence near Dixon's shop, across
the railway tracks to a fence at the bottom of the bank. 'I
climbed over first and May bunked the bairn over,' said
Norma.

'Look at that big tank, we'll get in,' Mary had said.
Norma had lifted the little boy up to the hole in the side of
the large tank and Mary, already inside, had helped him
in. 'It had a stinky smell, so we all got out again,' said
Norma. They'd go to the blocks instead, said Mary.

'Lift up your neck,' Mary told Brian when they got
there. Before anything more could happen they were

interrupted by children playing nearby. Brian's black and white dog, Lassie, which had followed them, was barking. 'Get away or I'll set the dog on you!' Mary told the children, and they left.

'Lift up your neck,' she told Brian again.

'She put her two hands on his neck,' Norma said. 'She said there was two lumps you had to squeeze right up. She said she meant to harm him. She got him down on the grass and she seemed to go all funny, you could tell there was something the matter with her. She kept on struggling with him and he was struggling and trying to get her hands away. She left go of him and I could hear him gasping. She squeezed his neck again and I said, "May, leave the baby alone." But she wouldn't. She said to me, "My hands are getting thick, take over."' Then, said Norma, she ran away, leaving behind on the grass the broken scissors which she had been carrying.

About twenty minutes later, Mary had found her playing with some other girls, and asked her to go back down to the Tin Lizzie. On the way, Mary found a razor blade on the path. That was the time, she explained, that she had tripped over Brian's head. She had lifted him up and patted him on the back, but his hand had fallen so she had put him down again. Mary, meanwhile, had lifted his jersey and cut his belly several times in the same place with the razor blade. The scissors were on the ground near his feet where Norma had left them.

Around tea time, Mary came calling again, asking Norma to come with her to see 'the bairn'. This time she had her Alsatian with her. When they got there, 'May said she would make him baldy,' Norma related, 'and she cut a lump of hair off his head. She pressed the scissors into his belly a few times, but not hard. That was when the man shouted at them kids and she hadn't cut any more hair off before we ran away.'

Dobson immediately called the pathologist, Dr Tomlinson, and arranged to view the body again. This time five faint but clearly visible marks, made visible through the process of decomposition, could be seen on the abdomen where nothing had been noticed during the post-mortem a few days earlier. Dobson and Tomlinson could not be sure whether the cuts formed the letter 'N' or the letter 'M'.

Wherever sudden death snatches away the life of an innocent child in working-class areas, whether in South Wales in the 1920s, Toronto in the 1930s, or Liverpool in the 1990s, we will find a great public outpouring of grief that focuses on the child's funeral. Brian Howe's funeral on 7 August, a hot, sunny day, was no different, with flowers piled high, more than 200 mourners massed at the house, and strangers weeping openly as the hearse went by.

Inspector Dobson was there that day, and what he noticed filled him with apprehension. Dobson, who has since died, told Gitta Sereny, author of the definitive account of the murders, *The Case of Mary Bell*, that he saw Mary Bell watching the coffin being carried out of the house. 'It was when I saw her there that I knew I did not dare risk another day. She stood there, laughing. Laughing and rubbing her hands. I thought, My God, I've got to bring her in, she'll do another one.'

By the time Brian Howe had been laid to rest, Mary Bell was once again sitting across from Dobson, this time looking distinctly nervous. Would she make a written statement? Her answer was yes. The inspector could not have imagined what would follow.

Yes, admitted Mary, they had picked up Brian when he was playing with his brother and two little girls. Only it was Norma, she claimed, who said, 'Are you coming to the shop, Brian?' 'I says, "Norma, you've got no money, how can you go to the shop?"' Mary wanted 'little Brian' to go home, but Norma kept coughing and drowning out her suggestions.

When they arrived at the big tank, it was Norma who said to Brian, 'Are you coming in here because there's a lady coming on the number eighty-two [bus] and she's got boxes of sweets and that.' They got inside, said Mary, 'then Brian started to cry and Norma asked him if he had a sore throat. She started to squeeze his throat and he started to cry. Norma said, "This isn't where the lady comes, it's over there, by them big blocks."'

It was Norma, Mary said, who made Brian lie down beside the blocks and told him, 'Put your neck up.' At that, 'she started to feel up and down his neck. She squeezed it hard because her fingertips were going white. Brian was struggling and I was pulling her shoulders but she went mad. I was pulling her chin up but she screamed at me.'

By this time, Mary said, Norma had banged Brian's head on a piece of wood and he was unconscious. 'His face was all white and bluey, and his eyes were open. His lips were purplish and had all slaver on, it turned into something like fluff.'

When Brian's dog, Lassie, whined, said Mary, Norma told it, 'Don't you start or I'll do the same to you.' On the way home, Norma's face was twitching and she was spreading her fingers. 'This is the first but it'll not be the last,' Mary quoted her friend as saying. It was Norma, she insisted, who had got a pair of scissors from her home and a razor blade and returned to prod and slice Brian's body, cutting off a piece of his hair. On the way home again, Norma had told her, 'May, you shouldn't have done [it] 'cos you'll get into trouble.'

'And I hadn't done nothing!' said Mary self-righteously. 'I haven't got the guts. I couldn't kill a bird by the neck or throat or anything, it's horrible that.'

The statement had been given in a flat tone with no sign of emotion beyond outrage at being accused herself of killing Brian. Yet it provided far more detail, even explanation, than Norma's had. If Dobson had his own view about the real culprit, he knew his duty: he charged both girls with the murder of Brian Edward Howe. 'That's all right with me,' was Mary's response.

On being told she was being charged with murder, Norma flared up: 'I never. I'll pay you back for this!'

More, perhaps, than any case I have come across, the Mary Bell affair reveals the confused emotions felt by those assigned to care for children who kill. The police-women, matrons and even the psychiatrists who were Mary's constant companions in the three and a half months leading up to the girls' trial felt themselves drawn frequently to a bright little girl reaching out for love, yet repelled by the knowledge of the crimes of which she was accused.

The very first night in the police cells, Mary proudly told a policewoman that Mr Dobson had bought them fish and chips for supper – as if he were a favourite uncle. The girls were awake half the night, shouting to each other from their cells. Mary's two worries: that she only had broken shoes to wear to court in the morning, and that she might wet the bed.

Later, eerily, the cells echoed to the sound of Mary

singing a favourite Cilla Black song that begins, 'Oh you are a mucky kid, dirty as a dustbin lid.'

Norma was sent to a mental hospital near Newcastle for examination, while Mary was sent initially to a remand home at Croydon, in south London. For Mary, the trip south was like a grand outing as she danced from one train window to the other. Then suddenly she became serious. 'I hope me mum won't have to pay a fine,' she said to one of the policewomen accompanying her. Her mother had finally made an appearance in court. She hoped, said Mary, that her mother wouldn't be too upset.

'She was upset this morning,' the policewoman said. 'She was crying.'

'I know she was,' said Mary. 'But if she loves me, why did she leave?'

At the same time an odd lack of feeling would sometimes emerge. 'Brian Howe had no mother,' she told one psychiatrist during her stay at the Seaham Remand Home on the coast fifteen miles from Newcastle, 'so he won't be missed.'

What would it feel like to be strangled? asked another psychiatrist. 'Why, if you're dead, you're dead,' Mary replied. 'It doesn't matter then.'

'Murder isn't that bad,' she would tell a policewoman guarding her during her trial. 'We all die sometime anyway.'

In a rare moment of introspection, she told Dr David Westbury, a forensic psychiatrist, 'I've got no feelings.' And to a woman psychiatrist to whom she opened up more than most, she said gaily of the day of Brian Howe's murder, 'I was full of laughter that day.'

There was only one subject she wasn't willing to talk about: her family. 'Me mum said for me not to say anything to you,' was a frequent response. Sometimes though she'd tell them that when it was all over she'd go and stay with her gran in Scotland. And then there were her disturbed nights: she'd sleep little, talking to herself when she did drift off, and sitting bolt upright at the slightest sound.

The trial opened in a small Victorian courtroom in Newcastle's Moothall on 5 December 1968. The only incongruity in those sombre surroundings was the two girls, pretty as pictures, Mary especially so, their hair sparkling, their faces shining, Norma wearing a yellow blouse with a frilly collar, Mary in a red dress. Quite soon after Rudolph Lyons QC, prosecuting, began his six-hour opening address to the jury of five women and seven men, a distinct difference was observed between the two girls, one that would hold true throughout the nine-day trial. Where Norma quickly lost interest in what was being said, indeed seemed not to understand a lot of it, Mary followed every word.

The girls were charged with the murder of both the little boys, but here's the difference: while in Brian Howe's case they both admitted being there and simply blamed each other, they both strongly denied having anything to do with Martin Brown's death. Mary's behaviour, harassing Martin's aunt and mother, had in itself been suspicious, but two pieces of harder evidence really pointed to their involvement. The notes found in the nursery break-in, which a handwriting expert would say had been written by both of them, amounted, the prosecution would claim, to a confession. And fibres found on Martin's clothes – similar to some discovered on Brian's clothing – were identical to those found in a grey woollen dress belonging to Mary.

Norma seemed to find the notes more upsetting than the murders themselves, and wept bitterly when asked repeatedly if she had not written the word 'murder' – to the point where Mr Justice (Sir Ralph) Cusack cautioned counsel: 'Neither I, nor, I think, the jury would be willing to sit here and have a weeping child plied with questions.' It was Norma's claim that the notes, some written at Mary's home, were Mary's idea of a game, and that her friend had then put them in her shoe. Mary's explanation for why the notes were written: 'For a giggle.'

The fibres were harder to explain. Mary had originally denied ever playing with Martin. But when the fibre evidence turned up, she suddenly remembered that, yes, she had pushed him on a swing shortly before his death. That didn't explain, said the prosecutor, how fibres came to be on Martin's vest.

Mary's technique, answering questions in her soft, singsong Geordie accent, was to wrap her lies – for undoubtedly she was lying a good deal of the time – in a cocoon of authentic detail. As when she was asked about the time they wrote the notes at her home: 'I was playing a recorder. I was playing "Go to sleep little brother Peter". I was playing that or "Three Blind Mice". I was playing one of those tunes and I just put it back in the box because too much playing, it makes the inside go rusty or something.'

And then? Immediately she was off on another rambling soliloquy about a stray cat for which she and Norma were trying to think of a name.

Mary was at her most imaginative on the subject of Brian's murder, ascribing to Norma details like the whitening of the fingers which, some would say, were simply observations of her own fingers as she squeezed the little boy's throat. Her accusation against her friend might have been convincing – if it hadn't been for an incident that had occurred just two weeks before Martin Brown died.

The mother of another Scotswood child, Pauline Watson, aged seven, complained to police that her daughter and two other little girls had been choked by either Norma Bell or Mary Bell as they played in a nursery sandpit. Interviewed by two policewomen, Mary and Norma both accused each other of putting their hands around the little girls' necks. But Pauline was quite definite: it was the smaller of the two girls, Mary, the one with the short, dark hair, who had done the choking, while the older girl was behind a shed playing. Mary and Norma were warned by the police at the time about their behaviour.

The judge for the most part showed the girls every consideration. His judgement though can surely be questioned when, on one occasion, he allowed Mary to be questioned for two and a half hours without a recess – an ordeal that would strain even the most competent adult witness and one which ended on this occasion in an ugly scene.

Mary was being pressed about her claim that Norma wanted to kill Brian and then run away from home. Her answers were becoming more and more incoherent. Did Norma say she wanted to run away? asked the judge.

'Because she could kill the little ones,' said Mary, her voice close to hysteria. 'And run away from the police.'

The judge took the hint and called an adjournment. Too late: 'I'll kick her mouth in,' yelled Mary, finally out of control.

Mary's mother, Betty, wearing a tatty blonde wig, and

her father, Billy, were there every day, but communicated little with their daughter. Norma's parents, by contrast, offered encouragement and reassurance at every chance they got. But even though the girls were accusing each other of murder, they seemed to draw their strength from each other, frequently exchanging meaningful glances. Their guards reported that, until they were separated later in the trial, they would chat away happily together during recesses, still the best of friends.

It would have been tidier for the jury if they could have believed that Mary was the little liar while Norma was telling the truth, but it wasn't that simple. Quite suddenly, under friendly questioning from her own lawyer, R. P. Smith, Norma admitted that she had lied about the razor blade in her final statement to Chief Inspector Dobson. Mary, she now insisted, had got it from her own scullery.

Didn't she remember telling Mr Dobson that Mary had found the razor blade on the path on the way to the Tin Lizzie?

'Yes,' she replied. 'I told a lie.'

Why? The question was repeated several times before she finally answered: ''Cos May wanted it found on the path. If we were caught, she wanted it found on the path.'

How did she know that?

''Cos May and me was talking together.' Mary, apparently, did not want the razor blade connected with her home. Why? Fear of her parents? It never became clear.

But even if the lie was originally Mary's, the jury now had to wonder how many other lies Norma had told.

After all the conflicting stories, after the pictures of the dead little boys that had made some of the women jurors feel sick, there was an almost palpable sense of relief as the psychiatrists were called to explain it all. But they could explain little.

Dr Robert Orton, using words with which we will become quite familiar in the cases that follow, testified: 'I think that this girl [Mary] must be regarded as suffering from psychopathic personality.' The symptoms, he said, included a lack of feeling towards other humans, a wish to damage things or people, a tendency to act aggressively on impulse, and a complete lack of remorse afterwards. Psychopaths, he added, neither learned from their experiences nor responded to punishment. Knowing little or nothing of her early years and her home life, Dr Orton could shed little light on why Mary Bell was the way she was.

Smith, eager to establish that his client, Norma, was very much under Mary's influence, got Dr Orton to agree that she was both a manipulator and a dominating personality.

The words didn't bother Mary. It was only when a second psychiatrist, Dr Westbury, described her as a bully that she reacted angrily. She shook her head violently, whispered to her counsel then, told to be quiet, turned to her mother and made an ugly face.

To some observers, there had from the start been a terrible incongruity in the might and majesty of the law being applied to two young girls. Yes, two beloved little boys had died, but issues of guilt or innocence seemed less important than the question of why it had happened – a question better asked in the psychiatrist's office. The inappropriateness of the court proceeding was finally laid bare when the prosecutor, Rudolph Lyons, used in his summing-up the kind of adversarial language you'd expect to hear if some vicious old lag were in the dock

35

rather than two children barely past the teddy-bear stage.

'In Mary,' he declared, 'you have a most abnormal child, aggressive, vicious, cruel, incapable of remorse, a girl moreover possessed of a dominating personality ... and a degree of cunning that is almost terrifying.' Norma, he allowed, was 'a simple, backward girl of subnormal intelligence' and Mary had wielded over her 'an evil and compelling influence almost like that of a fictional Svengali'. One waited for flames to issue from Mary Bell's nostrils, and sniffed instinctively for sulphur.

It took the jury something over three hours to reach their verdicts. Norma smiled and turned to her parents as she was found not guilty. Mary's mother sobbed hysterically as her daughter was found guilty on two counts of manslaughter. Mary cried quietly to herself. The judge allowed her to remain in her seat as he ordered her detained for life.

A cleaner, brighter Newcastle than the one Mary Bell knew as a child sparkled in the sunshine as I made my way on a spring morning to see Brian Roycroft, who has been the city's director of social services for more than twenty difficult years. Roycroft, on the point of retiring when I spoke to him, had just been appointed the city's children's officer in 1968, he told me, when he received a call from Chief Inspector Dobson. 'He was telling me, "Look, Brian, these are my suspicions [about Mary and Norma]. If I arrest them, can you put them somewhere?" I remember feeling at first a complete disbelief. It was logical [that a child could murder], but what do you do with them?'

Roycroft, an infinitely humane man, was shocked to discover that there was simply nowhere to put children involved in such serious crimes, either before or after their trials. One of the main differences today, he said, reflecting on the then-current James Bulger case, is that there are now several secure units in Britain where severely disturbed children can receive treatment.

'In 1968 people didn't actually talk about providing treatment for Mary,' he said. After much debate, she was placed in a special secure unit at the Red Bank approved school in Lancashire; the unit, until then for boys aged between fourteen and eighteen, was made coeducational for her benefit. At sixteen she was transferred to an open women's prison.

But at the start, following Dobson's call, Roycroft quickly made arrangements for the two girls to be kept initially in the comfortably furnished attic of a local children's home. Meeting Mary was his second surprise. 'She was a beautiful child, such lovely eyes,' he said.

It was only with the publication of Gitta Sereny's book in 1972 that people learned something of Mary's background. Her mother, Betty, had been disturbed as a child, refusing to eat unless her food was placed on the floor behind her chair. She had Mary when she was seventeen, and married Billy, the baby's father, the following year. But Betty had been so erratic, disappearing for periods of time, that one of her sisters had even offered to adopt Mary. Most disturbing: throughout her childhood, Mary had been the victim of mysterious 'accidents' when she would end up in hospital after taking pills left carelessly around the house.

Nowadays, said Roycroft, 'if these accidents occurred, there is little doubt that the police and social services would take action for child abuse.'

But nobody did anything, and Mary continued on her

doomed course, a naughty child at school, an unloved child at home, her only steady source of affection her unpredictable Alsatian.

With better treatment available now for seriously disturbed children, Roycroft worries still about the way we demonize children like Mary Bell. 'There are loads of parents who kill children,' he said, but when children kill – and he has encountered many cases – an unreasoning attitude takes over.

I had just come from reading the Mary Bell newspaper clipping file at the *Newcastle Evening Chronicle*. 'Child killer Mary Bell' is how she's always referred to in newspaper articles, even twenty-five years after the event. In 1974, when she was seventeen and had been transferred to a women's prison, James Dixon, head of the special unit at Red Bank where she had been for five years, who visited her regularly with his wife in the new setting, described her as 'lacking in hope. She must have hope that her treatment will continue and that some day she might be able to live a normal life again,' he said.

The wait was evidently too much for her: in 1977 she escaped from an open prison in Staffordshire with another woman. The escape, predictably, brought panic reactions. Margaret Howe, whose husband had been little Brian Howe's half-brother, announced that she was not letting her three-year-old, Alan, who had the same blond hair and chubby features as Brian, out of the house until Mary Bell was recaptured. 'Now that Mary Bell has escaped we are terrified she will come back and do something to Alan,' she said.

Mary had something else altogether more innocent in mind. She and her friend met two men and, after an evening at the funfairs and pubs of Blackpool, she checked into a hotel and spent her first night alone with a man. Following her recapture the next day, the men, in court for harbouring the two women, were said to have found her 'demure and pleasant, extremely attractive'. A 'wanted' picture, showing her looking defiant, with lank, unkempt hair, simply hadn't done her justice.

She was released finally in 1980 at the age of twenty-three; after her daughter was born she won a court injunction barring the media from revealing her new identity.

Her release was too long delayed, in Brian Roycroft's view. It is wrong, he feels, that high-profile inmates like Mary must be kept in prison long past the time when they are ready for release simply because the authorities fear the panic headlines that may result. 'But I hear she's adjusted very well,' he said.

Roycroft has reservations too about trying children between the ages of ten and thirteen for murder in adult crown court. 'When you are talking of children under fourteen you are talking about different mind processes,' he said. A child in those years, he believes, may not really understand that death is permanent. 'It's difficult to know when a child really understands that.' Television crime shows, where death is of little consequence, do nothing to hasten that understanding.

You have to wonder too to what extent the jury was influenced by the fact that one little girl behaved just as you'd expect a child to act in those frightening circumstances – by crying – while the other child, Mary, hardly shed a tear. Mary Bell certainly appears to have been the instigator, but what part Norma played will never be known.

According to Roycroft, Norma has had an unhappy

life, dogged by mental illness and guilt. Betty, who, with Billy, tried to sell the family's story to one of the sensational tabloids, has often been in the headlines and today, according to Roycroft, lives life on the edge, exposing herself to serious dangers. Mary has told friends she's had enough of being 'plagued' by her mother, and has no contact with her now.

There is still hostility towards Mary in some quarters in Newcastle. Pat Wheatley, Brian Howe's stepsister, who had gone searching for him the day he disappeared, still says Mary should never have been released from prison. 'I was very close to Brian,' she says. 'I was like a mother. She knew what she was doing, and I will never ever forgive her if I live to be a hundred.'

Martin Brown's mother, June Robinson (she has remarried since), can't forget either. 'It's not like a child has taken ill and died. This is like a life sentence. It's a terrible thought to live with.

'But I don't think anybody should be locked up for the rest of their lives,' she says. 'Especially children. A child that age [eleven], it's just a game to them.' As a result of what happened, June now finds comfort working as a volunteer helping prison inmates.

As I emerged from the civic centre, the square outside was bright with tulips. A mile away, in Scotswood, there were precious few flowers to be seen – only weeds. I remembered the words used about Mary by R. P. Smith, one of the lawyers at the trial: 'It's not her fault she grew up this way. It's not her fault she was born . . .'

BABY BUNTY
IS MISSING

It's been more than twelve years since I became interested in the Baby Bunty case, and in that time it's never been far from my mind. It always seemed to me the quintessential Great Depression story – the story of a pitifully poor couple who found consolation in the love of their child, only to see their happiness snatched away as a result of a bizarre crime. There's a little bit of *Les Misérables* and a little bit of *The Grapes of Wrath* in the tragedy of Baby Bunty, and her image has remained with me – a slightly faded snapshot that seems to go right to the heart of that far-off time.

And then a peculiar thing happened. As the tragedy of little Jamie Bulger unfolded in Liverpool in the early months of 1993, I began to see parallels. With important differences, it was as if the Baby Bunty murder was being re-enacted 3,500 miles away and sixty years on from the original crime. The similarities were uncanny: a beloved 'golden' child, snatched away in an instant, a public outpouring of love for the lost infant and the bereaved parents, a city in panic at young killers on the loose, and then a bitter anger directed at the suspected children.

The snapshot of Baby Bunty became sharper. Not only

the emotions but some of the issues that psychiatrists and public officials wrestled with in Toronto in 1933 were not much different to those confronting the authorities today. Questions like, how should a child be interrogated? How to handle children with fanciful imaginations. And, the hardest question of all, what to do with young children suspected of killing. The answers arrived at in Toronto were rough and ready. Officials did the best they could, and were severely criticized in some quarters for their handling of the case.

Today, no doubt, things would be handled better. But one thing hasn't changed: the huge anguish, private and public, that seizes a community when a child is killed, and the raw emotional conflict that is exposed when children are suspected. It's worth a visit to Boothroyd Avenue, a little cul-de-sac in Toronto's east end, to remind ourselves how little has changed.

Then, as in the early 1990s, times were desperately hard. Few of the men on Boothroyd Avenue, with its cheap, almost shanty-like houses, had full-time jobs; the best they could hope for was part-time employment. Alf Hillier at number six, for example, had recently lost his regular job when the firm went bankrupt. He counted himself lucky to have secured a part-time job delivering parcels. He received five cents for every parcel delivered, and it was a good day when he earned a dollar. It seemed a cruel fate for a man who had served in the British Royal Navy in the First World War, had fought at the Battle of Jutland and had been three times decorated for bravery.

But if Alf sometimes felt despondent, he could always look forward to that special moment when he came home through the door of his little two-bedroom house. 'Dimme tiss, Daddy!' his eighteen-month-old daughter,

Alfreda – whom everyone called Baby Bunty – would cry, throwing herself into his arms.

Both Alf, thirty-four, and Bunty's mother, Florence, slim and girlish and looking closer to seventeen than her actual age of twenty-four, had been involved in unhappy marriages. At a time when these things mattered, they called themselves Mr and Mrs Hillier, and tried to keep their unmarried status from the neighbours. Florence, who had emigrated to Canada from Glasgow in 1923, found it difficult to believe, after her disastrous marriage, that things had turned out so well. Never mind that they had no money – Alf was quiet and considerate, and Bunty made everything else seem unimportant.

When the baby was seven months old, her mother felt moved to write a poem entitled 'Miss Bunty':

> We have a little baby
> Who is playing on the floor.
> Her daddy, he's just gone outside
> So her eyes are on the door.
>
> She's one of the happiest little souls,
> And always wears a smile.
> One wonders what she thinks about
> To be smiling all the while.
>
> She's a regular little roughneck.
> We call her 'Bully Beef',
> And when she finally falls asleep,
> It is a sweet relief.
>
> Miss Bunty is our baby's name,
> With her we'd never part.

43

She's her Dad and Mummie's honey bunch,
God bless her little heart.

We come to Wednesday, 25 October, a bright, sharp
autumn day with the children on Boothroyd Avenue
shushing their feet through the brittle leaves on their way
back to school after lunch. Florence tiptoed into Bunty's
room, but the little girl already had her eyes open after
her midday nap and a big smile on her face.

'Time to go out and get some sunshine, pet,' said
Florence, and as she dressed her, she sang one of Bunty's
favourite songs, 'Who's afraid of the big, bad wolf?'
Bunty couldn't wait for the end of the verse. 'Wuff, wuff,'
she cried, screaming with laughter.

All Florence's love and concern went into making sure
Bunty wouldn't be cold: a vest and pants, a white
sleeveless sweater on which her mother had embroidered
'Alfreda', a white dress, a green sweater, brown pullover
leggings, a pink and white bonnet, white scarf, and a pink
coat on to the sleeves of which were pinned her red mitts.

'You'll be warm as toast,' Florence promised as roly-
poly Bunty trotted out of the door at 2.30 p.m. Half an
hour later, just as the newspaper boy arrived with the
paper, Bunty came in briefly for a biscuit and a glass of
milk. Fifteen minutes later, Florence, doing the ironing,
heard Bunty's distinctive laugh on the front veranda.
Around 4.30 p.m., Florence went out to take in the washing and to call Bunty in because the afternoon was getting
cold. 'Time to come in!' she called. There was no answer.
'Bunty!'

No need to panic. Everyone knew Bunty. She was
always playing with the neighbourhood children. Florence
checked the alley behind the house, then walked down

Boothroyd Avenue to Boultbee Avenue at the end, calling all the way. 'Have you seen Bunty?' she asked several children. They all shook their heads.

She could feel the cold penetrating her thin burgundy dress now, so she hurried home, slipped on a coat and started knocking on doors, asking if anyone had seen Bunty. It was already getting dark as she heard a locomotive pant by and the rumble of boxcars on the main Canadian National Railway line behind the houses on Boultbee Avenue. Her hand went to her mouth.

She remembered a dream she'd had two months earlier. She and Alf and Bunty were in a truck. As they went over a railway crossing, the truck stalled. A locomotive was bearing down on them. At the last instant, she threw Bunty free.

Bunty loved trains. Only a few days earlier, they'd taken her down to the tracks to see the big black steam monsters thunder by on their way to Montreal. Could she have . . . ? With children and neighbours helping in the search now, she stumbled along the gravel beside the track. But no sign of Bunty.

Florence phoned Alf's work and left a message for him, then resumed knocking on doors. At the Every house on Boultbee Avenue, the door was answered by seven-year-old Howard Every. 'Have you seen Bunty?' Florence asked. Howard made no reply, but went straight away and put on his coat.

'What are you doing, Howard?' his mother, Muriel, asked.

'I'm going to look for Bunty,' said little Howard.

He went out of the door, but came back in a few moments. 'It's dark, I can't find her,' he said. 'I'll look for her in the morning.'

The message did not get through to Alf. He arrived home at the usual time of 8 p.m. to find the little street filled with police cars and Florence crying on the veranda.

The topography of the neighbourhood was remarkably like that of Scotswood in Newcastle, where, thirty-five years later, a very similar search would take place for little Brian Howe. Down the hill from Boultbee Avenue and alongside the railway track was a large piece of wasteland littered with bricks and chunks of concrete, very much like Scotswood's Tin Lizzie – and the spot where Jamie Bulger died in 1993.

The wasteland was the natural place to look. When he got there Alf found it was a scene of blazing activity. Cars ringed the site, their headlights illuminating policemen in their tall 'bobby' helmets, scouring the rubble and debris. To one side, Inspector William 'Chesty' Johnson (named for his parade-square posture) was barking orders and organizing civilians and officers into a line to sweep the area. Alf, shivering from cold and apprehension, stood at the top of a forty-foot drop, looking down over the rubbish dump below and swinging the beam of a torch back and forth along the bank beneath him.

'Bunty!' he cried suddenly. 'There she is. She's dead . . . she's dead!' Slowly, too slowly for Alf, an officer with a torch made his way through the rubble and debris towards the spot he was pointing to. 'I'm coming, Bunty!' Alf called, lunging towards the edge of the drop. Two policemen held him back. 'Bunty. She's down there!' he told them. 'I've got to get to her. Let me go.' He wouldn't believe them when they told him it was only a box that, in the shadows, had looked like a child. Finally they had to bring it up to show him.

A few minutes later a detective came puffing up the slope to announce that he'd found signs of a fresh cave-in below the railway track. 'We need shovels!' he said. 'Let me come,' Alf said as the policeman returned to the cave-in carrying the tools. When he got there, not waiting for digging to start, Alf fell to his knees and began scrabbling at the yellow clay with his bare hands. Only reluctantly did he pull back and allow officers with shovels to move in. They dug for twenty minutes before giving up. There was no sign of Bunty. Attention turned to half a dozen deep holes filled with water from recent rains, and drag irons were called for.

The steadily falling temperature added urgency to the search. By the early hours of the morning, the thermometer was registering ten degrees below freezing, and ice was forming on the ponds. Lights were on in every house on Boothroyd Avenue as people made tea and coffee for the chilled searchers and answered the same questions for the umpteenth time.

'Bunty used to be my special friend,' said Mrs J. E. Boardman at number eighteen. 'Ever since my own little girl died of pneumonia a year ago. But I walked down the street at twenty after three and I didn't see her.'

'Perhaps someone took her in,' said Florence when Alf returned, tired and frozen, after midnight, 'and they don't have a phone to let anyone know.'

Just before dawn, Florence fell asleep in the chair. When she woke half an hour later, Constable Frank James was at the door. 'I believe I've found her,' he said. She let out a wail. Alf, feeling that his legs might give out at any moment, followed the officer out of the door and towards the wasteland.

James had come on duty at 6.15 a.m. Picking his way

through old bedsprings, tin cans and bricks at a spot which had already been searched in the night, he came across a rusty car door covered in hoar frost and half hidden under bushes. Something pale caught his eye in the bushes. He pulled aside the door, and there she was. Bunty was lying face down on the brick rubble, the door covering the lower part of her body. She was naked and icy cold – frozen in fact – to James' touch. A few feet away he saw what he thought was a rag, covered again with the glistening frost. As he reached for it, though, he realized it was a six-quart wooden fruit basket in which were neatly folded Bunty's shoes and clothing.

Alf Hillier was told he couldn't approach the body until the city's chief coroner, Dr M. M. 'Mac' Crawford had inspected the site and the police photographer had finished his work. 'Oh God! Oh God!' sobbed Alf, glimpsing her whiteness in the bushes. 'She was only a little kid; she couldn't hurt anybody. Why should this be done to me?'

The policemen and officials stood awkwardly in a circle in the stillness of the early morning, the only sound the whirr of the photographer's Speed Graphic camera. Alf's voice came harsh and strident: 'Somebody has done this! She's all I had in the world!'

The coroner was walking back to his car. Someone signalled Alf forward. He took off his mechanic's cap, sank to his knees and reached out a tentative hand to touch Bunty's bare back. He said nothing else, only crossed himself and seemed to be praying.

'It was just...' he said to reporters as he went home, 'just like she was undressed ready for her bath.'

When James Bulger's little body was discovered horribly mutilated on the train tracks in Bootle in 1993, his parents soon found themselves guarded from the curiosity of the media by round-the-clock police protection. In the less sophisticated 1930s, the press had free rein, and the Hilliers had few moments of privacy once their baby went missing. A reporter was in their kitchen to hear Florence ask Alf when he returned, 'How did she look?'

'She looked as if there were red welts all over her body,' he said.

'She's been hit with a strap,' said the young mother with certainty. 'Did you notice if her little feet were dirty, as if she had been walking? Walking in her bare feet, I mean?'

'Oh no, they were clean.' He turned to the reporter: 'This neighbourhood is like a large family. We know everybody and everybody knows us. There is nobody around here who would do a thing like that.'

'It was someone from another district and he must have enticed the baby away,' said Florence. 'It was probably a degenerate, a fiend of some sort, and when he took her clothes off, she probably cried and that frightened him.'

At the city morgue, a handsome red-brick building with tall windows on downtown Lombard Street, pathologist Dr William L. Robinson was making an urgent preliminary examination of the baby's body. The results were, in one sense, reassuring to the public. And mystifying.

Bunty had a wound on her forehead, but this had not caused her death. In fact, Mac Crawford told the press that afternoon, 'There are no gross lesions that would in any way account for death. There are also no signs of violence to lead one to think the child had been violated. From what has been learned so far, it would appear that the child probably died of exposure.'

Was it murder? It was undoubtedly peculiar that Bunty had been found undressed and with her clothes in a basket several feet away and at a higher level, he said. The red blotches on her body could have been caused by the frost, but there were also scratches on the lower part of her body that could not be accounted for.

If Bunty's death had not been as violent as had at first been thought, there were plenty who shared Florence's fear that a fiend was on the loose. People still remembered the atmosphere of panic the previous year, when aviator Charles Lindbergh's baby had been kidnapped and murdered in the United States. Women in the east end of Toronto announced that they weren't letting their children out of the house until the beast was caught, and stories spread about strange men seen in the neighbourhood.

Ten-year-old Isobel Miller told how she and other girls were chased by a man as they came out of gym class at a local school. 'He was old and wrinkled, and he had his cap pulled down over his eyes,' she said breathlessly. 'He didn't catch me, but he caught some of the other girls and started kissing them!'

Even some professionals added to public fears: 'It's likely to be a chronic mental case of the lowest animal type,' speculated neurologist Dr Goldwin Howland. The man, he added, would be likely to have 'scarcely any mind at all and, this being the case, he is apt to repeat his crime'.

A man convicted of several counts of indecent assault on young children, who had escaped from prison that summer, seemed, in the public's imagination, to fit the bill.

The police were less impressed by all the talk of a fiend. The investigation had uncovered a witness, a woman living at 60 Boultbee Avenue, who said she had seen Baby

Bunty with two boys, Howard Every and a four-year-old, Jackie Marland. 'They had her by the hand, and she was crying. I told them to take her home,' said the woman.

She didn't know the child, and only learned it was missing when Alf called at the door later that evening. Why the woman didn't tell Alf at that point what she'd seen, we'll never know. Perhaps it was because she put the time she saw the baby at around 2.30 p.m. – well before she disappeared. Could she have been mistaken about the time?

Sergeant Nelson Silverthorn and Mac Crawford were soon at the Everys' door on Boultbee Avenue. Arthur Every, out of a regular job and trying to make a living collecting and selling waste paper, called his son, Howard, to talk to them. The boy who hung shyly to the banister was small for his age, with narrow, dark features. When he spoke, a cleft palate made it difficult for them to understand him. Yes, he told them, he and Jackie had been playing with Bunty when the baby tumbled down the slope into the dump.

'She fell and I went down to her,' he said. 'She wasn't moving, so I went home and I didn't go back again.'

Would he be willing to show them where it had happened? Howard cheerfully led the two men and his father to the lane off Boultbee Avenue leading to the bank at the foot of which Bunty's body had been found.

'That's where she fell,' he said, and started rolling down to demonstrate until his father called him back.

'Did you touch her clothes?' asked Crawford.

'No, I did not,' replied the boy.

'Thanks very much, Howard. Run along now,' said the coroner.

Jackie Marland would give a very different account.

At the morgue a little later, Alf returned to Mac Crawford's office supported on a policeman's arm after making the official identification of the body. 'I've got to keep up face,' he said. 'If I go, my wife goes too.'

'I don't want to seem to be prying into your affairs, my boy,' said Crawford, fingering his gold watch chain, 'but how are you fixed?'

'I've only got a few cents between me and starvation,' replied Alf.

'Don't worry now, my boy,' said the coroner. 'I'd advise you to leave your little girl here for the night. It's just the same as if she were with an undertaker. Then tomorrow we'll see what we can do. I could apply for a city burial.'

'No, no, we don't want that,' interrupted Alf. 'We don't want a pauper's burial.'

By the next day Crawford would announce that six undertakers had offered to provide their services free, and several people had offered to donate burial plots.

Meanwhile Crawford had an appointment to keep at police headquarters, where Howard Every and his little friend, Jackie Marland, had been summoned with their parents. Howard sat with a stubborn expression on his face as Jackie told his version. Bunty had been crying, he said, when Howard rolled her down the bank into the dump.

'I did not!' insisted Howard.

Yes he had, said Jackie, and then Howard had taken the baby's clothes off. After Howard had put the car door on the baby's back, they'd gone home, leaving her there, he said. Howard vehemently denied it. It was Jackie, he insisted, who had taken off Bunty's clothes.

A few minutes later the boys were running up and

down, laughing and playing, in the detectives' office. Jackie came out of the police station snug in his father's arms. Howard came dancing down the steps between Mac Crawford and his parents, chattering excitedly. 'Here, lad,' said Crawford as he stopped at the blind man's confectionery stand and bought Howard a bar of chocolate.

What we would find shocking today is that from this time on Howard and Jackie were constantly exposed to questioning by their parents, by neighbours dropping by, and by reporters who all but took up residence in the Every and Marland kitchens. It was hardly surprising that the boys frequently changed their stories.

Muriel Every was making supper for her five children when the reporters arrived that evening. 'Such sorrow!' she said. 'I am so sorry for Mrs Hillier. If I could only buy a wreath for the little girl, but I haven't enough money.'

She couldn't understand why Howard hadn't told her about Bunty being left in the dump when he'd come home that day. 'Even though it's hard to understand what he says and he's had a lot of sickness, he's much sharper than the others were at his age. Come here, Howard,' she ordered. 'Did you see little Bunty fall?'

'Yes.'

'Did she cry?'

'Yes.'

'Did you see her with her clothes off?'

'No, I didn't.'

'Wasn't Bunty cold with her clothes off?'

'Yes, she was cold.'

'Who took her clothes off?' his mother asked.

'Don't know,' he replied sullenly, and went into the next room.

Howard simply wasn't the sort, his father insisted. 'He plays with boys – not girls. Even though he's not very strong, he isn't a sissy. He doesn't like to play with dolls or toy animals.'

'He'd go a mile to see a fire engine,' said his mother.

An hour or so later Howard was telling the reporters: it was Jackie who had taken Bunty's clothes off.

At the Marland house, two doors away from the Hilliers, Glen, Jackie's father, apologized to reporters for the untidy state of the kitchen. His wife had died a few months before, and a neighbour was now caring for Jackie when Marland went to his job as a night caretaker. The kitchen seemed cosy enough, though, with a pot of soup on the stove, a comfortable rocker, toy trains on the table, and a kitten playing with a spool of thread. Jackie had been playing out at the front of the house with his wagon when his father had left for work at 4 p.m. the day Bunty went missing. It was only the following afternoon, after sleeping all day, that Glen heard what had happened. Jackie told him later, 'Bunty's dead, Dad. She's gone. Where did she go?'

'Bunty's gone to be with Jesus,' his father explained, 'just like Mamma.'

Jackie, carrying one of the toy trains, answered a reporter's questions. Did he see Bunty fall? 'Yes.'

Did she cry? 'Yes, she cried a lot.'

Wasn't she cold with her clothes off? 'Yes, she was cold.'

Did she have her clothes off? 'No, but she was cold.' At that point his attention switched to the kitten and he showed no further interest in answering questions.

Glen Marland too didn't want people to think his boy was the sort that played with girls. 'He thinks any boy who plays with girls is a sissy,' he said. 'Are you a sissy, Jackie?'

'I am not!' declared Jackie, glaring at his father.

'He's a real boy,' said his father proudly. 'Even if he is so young.'

Outside, the street was filled with cars. Obscure little Boothroyd Avenue had become suddenly a magnet for the curious and the morbid. Crowds walked first past the Hillier home, then past the homes of the two boys, Howard and Jackie, whose photographs had appeared in the evening newspaper. In the picture, the boys are standing on the bank and pointing down to where Bunty had fallen. Finally, the sightseers trooped down to the dump to view the exact spot where the body had been found.

The next day an even more remarkable phenomenon occurred. The street was lined with hundreds of people waiting their turn to enter the little Hillier parlour where Bunty, doll-like and wearing a dainty white dress trimmed with pink satin rosettes, lay in an open coffin. Beside her lay her favourite doll, and on a pillow of red and white roses rested a card inscribed, 'In loving memory, from Dad and Mummie.' From the flowers floated a wide white chiffon ribbon with the name 'Bunty' spelled out in gold lettering. The small brass plate on the lid of the coffin, which was supplied free of charge by a local funeral home, was inscribed, 'Our Darling'. The Baby Bunty mystery had become one of the great folk events of the Depression era in Toronto.

The crowd, which the newspapers numbered in the thousands, and which mostly consisted of women, shuffled past the coffin all day while Florence, a tiny figure in black crêpe, stood beside it accepting condolences. When one woman reached out and tried to give the baby's cheek a pinch, Florence let out a stifled scream: 'Wait! Oh, don't!' Even when the crowds were turned away so that the couple could eat, people banged on the doors and peered in through the windows.

The crowd scenes were repeated when, five days after she disappeared, and with six little girls as pallbearers, Bunty was buried at Park Lawn Cemetery. Beside her in the coffin lay a new, fair-haired doll that her mother had bought her as a final present.

The authorities now faced a ticklish problem: because the boys involved were so young, there would be no trial to establish once and for all who was responsible for Bunty's death. But the public, at the same time, needed to be reassured that there was no loony on the loose. The solution would be a far-reaching inquest inquiry under the fatherly patronage of Dr Crawford. Inquests traditionally are more open-ended and less bound by legal restrictions than trials, and the coroner's courtroom at the Lombard Street morgue seemed the ideal forum for getting to the root of this death that had so captured the public imagination.

There would be some who would say that the inquest was a travesty. Almost from the moment an eight-year-old boy named Stanley Lott breezed into the witness box wearing a red sweater, it was apparent that there would be problems with the 'open-ended' approach.

Oh yes, said Stanley, his pink elfin face just visible over the edge of the box, he had seen Jackie and Howard with Baby Bunty at the dump. He had seen Howard put the baby's clothes in the basket. He was so concerned, he'd gone up to them, and put his own coat under the baby. Then a man had come along the railway tracks and put his coat over Bunty. By then Howard had put the car door over Bunty. 'I tried to lift it off, but I couldn't. I'm as weak as a door knob,' he said, offering to let anyone feel his muscles.

That evening, reporters calling at the Lott house were told that Stanley had been sent to bed, 'until he learns to tell the truth'. Next day, the boy's mother went into the box to brand his story 'a lot of nonsense and rubbish'. Stanley, shamefaced, admitted he'd made it all up. 'I read story books about murdering and things and I get stories out of them,' he explained.

Jackie Marland was wearing a blue sailor suit trimmed with gold as he arrived at the courtroom holding his father's hand. Dr Crawford, dispensing with formality, lifted the boy on to a table and put his arm around him. Where had he gone on the Wednesday afternoon with Howard and Bunty? the coroner inquired. Jackie looked up at the crowded courtroom, then down at Dr Crawford. He twisted his feet together and tore a paper cup into shreds.

'Tell me, Jackie. You don't need to be afraid.' Crawford took the torn cup from Jackie and dropped it on the desk behind him. Jackie wriggled, toyed with the yellow cord around his neck that was attached to a whistle and looked out of the window.

'Where?' To the dump, he finally admitted.

'What happened to Bunty?'

'Howard threw the door on her.'

'Before that?'

'Howard threw rocks at her.'

'What did Howard do then?'

'He took her clothes off.'

'You are telling the truth?'

'Yes.'

'What happens to little boys who tell lies?'

'They die,' said Jackie, twirling the whistle.

As the questions continued, Jackie, who had now discovered the court official stamp, and was stamping his knee, his clothing and any papers he could reach, gave them at best half his attention. After a particularly loud bang, Crawford removed the court stamp from him. Jackie immediately fastened on the Bible, flapping the cover back and forth. Plainly he was tired. Plainly there would be no further answers.

Howard Every proved equally elusive when, after sitting him on the table, Crawford asked: 'Tell us what happened to Bunty.'

The boy, wearing a black armband on the sleeve of his brown jacket, squirmed and remained silent. 'Will you tell your father?' Still silence. With his father acting as interpreter, Howard claimed that Bunty, playing on the sand bank, had fallen down the slope.

Did anyone push her? 'No, she fell and slipped, and Jackie undressed her.'

Yawning, his attention caught by a clock chiming outside the window, he didn't seem to hear a question from J. W. McFadden, the crown attorney. 'Howard!'

'What!' he exclaimed, suddenly coming to life and causing general laughter.

'Did you help Jackie undress her?' persisted the lawyer.

'No.' The answer was always the same. It was Jackie who had pushed Bunty into the bushes, Jackie who had pulled the car door on top of her, Jackie who had thrown stones at her. As the questions kept coming, Howard, his finger stuck in his mouth, became bored, his answers close to incoherent.

It was only fair, said Crawford when Howard had been lifted down, that Jackie should have a chance to answer these accusations in the presence of his father. Jackie, placed on the table again, was munching a bar of chocolate, and the proceedings were halted until he had finished it. 'Howard said you hit the little girl,' said McFadden.

'It's a lie!' said Jackie, wiping his chocolate-stained fingers on his father's handkerchief.

'He said you took her clothes off.'

'Aw, I never.'

'Did you put the door on her?'

'No.'

'Did you throw stones at her?'

'No.'

Leaving the courtroom with his father, Jackie stopped in front of the rusty car door, an exhibit in the case, which was lying on the floor. Jackie couldn't resist. He pulled away from his father, grasped the eleven-pound door, and lifted it up to show how strong he was. 'Watch it, Daddy. Watch it!' he said.

Some experts thought the whole inquest had been an object lesson in how not to question children. 'It was ridiculous,' fumed Dr C. B. Farrar, a University of Toronto psychiatry professor. 'Now the story is all mixed up in their minds by the constant telling.' As soon as it was discovered that the two boys were connected with the baby's disappearance, he said, 'they should have been brought to specialists, put at their ease in protected surroundings, and an attempt made quietly to see what it was all about.'

The doctor was particularly incensed at the way the two boys had been questioned in open court to general laughter. 'You don't take them to a public place, sit them on tables and ask them more or less irrelevant questions and ever hope to get at the truth,' he said witheringly.

The evidence of the two boys, nebulous and contradictory though it was, was the centrepiece of the inquest. Beyond that, only clues were offered: Dr Robinson, the pathologist, said Bunty should have been able to wriggle out from under the car door. That she didn't suggested she might have been unconscious from the blow to her head. In the cold that day, she would have died in about three hours, he estimated.

Muriel Every recalled her son's suspicious behaviour the afternoon Bunty went missing. He had come in early – 3.30 p.m. 'Why don't you go out to play?' she'd asked him. 'Too cold.' 'Where is Bunty?' This is the first time we learn that Mrs Every knew Howard had been playing with Bunty. 'Bunty has gone home.' Said his mother: 'He did seem – I don't know whether he was afraid or not. He just sat around.'

Florence Hillier, whose real name, as they were not married, was given as Florence Campbell, told how Alf's original wife, Emma, had visited them once, making a point of telling the neighbours that she was the real Mrs Hillier. Florence had left her in the living room while she went down to the basement. On her return, she had found Emma, who had a cold, leaning over the baby and breathing heavily in its face. She was certain, Florence said, that the woman wanted to give Bunty consumption. But there was nothing to suggest that Emma, the bad fairy, had anything to do with Bunty's death.

And then, just as the inquest was coming to an end, the jury got a glimpse of another side of Howard Every. A neighbour testified that, one day, Howard had removed her grandchild's pyjamas on the street. Another woman said that, while on holiday at Port Perry the previous year, she had only just managed to save her baby after Howard took off its clothes and put it in the lake. The next day, she said, Howard had pushed the pram with the baby in it into the lake. Wilfred Scott, a psychiatrist with the Children's Aid Society, said he'd examined Howard and found him 'markedly defective' in intelligence. But he had no antisocial tendencies beyond quarrelsomeness, Scott said.

The coroner's jury found that Bunty's death had been caused 'by a child or children of irresponsible years', and recommended that Howard Every be placed under supervision. No mention was made of Jackie. A few days later, the Every family, hounded by threatening anonymous letters, were ordered out of their home by their landlord.

What happened to Howard? In 1981 I knocked at the door of an apartment in a senior citizens' building only a couple of miles from Boothroyd Avenue. Alec Every, Howard's oldest brother, invited me into the sparsely furnished living room. He looked older than his sixty-five years, a man ravaged by life. And still angry.

Howard, he said, had been made a public ward and sent to the Orillia Hospital, a large institution a hundred miles north of Toronto, ostensibly for the retarded, but used at that time as a dumping ground for many of society's misfits. What outraged Alec was that he, seventeen years old at the time, had been sent along ostensibly to help look after his brother. 'Bitter? Oh yes, we were bitter about it all right. We've always felt it was a terrible thing in our family.'

He was quiet for a few minutes, rolling himself a

cigarette. 'Howard couldn't speak properly,' he recalled. 'He had that cleft palate. He was, well, a bit retarded, I guess you'd say. But he couldn't have been so bad. He did better than me. We got out after a few years, and he moved out west, got married and raised four kids. Me, I went into the army and fought all through the war.'

He was looking for words to express that old anger. 'It was a terrible thing they done to us,' he said. 'We was inside – I knew that because they locked every door behind us. And I done nothing.'

Bunty's parents too moved away from Boothroyd Avenue within a few weeks, perhaps unable to bear the associations or, more likely, unable to pay the rent. Alf went from job to job, finally working the last years of his life in the workshop of an engineering company. He was living at the Eton Hotel, a run-down joint not far from Boothroyd Avenue, when he died around 1970. It looks, from the records, as if he had parted from Florence years before. There may be an explanation.

Examining again the times cited for the day Bunty disappeared, there was a significantly long gap between about 3.15 p.m., when Florence heard Bunty laughing, and about 4.30 p.m., when she went looking for her. Evidence at the inquest showed that a friend had been with the Hilliers, working at a crossword puzzle, until close to dawn that day. It's my suspicion that Florence sat down for a moment that afternoon and fell fast asleep. Some evidence suggests that it was even later than four thirty when she sounded the alarm. What I'm left wondering is: was it the corroding guilt she would have felt, and Alf's understandable recriminations that finally drove them apart?

The loss of any child leaves a wound that is hard to

heal. In Baby Bunty's case, no child was ever more loved, and her loss, I believe, may have been simply too much to bear.

THE LONG DYING
OF SHANDA SHARER

It was the kind of conversation no God-fearing mother in a small Midwestern American town would ever expect to have with her twelve-year-old daughter, and Jacqueline Vaught handled it rather well.

She had found a letter addressed to her daughter, Shanda, from a fifteen-year-old school friend, Amanda Heavrin, which had distinct sexual overtones. 'There was, I won't say a romantic tone to it, but there was a tone that was not normal,' she would say. 'There were things there that alarmed me.' She was right to be alarmed: Shanda's affair led to a murder that ruined the lives of several families and caused parents in three small Indiana towns to wonder just how much they really knew about their children's lives.

Shanda should have been the last girl to give her mother cause for concern. At St Paul's Catholic School in Louisville, Kentucky, she had always shone, a gorgeous little girl with fair hair and an outgoing manner. Athletically active, a cheerleader, she had been involved in Girl Scouts and the 4H youngsters' farm club – just the kind of girl who would one day be a homecoming queen. After her parents were divorced, she moved with her mother a few miles away across the state border to the little town of New Albany, Indiana. At that point, Shanda complained that she was tired of wearing a school uniform and pleaded to be allowed to attend Hazelwood Junior High School, the local state school. She could go, her mother said, only as long as her marks remained good.

Shanda, who used her father's last name, Sharer, was an immediate social hit at her new school; the boys – and some of the girls too – sat up and paid attention to the attractive newcomer, and it wasn't long before one of the boys gave her his ring as a token of his affection. It was when she had a change of heart and gave back the ring that something quite unexpected happened. The boy's cousin, Amanda Heavrin, goaded by her close and good friend, Melinda Loveless, attacked the surprised Shanda, wrestled her to the ground and got in a few good blows before teachers separated them. For Shanda, always Miss Popularity at her well-disciplined parochial school, it was a tough introduction to the rude, rough ways of public education. And she probably didn't even suspect the intrigue that lay behind the attack.

Melinda, sixteen, an attractive, petite girl with dark, flowing, Botticelli-style curls, was jealous when she noticed that the slight, boyish-looking Amanda, with whom she was having a lesbian relationship, was attracted to the new girl. The fight had the very opposite result to the one Melinda intended. Ordered to serve periods of detention for a week as punishment for the fight, Amanda and Shanda were soon passing notes to each other. In detention too one day, Melinda was furious at the growing intimacy she observed between the two girls.

At home, Shanda's mother noticed an alarming change. The girl who formerly took such pains to look attractive now wore scruffy jeans and sweatshirts, and didn't seem to care how she looked. 'She went from this robust child that could never do enough, to this child that didn't even want to talk, that would close the door to her room and not come out all night,' said Jacqueline. 'She changed completely within a matter of a month.'

Her marks dropped, and when Jacqueline went to the school she learned Shanda's big problem was that she was mixed up with girls who were nothing but trouble. 'Her teachers said that if she continued to hang around with them, she would find herself on a road where there was no way of getting back,' Jacqueline would say.

'I want to get free of them,' Shanda told her mother. 'But you don't understand. It's not that easy.' What she meant was that she was now part of a triangle: Melinda would harass her in the school hallways, warning her to stay away from Amanda. But Amanda would pursue her, defending her against Melinda and making Shanda feel she owed Amanda a debt of gratitude.

At that point Jacqueline found the letter from Amanda and was no longer under any illusion that this was just a schoolgirl crush. She acted with commendable determination, forbidding Shanda from seeing the girl again and, with financial help from her ex-husband, an air-conditioning engineer named Stephen Sharer, transferring Shanda to Our Lady of Perpetual Help, the Catholic school in New Albany that she, Jacqueline, had once attended. But the letters from Amanda kept coming.

Again Jacqueline acted resolutely. She went to Amanda's home, spoke to her father and invited him to come over that evening with his daughter to talk things out with herself, Shanda, and Shanda's father. In the end, Amanda and her father didn't turn up. 'I had never in my life dreamed I would be in a situation where I would have to deal with something like this,' Jacqueline said much later, when it was all over. 'I worried, "How do I do this so I don't hurt her, and let her know that I'm here for her, and no matter what she's done, it's going to be okay?"'

Many modern parents would have been squeamish, would have avoided the subject. Jacqueline told Shanda, 'We will always love you. Whatever you have done is not unforgivable. You are twelve years old. You are just a little girl.'

Shanda insisted that it was still just a friendship and that there had been no sexual touching. But the wall had been breached – the subject was out in the open. They had many talks, and one evening in the kitchen, Shanda told her mother that she felt she'd been given a second chance. 'I did so many bad things that I had never done before, and I just couldn't find my way back,' she said. Then, as they cried together: 'You helped me find my way back.'

Shanda couldn't know that, by then, there was really no way back. No way to reach home again.

The three towns of New Albany, Jeffersonville and Madison, all on the banks of the Ohio River, are the three jilted sisters of southern Indiana. At one time the burghers of all three had grand plans for development, but Louisville, on the opposite bank of the river, eloped with the bridegroom by securing an important canal. It went on to become the largest city in Kentucky, while the three small towns remained just that. With their handsome old buildings, their Stars and Stripes flying from the flagpoles, you could call the three towns essential America, and Madison, with a population of 12,600, was even picked as 'the typical American town' for a World War II propaganda film.

Mayor Morris Wooden still describes Madison as 'the ideal small town – good schools, low crime rate [a euphemism for 'few blacks'] a strong sense of family, and a confident, optimistic approach to life.' These are the sort of places people like to say are perfect for bringing up kids, which is to say they are the very last places on earth most kids would want to be. As one eighteen-year-old put it to a British reporter who arrived in town following the murder, 'There ain't much to do around here but drink and fuck.' Local teenagers, disdaining the Currier and Ives prettiness of Madison's carefully preserved down-town, would rather cruise the neon strip of fast-food joints, supermarkets and gas stations on the hill above the town, hang out at Hardee's restaurant parking lot, or shuttle back and forth aimlessly in their cars between the bright lights of Louisville and the two other sister towns.

Booze, drugs and sex were the norm for these kids, but when it came to lesbianism their values were still small town. Which made Mary Laurine 'Laurie' Tackett, a chunky but not unattractive girl who described herself as bisexual, very much a shunned outsider at the local high school. No one could envy Laurie her upbringing. Her mother, Peggy, attended the Lighthouse on the Hill Pentecostal Church and had decidedly conservative views about standards of dress and behaviour for her daughter. When she was younger, Laurie's mother had forced her to wear only long dresses to school and to skip physical education which would have required her to wear tracksuit trousers or shorts. The only music she was allowed was gospel music and, after making a pledge to the Lord, her mother sold the family television set. Her father didn't seem to have much say in all this. 'Other kids joked about me and teased me because I was different,' Laurie would say.

Sullen resentment turned into outright rebellion as Laurie grew older. One day her brother stole her diary and gave it to her mother. In it, Laurie had written that she wished she was a boy. Marched to church, she was forced to listen to a sermon on the theme 'Why homosexuals will go to Hell'. She never returned to the church.

By the time she was fifteen, Laurie, who dyed her hair wild colours and once cut it all off to antagonize her mother, was calling the police to ask if trying to force a youngster to attend church constituted child abuse, and a neighbour's report that she had been beaten by her parents was investigated by welfare officials. On one occasion, Laurie, who was dabbling in occult beliefs, and who would cut her wrists and bleed herself slowly to relieve emotional pressure, was taken to a hospital emergency department after cutting too deeply. After that, her mother invited her pastor to the house to pray for her wayward daughter. Laurie's answer was to run to her room, slam the door, and bleed herself using a razor while the hapless cleric stood outside the door bidding the devil begone.

Several times she ran away from home, the last time to New York City. Out of school now, and seventeen, Laurie decided once again that she couldn't take Madison, and in October 1991, a friend from New Albany, Carrie Pope, also aged seventeen, drove over to pick her up and have her stay for a while. In the car Carrie introduced her to a girl with long dark curls, Melinda Loveless.

If someone had been listening, there were several warnings of the tragedy about to occur. Amanda Heavrin's father may not have had the guts to take his daughter to talk to Shanda's mother, but he did discover letters from Melinda Loveless to Amanda, the sexual tone of which alarmed him. He turned them over to the local probation department, and a probation officer actually warned Melinda to stay away from Amanda. In one of the letters she'd written, 'I want Shanda dead.' No one thought to tell Shanda's parents.

At school, Melinda told fourteen-year-old Kristina Brodfuehrer that she wanted to beat Shanda up, or maybe kill her. 'Why her?' asked Kristina. 'She's not the one you should be mad at. It's Amanda that's messed you about.' Right, agreed Melinda, whose intelligence we can't have the greatest respect for – she had already dropped behind a year or two in school. So she and Kristina worked out a plan to abduct Amanda from her home in a car. One hitch; they didn't have a car. No problem: they'd persuade a couple of boys with a car to help them. Only the boys had a different idea, and took the two girls to an apartment. By the time they all got to Amanda's house, it was four in the morning. No one answered the door.

In those final days danger was in the air. 'Wouldn't it be fun,' Laurie Tackett said to her friend, Carrie Pope, one day, 'to kill someone. Wow! Maybe burn them alive! And then get all that publicity.' When Carrie made some complaint about her grandmother, Laurie offered to kill her. Maybe Carrie was beginning to have her doubts about Laurie. She'd seen her friend 'channelling', or talking to spirits, while calling herself 'Diana the Vampiress'.

Another time she'd seen her cut her own wrist and drink the blood. At times, she'd say, she felt Laurie was controlling her mind. They had words, and Laurie went back to live with her parents in Madison.

By then Laurie and Melinda, she of the curls, were close. They were a perfect match. As the prosecutor would say a year later: 'Loveless wanted somebody killed, and Tackett wanted to kill somebody. They each got what they wanted.'

There was no secret about it either. On the evening of 9 January 1992, Jeffrey Stettenbenz, a friend of Amanda's, got a call from Melinda. 'We're going to kill Shanda,' she said. He thought she sounded drunk. He didn't tell anyone.

The following afternoon, a Friday, Amanda too got a call at home from Melinda. A boy who was there heard Amanda say, 'Don't do it. You'll get arrested. Don't kill her.' He knew they were talking about Shanda, but he did nothing to warn anyone.

In Madison, two fairly ordinary teenagers, Toni Lawrence and Hope Rippey, both aged fifteen, were pretty happy as they came out of Madison Consolidated High School that afternoon. School was over for another week, and their friend Laurie Tackett was waiting for them in her dad's big grey Chevrolet to take them to a slam dance that evening at an indoor skateboard rink called Skaters Unlimited in Louisville. A slam dance involves a lot of bumping and thumping into your partner to the beat of a punk rock band, and it promised to be a rousing night. Laurie? When she was at school she'd been shunned as a lesbo weirdo; now, with her spiky hairdos, her black clothes and her witchcraft mumbo-jumbo, she had become . . . interesting . . . to the younger girls. Besides, she had access to a car.

On the way to New Albany to pick up Melinda Loveless, there was something especially titillating to talk about: Melinda wanted them to kill a little girl, a little girl none of the three of them had met. 'I didn't believe it,' Toni would say.

About that time Shanda Sharer was on her way home to her mother's apartment in New Albany from where, as usual, her father, Stephen, collected her and took her to his home in Jeffersonville where she was to stay the weekend. Shanda was helping him with the chores at supper time when there was a knock at the door of the modest single-storey house. She answered the door. 'Is Shanda in?' one of the two girls standing there asked. Her father, eavesdropping, thought it odd that the girls, in fact Toni Lawrence and Laurie Tackett, didn't even know Shanda.

'Oh, you're Shanda!' one of the girls said. 'Do you want to come to the mall with us? There's someone wants to see you.'

'Who?'

'Amanda. She says she's really got to see you. It's important.'

Shanda flushed. 'I can't. I'm not allowed to,' she said. And then, hoping her father couldn't hear: 'Why don't you come back later on. I'll try and slip out.'

Her father had heard enough to be annoyed. He was under the impression, he told Shanda when she returned to the kitchen, that the whole Amanda episode was over. They had a few words, but soon it was time for Shanda to leave for a party at a girl's house nearby.

She was home by eleven o'clock, and asked her father if the friend at whose house she had been could sleep over. 'No, Shanda,' he replied. 'I have to be up early to do some work on the house, and we've got some people coming tomorrow. It's not convenient.' Stephen Sharer will spend the rest of his life wishing he had said yes. If he had, probably nothing would have happened. Instead, he told Shanda she could stay up for half an hour watching television and he went off to bed.

At about four in the morning he woke and went to the kitchen. To his surprise, the back door was ajar. He shut and locked it, then checked on Shanda. She wasn't in the bedroom where she usually slept. He assumed she'd gone downstairs to sleep on a bed in the basement as she sometimes did, and went back to bed. When he and his wife, Sharon, woke at seven o'clock, he checked the basement.

'She's not here,' he called.

'Not there?' said Sharon.

'Oh God, maybe I locked her out when I shut the back door last night.'

The icy air hit him as he dashed outside. He peered through the frosted windows of the cars in the driveway. No sign of her. Back inside, he noticed her handbag and coat were still there. She never went out without her handbag. For the next couple of hours he and Sharon called every friend and neighbour they could think of, seeking news of Shanda, hoping she would walk in the door any minute. Finally Stephen faced up to making the hardest call of his life. 'Shanda's missing,' he told Jacqueline.

Donn Foley and his brother Ralph were up early that

morning. The sky was clear – a perfect morning for shooting a few quail. Their hunting dogs jumped eagerly into the back of the pick-up truck and stood, tongues lolling, heads into the wind as the brothers drove slowly down a gravel road some ten miles north of Madison.

'What's that there?' Donn said, pointing to a dark object about ten yards off the road in a soya bean field.

'Looks like a body, don't it?'

'Naw. Somebody fooling around. It's one of them blow-up dolls. What some people will do for a laugh!' he said as they climbed out of the truck to take a closer look.

'Oh God,' Donn said a moment later as they stood looking down at the charred object at the centre of a circle of blackened earth. To one side they noticed a half-melted plastic bottle. 'Better call the sheriff.'

Amanda Heavrin was shopping at the River Falls mall that day when she was paged over the public address system. When she picked up the emergency phone, it was Melinda. 'Listen, Shanda is dead,' she said. 'We've got to talk.'

'Amanda was crying on the phone,' a boy who was with her was to report. A short time later Melinda and Laurie arrived to pick Amanda up from the mall in the big grey Chevrolet.

'Dead? I don't believe it,' Amanda sobbed in the car. 'You're just trying to fool me.'

'Stop the car,' Melinda told Laurie. 'I'll show her.'

Melinda opened the boot. All Amanda could see was the blood on the floor.

Toni too couldn't stop talking about it. At a bowling alley in Madison that afternoon, she told a bunch of friends. Finally someone thought something should be done. A fifteen-year-old boy in the group later went to the police.

About that time Toni was arriving home. Her father, Clifton Lawrence, was surprised to see that she had her friend Hope Rippey and Hope's parents with her. 'Daddy,' she said, 'you're going to hate me.'

'She was crying so much,' Lawrence would say, 'I thought she was going to tell me she was pregnant. I guess that's the worst thing a father can think his daughter will tell him.'

It was Hope's parents who, having heard the story from their own daughter, told him what had happened. 'We've got to go to the police,' was Lawrence's instant reaction. 'There may be a chance she's still alive. We can't waste a minute.'

Hope's parents saw it differently. They had already spoken with a lawyer and had made an appointment to see him the following Monday. Meanwhile they were going to hide out with their daughter in a motel.

Sheriff's officers, who had been busy earlier collecting footprints, tyre tracks and the half-melted Pepsi bottle from the spot in the soya bean field where the body had been found, had just finished questioning the fifteen-year-old boy at close to 9 p.m. when Toni arrived with her parents. She was crying, Jefferson County Sheriff Buck Shipley would remember. Her story came out all jumbled in bits and pieces. 'It's hard to put into words what I felt when I learned what had happened,' said the sheriff.

In the reconstruction that follows, there is one fact we need to keep in front of us:

Shanda Sharer is twelve years old. A child.

Nearly all the lights are out in the Sharer house as the

grey Chev pulls up outside around midnight. Shanda, in spite of everything, intrigued and excited that Amanda wants to see her, has been waiting for the knock. She is at the back door in a second.

'Shall I bring my coat?'

'You won't need it,' says the older of the two girls, the one with the spiky hair. 'Amanda's in the car. You'll only be a few minutes. Hurry!' Shanda leaves the back door a little ajar, afraid of locking herself out. She reaches for the handle of the car's rear door, believing the girl inside is her friend. Then she realizes it's not Amanda.

'You get in the front,' the girl behind her says. By now the one with the spiky hair has moved around to the driver's door. The other girl pushes in behind Shanda, who finds herself wedged in the middle seat.

'Where's Amanda?'

'Not far,' says the driver, switching on the engine. 'You'll see her in a minute, don't worry.' As the car rounds the first corner she turns up the heavy metal on the radio.

Shanda feels hemmed in between the two. Maybe this wasn't wise.

Suddenly she feels her hair grabbed roughly from behind. 'Surprise!' Melinda Loveless, who has been hiding under a blanket in the rear seat, has her face close up to Shanda's. Something cold is against her throat. Shanda can smell Melinda's perfume, feel the softness of her hair against her cheek. There's nothing soft about Melinda's voice. It conveys pure malice: 'I guess you didn't know I was here, eh, sweetie pie? Thought you were going on a date with your dear Amanda!'

'Let me go home, please, Melinda. I promise . . .'

'You promise! You promised before. You promised

you'd stay away from her. But you can't, can you?'

'I never . . .'

'What did you two do? Did you kiss? Did you feel her up? Tell me!' Shanda felt the flat of the knife blade pressing harder against her throat.

'We didn't do nothing. Nothing! Melinda, please let me go. I'm sorry.'

'We got to teach you a little lesson first, Shanda. Just so you don't forget again.'

'Don't hurt me.'

'Oh, I'm not going to hurt you. Honest.'

The car stops. Shanda has never been here before. But the others know it well. It's a deserted building on the Utica Pike that the kids call the Witches' Castle. 'Get out,' says the driver, giving Shanda a shove. She falls sprawling on the rock-hard frozen earth.

In a second she feels herself pulled to her feet. 'Grab her other arm, Laurie,' says Melinda to the driver. Laurie grabs, then twists her arm up behind her back. Shanda cries out in pain.

It's dark inside the building, and one of the girls lights a match. The place smells of human excrement. 'See down there,' says Melinda, jerking Shanda in the direction of what appear to be basement stairs. 'You want us to leave you down there?'

'No, please, Melinda. Please,' she weeps.

'There's bones down there. Human bones. Yours are going to be next.'

'Oh, please, please.'

'What do you guys think?' Melinda asks the others. 'Shall we throw her down there and leave her?'

'Naw,' says Laurie. 'It's early. We can have lots of fun yet. Let's take her for a ride.'

Back at the car one of the girls pulls off Shanda's watch, her earrings and the ring on her finger, while another ties up her wrists and ankles. Melinda yanks her blonde hair, twisting her head around. 'I should cut your hair off, bitch. I know you just do it that way to look like Amanda. Get your ass in there!' Shanda feels the boot from behind, and tumbles into the back seat.

Shanda Sharer is twelve years old.

To Shanda it seems as if they are driving all night. For a second she allows herself to think of being home and safe in her father's house. But only for a second. 'Maybe we'll kill you,' Melinda is saying, flashing the knife blade in front of her eyes. 'Stop here, Laurie. This should be okay. You get out, and stop snivelling.'

They are on a dark, empty country road. When Laurie turns off the motor, the silence presses in like a wall. 'I'll stay in here,' the girl the others call Toni says.

Laurie is coming around from the other side of the car. Shanda's wrists and ankles are no longer tied. 'Get your pants off,' rasps Laurie.

'Oh, please, no.'

'Get them off.' In a few minutes Shanda is standing shivering in the snow wearing only her tee shirt and panties. She senses Laurie moving around behind her. Then quickly the girl's strong arms seize her from behind. 'Hit her, Melinda,' Laurie grunts. 'Hit her good.'

Shanda feels the air expelled from her stomach as if from an explosion as Melinda punches her. 'Oh, stop!' she gasps. 'I have asthma. I could die.'

'Die then.' Melinda holds Shanda's head and brings her knee up hard into the younger girl's face. She's seen them do that on wrestling shows on television. The blood gushes. Groggy, Shanda hardly knows what they're doing, only feels Laurie putting something rough around her neck. 'Melinda,' she cries. 'Don't let her do this to me. Help me.'

'Shut the fuck up,' Melinda tells Shanda.

Laurie is tightening the rope around the girl's neck. 'Grab it!' she cries. She and Melinda pull on the rope as Shanda's long, pale legs thresh in the snow and then are still. That's when Melinda gets out the knife again and stabs the girl in the neck.

'She's dead now for sure,' says Laurie. 'Give me a hand.' Together the girls lift the body, dump it in the boot and slam down the lid.

Shanda Sharer is twelve years old.

It's some time early in the morning when the grey Chev pulls into the Tackett driveway in Madison. 'Shhh!' Laurie says, letting them in. 'My parents are sleeping.' The girls are on a high now, giggling, joking as Laurie fetches a bottle of Pepsi.

Until they hear sounds from outside. Muffled screams and banging. 'I'll go check,' says Laurie. When she returns the noise has stopped. She'll say later that she put a blanket over Shanda and left the boot lid open so that she could escape. That's her story. When she comes back they notice blood on her that wasn't there before.

'Let me do your stones,' she says to Melinda. And when she tells Melinda's fortune, surprise, it shows it's all going to turn out well.

At one point Laurie and Melinda whisper together in the kitchen. 'Why don't you guys bed down for a while,' Laurie suggests to the other two. 'Me and Melinda are going country cruisin'.'

It's a bright, starry night as Laurie and Melinda cruise the back roads. But when they stop every once in a while, it's not to admire the velvety sky. It's because Shanda is screaming again. They've got out the tyre iron now, a heavy steel bar. They give her a few whacks with it, then she's quiet for a while. Only once does she speak, and then a single word: 'Mommy.'

'Why don't we leave the trunk open so she'll make a run for it,' Melinda suggests. 'Then we can run her down.' Looking at her, though, they decide she doesn't have the strength to run.

Then one of them – we'll never know which one because they never tell – has an idea. Shanda is in a foetal position. One of them pulls down her panties at the back, and shoves the tyre iron home. We can't – don't want to – imagine Shanda's screams. They must echo yet in that cold Indiana countryside,

Shanda Sharer is twelve years old.

Finally Shanda, covered in blood, her eyes rolled back with only the whites showing, seems as dead as anyone could be, and Laurie and Melinda come home like dogs from the hunt, their hands, their clothes smeared with blood. 'Where've you been? What happened to the little girl?' one of the other two asks, just waking up.

'Don't you worry,' Laurie tells her. 'You just had a nightmare. There was no little girl.'

It's a fiction, of course. They know they have a body on their hands. 'We'll burn her at the dump out back,' says Laurie. They're just trying to light the fire when a window opens. 'Laurie, what's going on out there? Don't you know it's only four in the morning!'

'Nothing, Mom. You go back to bed.' Peggy Tackett has no plans to go back to bed. What does Laurie mean, bringing all these girls here in the middle of the night? Mother and daughter argue. 'For Chrissake!' Laurie grabs up the two-litre Pepsi bottle they've been drinking from and storms out. 'I've got a different plan,' she tells them as they all get into the car.

At that time of the morning, the guy at the Clark self-service filling station on the hill above town isn't paying much attention anyway. So sure they spill half the petrol trying to get it in the narrow neck of the bottle. He doesn't care. It's just money to him. (Shanda's parents are now considering suing the oil company for selling petrol in an improper container.)

They drive about ten miles north of town, pull off into the soya bean field, lift the body from the boot and lay it on the ground. Only it's not a body. Shanda is semi-conscious, trying to say something. 'Pour the fucking gas on her!' Laurie tells Hope, who is hesitating. The girl splashes it on her legs, her tee shirt, but stops short at her blood-smeared hair. Laurie, smoking a cigarette, kneels beside Shanda. 'What you wanna say, baby?' she asks. 'You wanna see me light the match? Okay.' Is that the way it happens, or does the cigarette start the fire? There will be conflicting accounts.

Perhaps it's panic that makes them all jump into the car and drive off, leaving the flaming pyre in the field. 'Shit!' exclaims Hope, at the wheel, as the bottom of the car hits the ground, damaging the muffler. 'Wait,' says Melinda when they've driven just a short way. 'What if she doesn't burn. We got to make sure.'

Hope turns the car around. This time, while the rest stay in the car, it's Melinda who pours the rest of the petrol on the body, throwing down the empty bottle. She's laughing as she gets back in. 'She's out of my life. I'm glad she's gone,' she says. 'Now if we all stick together, we'll be okay.'

The dying of Shanda Sharer, since the time she was picked up, has taken some eight hours. Now it's done. 'I'm hungry,' says Laurie. 'Anybody want breakfast?' There are only a few people at McDonald's in Madison as the four take their orders to a table. Laurie has ordered sausage and eggs. 'Hey,' she says, poking a well-browned sausage with her fork, 'that looks like Shanda.' And they laugh.

Shanda Sharer is twelve years old.

Along the strip in Madison the news, which some teenagers had heard from Toni Lawrence even before the police knew, was greeted with a thrill of horror – and a profound awe. In the days that followed, kids would make their way to the famous soya bean field, duck under the yellow police tapes and stand around the circle of blackened earth, smoking joints and fancying they could still smell the burning flesh. It was, they said, 'a pretty spooky buzz'.

'Ain't this a trip, man?' a teenager named Gary Williams said to Richard Grant, a writer for *The Independent*. 'We're standing on the exact same spot where a girl was beaten, raped with a crowbar and caught on fire. Unfuckingbelievable! She was a nice-looking girl too, man. She was going to be a babe when she growed up.

'I could maybe see Laurie Tackett doing something like this – she is one weird bitch – but I can't believe Hope and goddamn Toni Lawrence went along with it. Hell, Hope ain't but ninety pounds soaking wet, and Toni Lawrence, she's just a little kid. They was all just kids, man.'

It would be almost a year later and the shops along the

strip would all be playing 'Joy to the World' when Melinda Loveless, the first of the four, came before Judge Ted Todd at the handsome old Madison courthouse. By then citizens of the town had grown used to the big TV station vans turning up with every new legal development, although the older people could never accept the notoriety that now attached to their bucolic little community. 'If that poor girl had been killed in New York instead of Madison, Indiana,' Donna Jackson, the clerk in the courthouse, would complain as yet another out-of-town reporter would arrive to examine the grisly documents in the case, 'none of you fellows would have batted an eyelid. We've got a nice little town here, and I think it's a shame that it takes something like this to get us noticed.'

The Jefferson County Prosecutor, Guy Townsend, had anguished long over what approach to take. Under Indiana law, he could have sought death sentences for the four. 'But you have to be realistic,' he said. No one had been executed in Indiana in thirty-one years, juries don't like imposing the death penalty, and with only Toni Lawrence's testimony to go on, it was quite possible that by blaming each other, the others could so cloud the issue that juries might set them free. In the end, Laurie and Melinda agreed to plead guilty to murder, arson and criminal confinement, charges carrying a maximum sentence of sixty years, in return for the state not seeking the death penalty. Toni Lawrence, after agreeing to testify against the others, pleaded guilty to criminal confinement, a charge carrying a maximum sentence of twenty years, while only Hope Rippey pleaded not guilty to murder.

Even if the results were a foregone conclusion, with

only the sentences to be determined, the curious who crowded the courtroom for a look at the notorious girl killers during the hearings in December and January were rewarded with unforgettable images of the gothic and the gruesome.

Like Dr George Nichols, Kentucky's medical examiner, testifying that Shanda had been alive when she was doused with petrol and set alight. The cause of death was burns and smoke inhalation, but her legs had also been cut and she had been severely beaten. She had been sodomized with the tyre iron, which had penetrated about four inches into the colon, he said. Even then, with careful surgery and a temporary colostomy, the damaged blood vessels could have been repaired. Shanda would have lived.

Like Crystal Wathen, describing how, as she drove around with her friends, Laurie and Melinda, a few hours after the murder, Laurie pulled out the tyre iron and started beating the dashboard with it to show how she had hit Shanda. 'She stuck it in my face and told me to smell it,' Crystal said. She told too how, a few months before the murder, Melinda had asked her how she would dispose of a body if she killed someone. 'I'd put it in with some leaves and burn it,' Crystal advised her friend.

Like Prosecutor Townsend, lighting a match, holding the flame in front of Laurie Tackett and asking, 'Isn't it true you were going to show that match to Shanda before you set her on fire?'

'No!' was the angry response. She had only knelt down holding a lit cigarette and was trying to talk to Shanda when 'the fire just went up'.

'What were you going to say?' asked Townsend, going down on his knees as if he were leaning over a body.

'I don't know. I wanted to get her to talk to me.'

'Some famous last words – is that what you wanted?' he asked with deadly irony.

As Townsend had expected, each of the girls tried to blame the others. Both Melinda and Laurie's lawyers called psychologists who swore straight-faced that each of the girls was a follower rather than a leader. And much of the life-and-death testimony still seemed influenced by lovers' spats and infatuations.

'What did you say to Melinda when you gave her that long embrace by the water cooler [during court recess]?' Townsend asked Carrie Pope, who had just given damaging testimony against her one-time friend, Laurie.

'I told her that I loved her and she would always have a place in my heart.'

'What else did you say?' Townsend persisted.

Carrie hesitated. 'I told her I hope Laurie fries for this.'

Spectators could only be intrigued by the way the carefully created images of the girls as submissive victims, who just went along with what was happening and who were now desperately remorseful, seemed so often at odds with the evidence.

'I did what I did because I was scared of [Laurie],' Melinda testified.

'You say you were afraid of her,' said Laurie's lawyer, Ellen O'Connor. 'Yet you climbed in the same bed with her and that's where you were when the police arrested you!'

Turning to Shanda's parents in the courtroom, Melinda said in a breaking voice: 'I'm so sorry. If I could trade places with Shanda, I would,' and then collapsed sobbing in her lawyer's arms.

Two inmates confined with Melinda in the county jail

said she revelled in her notoriety, gave autographs, and kept a picture in her cell of Shanda under which she'd written, 'So young, so pretty, had to die early.'

When Laurie described the torture and killing of Shanda, Melinda moaned and cried out, 'It's sickening.'

'Poor thing,' came a voice from the body of the court.

In an unusual, if somewhat oblique defence, Melinda's lawyers put on the stand two of her grown-up sisters, who testified that, as children, they had been sexually molested by their father, although they admitted they had never seen him molest Melinda. As a result of their evidence, the father, Larry Loveless, was brought back from Florida, where he was then living, and charged with child sex abuse.

Laurie too claimed she had been sexually abused and raped, although the boy she accused of raping her gave evidence that she had consented to sex, and there was no other evidence to support her abuse allegations.

Only Toni Lawrence's claim of remorse seemed to hold some credibility: she had tried to commit suicide in August by taking antidepressant pills in her jail cell. Lloyd Trotter, a Louisville teenager, said that the night Shanda was abducted, Toni Lawrence and Hope Rippey spent some time in a car with him and a boy called Jimmy outside the slam dance. Toni told them that Melinda and Laurie were going to kill someone.

'We'll take you home if you like,' he offered. Toni accepted initially, but Hope refused, so Toni returned with her to the dance.

Toni, slight and bird-like in the witness box, a girl whom the husky Laurie had dismissed at one point as 'a prep', claimed that during the death drive, when she was often crying, she had told the others to take Shanda

home. They told her to shut up. But, as with Melinda and
Laurie, Townsend made the point that there were any
number of opportunities for her to notify someone of
what was going on. She phoned a boyfriend at one point
that night, and went into a shop to buy something. But
she'd said nothing.

Who was the real instigator? Michael Quinlan, who
followed the case for more than a year and who attended
all the hearings for the Louisville *Courier-Journal*, told
me, 'I don't think we will ever know the entire truth. In
my opinion, Melinda intended to scare Shanda. But then
Laurie Tackett took over. Tackett had a coldness in her.
She's very unemotional. There's a Charles Manson look
in her eyes. I think she saw in Shanda all the things she
never was and never could be.'

When Shanda's mother, Jacqueline Vaught, took the
stand at the final hearing, her patience was exhausted. 'I
have seen three girls lie and put on acts that are worthy of
an Oscar,' she said. 'I've heard lawyers cry child abuse
and rape and try to persuade everyone that these girls are
all victims. The victims here are Shanda and her family.'

There was some small consolation for the family when
Circuit Judge Todd gave all three girls the maximum
sentence available to him: sixty years each for Laurie and
Melinda, twenty years for Toni. The two with the longer
sentences must serve thirty years before they are released,
and Toni, after being held for a year in jail, could be
released when she is twenty-five.

There was to be a final footnote. In June 1993, six
months after the fate of the other girls had been settled,
Hope Rippey appeared before Judge Jeanne Jourdan.
Originally Hope's lawyer had intended her to plead not
guilty. Hence the delay. In the interval she had decided to

plead guilty to the same charges as the other girls. It wasn't surprising: she had admitted to the police that she had been the one who poured the petrol over Shanda on the first occasion.

By the time of Hope's appearance in court, it seemed impossible to imagine that any further horrors could be piled on top of what was already known. It was not so. Hope, the court was told, had admitted to the police that when she and the others opened the boot the final time to get Shanda out, the little girl sat up and was rocking herself and moaning, Indian style. Why did Hope pour the petrol on her? 'I felt she was already as good as dead,' she replied.

Prosecutor Townsend pointed out too that Hope, more than anyone, had been given a chance to save Shanda's life. It was she who had gone up to the Sharer house with Laurie to fetch Shanda to the car on the night of the murder. Laurie had even left her there for a few moments on her own. It would have been the easiest thing in the world for Hope to warn Shanda. But no warning was given.

Hope wept as Judge Jourdan sentenced her to sixty years in prison, with ten years suspended and ten years' probation. If Hope is an old age pensioner by the time she gets out, the ten years' probation seems academic. In fact like the others, she will only serve half her sentence before being eligible for release. That could see her on the street again by the time she's forty.

Which leaves begging the question: Why would four teenage girls, living in 'the ideal small town', none of them in trouble with the law before, indulge in an orgy of violence that would horrify even those hardened to big city crime?

There are many answers, but one, it seems to me, goes to the heart of this particular crime. In all the self-serving psychological flummery heard in the Madison courtroom, one phrase stands out. Psychologist Eric Engum, testifying for Laurie, said that the murder had the characteristics of 'sharks in a feeding frenzy'.

For some elaboration, I called on Charles Patrick Ewing, a forensic psychologist and law professor at the State University of New York, in Buffalo, who, since the publication of his book, *Kids Who Kill*, has become America's most frequently quoted expert on child killers. Murders by girls, he said, are still extremely rare, but increasing. In 1991, the latest year for which figures are available, 247 out of 4,335 teenage murders in America were committed by girls.

Most commonly, he said, girls kill family members, and abuse is generally the reason. They also rarely kill unaided, said Dr Ewing. A common pattern is for one girl to assault the victim, at which another pitches in, each topping the other – until the victim lies dead. Occult practices, such as witchcraft, are also a not unusual feature of such murders. He sees more violence among girls than used to be the case. 'Girls are becoming more like boys,' he said. 'It seems to me the goal of society should be to feminize boys instead.'

For Shanda's family, it's too late for explanations. During the sentencing hearing for Melinda, Shanda's mother showed the judge videotapes of her daughter growing up. 'Listen to her laughter,' said Jacqueline Vaught. 'Her laughter was something we cherished.' At Shanda's funeral the family was not able to say a proper goodbye, she said, because the coffin was closed. 'She was so mutilated you couldn't tell she was a human being. She

90

had no face. We couldn't put clothes on her, so we covered her with a blanket of roses. She would have wanted something pretty. Shanda was so pretty.'

Her death has left a void in Jacqueline's life: 'I used to have a reason to come home every night from work – someone to cook for, someone to clean clothes for. Now there's no one to kiss good night. I want her home for Christmas, but there are no presents for her under my tree. I don't think there's anything worse than burying your own child.'

Shanda's father, Stephen Sharer, had anticipated the worst when, the evening of the day Shanda had gone missing, the police came asking for his daughter's dental records. Now, he said, he feels a pain inside every time he sees a school bus, realizing his daughter is never on it. 'My mother said it well. She says when she gets up in the morning she's one day closer to seeing Shanda in Heaven.'

Several weeks after Shanda's funeral, her mother, clearing out her daughter's bedroom cupboard, found a shoebox on which Shanda had written: 'For my eyes only. Please do not open.'

It contained all the letters sent to her by Amanda Heavrin. 'She would compliment Shanda and tell her how pretty her hair was and how pretty her clothes were,' said Jacqueline. 'You could just see how manipulative she was, and how she was just working her and reeling her in.' In the letters, Amanda was soon writing, 'I think it's okay to touch. Have you ever touched another girl?' and then she wrote that she was afraid Melinda was going to hurt Shanda. 'It was all there in the letters,' said Jacqueline, a bright, intelligent woman who, at the time of writing, had been unable to return to her administrative job with a barge firm because of her emotional turmoil. 'It was everything.'

And, Jacqueline told Michael Quinlan, there was one thing she wanted to say to other parents: 'Parents blind themselves. They don't want to believe that this could happen to their child, or that their child could ever be subjected to this. Well, I'm here to tell you, as a mother who has had her child murdered, brutally murdered by girls, it did happen. And it could happen to your child.'

THE BAD BOYS
OF ABERTILLERY

They were strung across the road like a flock of rather scruffy birds of paradise, their satiny pink, apple-green and black nylon tracksuits catching the late afternoon sun. I'd put their ages at between eight and ten, and this Saturday afternoon the boys of Abertillery, one of the legendary coal towns of the Welsh valleys, were relieving their boredom by throwing stones at a disused industrial building. As I slowed the car, I heard the unmistakable sound of shattering glass, followed by laughter. They moved hardly at all from the middle of the road as the car approached, looking insolently at me with expressions that said, 'So what are you going to do about it!' The message was clear: if I stopped to tell them off, I could expect a smashed windscreen.

Harold Jones would have had nothing to do with the modern-day bad boys of Abertillery. The Abertillery where he grew up was a gritty, hard-working town where life was governed by the steam whistle summoning the men to work in the pits, and where children were expected to earn their keep as soon as they were able. It was a town where hymns echoed up and down the valley from the numerous chapels on Sunday morning, and where school for many was seen as the golden first step to a career in the law or the ministry – callings ideally suited to the silver Welsh tongue. It was a town proud to produce a lad like Harold whom his schoolmaster would describe as 'an exemplary boy, honest, clean-living, clean-minded, truthful and,' the teacher added with a tiny inward shudder, 'never familiar with the girls.' Breaking windows? Harold wouldn't have dreamt of it. In the little spare time he had, he enjoyed reading a good book, or practising on the organ his doting parents had bought for him. Which just goes to show how misleading appearances can be.

I have included the story of Harold Jones to show again that juveniles who murder are not necessarily the products of broken homes and dysfunctional families; they are not simply hell-raisers from hideous big city housing estates or products of drug-scarred American black ghettos. And to show too that the past was not Camelot, that even in a tight-knit Welsh mining community, where social cohesion reached in the early part of this century a level unthinkable today, hideous crimes could happen. It was, of course, because the people of Abertillery put such faith in their town's solid values that Harold Jones was able to fool them for so long.

Come with me to Abertillery on the morning of 5 February 1921. The grimy air is filled with the sweet, insidious smell of coal fires as children fetch scuttles of coal – every miner gets a free supply – from the sheds behind the grim terraced houses that line the mountainside. Down in the town, at 9 Earl Street, Freda Burnell, who is eight, is being a very good girl. It's Saturday, so no school. But Freda has already been to the barn not far away with the shiny metal milk can to buy milk, and now she's amusing herself drawing on her blackboard with coloured chalks, pausing now and then to wipe away a mistake with her handkerchief.

'Go down the corn shop for me, there's a love,' says her father soon after nine o'clock. 'I need some spice [a food additive] for the chickens and a bag of grit. I'll give you a penny when you get back,' he promises.

Freda slips the handful of change her father has given her into her pocket and draws her wrap around her against the chilly February morning fog. Mortimers', the corn shop, is only a few minutes' walk away. The bell jangles as she opens the door. A few moments later Harold Jones, fifteen, comes up the stairs from the kitchen below, wiping his hands after fetching coal. 'Hullo, Freda,' he says. 'What can I get you?'

'A bag of poultry spice, please, Harold,' she says, and gives him the twopence-halfpenny. 'Oh, I nearly forgot. My da wants a bag of grit too.'

A few minutes later, the Mortimers' ten-year-old son, Frankie, sees Freda coming out of the shop. With the exception of her murderer, he is the last one to see her alive.

When Freda had not come home within half an hour, her parents quickly became alarmed. Her mother, Susan, went straight to Mortimers'.

'Yes, she was in here,' Harold said in reply to her question. 'She came in about quarter past nine, Mrs Burnell. She bought some spice and then she said she wanted some grit. I told her we didn't sell it by the bag any more. We only sell it loose. So she said she was going home to ask you about it before buying some. Didn't you see her?'

'No. When did she leave here?'

'Oh, it must have been about twenty past nine.'

By that afternoon parties of men were being organized to search the woods and the mountainside for miles around. When it became dark, miners' safety lamps dotted the mountainside like flickering stars.

It was only the next morning that Edward Lewis, on his way at twenty past seven to his job caring for pit ponies underground, noticed what he thought was a bundle of clothing in a back lane about fifty yards from the corn shop. As he came up to it, he saw to his horror that it was the little girl's body. Her arms and legs were secured with string while her wrap had been used to gag her. Her clothes were dry and there was little sign of blood.

The police surgeon, Dr Thomas E. Lloyd, following a post-mortem, gave the cause of death as nervous shock and exhaustion. Freda's underclothing had been interfered with, and there had been an attempt at rape. She had been choked and then stunned with a blow to the forehead from a blunt instrument, but neither of these attacks had been sufficient to cause death. The doctor estimated she had died about 1.30 p.m. on Saturday, although the attack would have taken place earlier.

That such a terrible crime could occur in broad daylight in the centre of a busy town seemed incomprehensible. The murder caused a sensation throughout South Wales, and within a couple of days Scotland Yard's Chief Detective Inspector Albert Helden, accompanied by an assistant (and to be followed shortly by two other Yard officers), arrived from London to take charge of the investigation. It seems, though, to have been a surprisingly inept operation.

Not until 11 February – six days after the murder – did Henry Duggan, whose back garden abutted the large shed in which Henry Mortimer kept his prize fowl, recall a significant incident the morning of the murder. He'd just finished his morning cigarette when he heard a short scream coming from the direction of the shed. It sounded like a child, and the sound ended abruptly, as if the scream had been choked off. He stood outside the boarded-up window of the shed, listening, and when he heard no more, thought nothing of it. He had completely forgotten the incident until his mother, who had also heard the sound, reminded him of it. Amazingly, two other women at that point recalled the scream coming from the shed.

Chaff – the husk of the grain – had been found in Freda's clothing and even in her vagina. Yet it was only now, with Duggan's revelation, that the police thought to search Mortimers' shed where chaff was stored. 'Hello, what's this?' said Chief Inspector Helden, stooping down as he entered the shed. Sticking out perhaps an inch from under a box was the corner of a white handkerchief. Freda's sister, Ivy, would say it was hers, although she'd loaned it to Freda. It had holes where Freda customarily chewed her handkerchiefs and, most telling, it still bore the coloured chalk marks where the girl had used it to wipe her blackboard.

Whether or not the Yard men had suspected Harold Jones prior to this discovery, he was now certainly the chief suspect. The reason: it was his job to unlock the shed every morning around nine thirty to feed his employer's prize chickens. But when Helden tried to pin down the exact time when Harold would have had a chance to attack the girl, he found there were witnesses to

account for the boy's movements for almost the whole of
the crucial hour during which the attack must have
occurred.

It went like this: Harold had awoken at about quarter
to nine in the bed he shared with a lodger, William
Greenway, in his parents' home on Darran Road, high
above the town. By five past nine he was at work, and was
just getting the coal for the stove in the shop when Dolly
Hathaway, the Mortimers' maid, told him there was a
customer upstairs – Freda.

Henry Mortimer was in a fluster that morning, due
to leave the house by five past ten to be in time to
catch a train down the valley so that he could be a
judge at a poultry show. He came clattering down the
stairs at, he estimated, nine seventeen, and glimpsed
Harold in the shop as he went on down to the kitchen to
have his breakfast. Mortimer, his wife and the maid
remembered hearing Harold's heavy boots scuffing the
floor overhead as they ate. By nine forty Mortimer was
dashing up the stairs again to get his collar from the room
behind the shop, and after that he went upstairs to
retrieve his wallet before leaving the house at five past ten
as planned. Each time he passed the shop, he saw Harold
in there.

But there was an inconsistency: Harold at first insisted
he had never left the shop during the crucial period. But
Mrs Mortimer and the maid heard him shout downstairs
to say he'd left the twopence-halfpenny he'd collected
from Freda on the shelf. Why tell them if he wasn't
leaving the shop? Oh yes, recalled Harold, he had after all
slipped out for a few minutes to buy some cigarettes.

Chief Inspector Helden encountered an equally puzzling set of facts when he spoke to some of Harold's

friends about the events of Saturday night, a few hours after the murder. Ted Clissett said he and Harold had gone to visit Freda's parents, apparently for news of the search, and had then gone to Ted's house where, oddly to our ears, Harold had sat reading a book for a while. At ten twenty he'd announced, 'I'm going home now,' and bidden them good night. A little later Ted's father, obviously a late-night gambler, asked Ted to go over to Harold's house to borrow a pack of playing cards. On the way, to his surprise, Ted met Harold on the street.

'Where've you been?' he asked.

'I went to the fish and chip shop,' replied Harold.

They ended up at the Clissett house again, where Harold suddenly realized he had forgotten to lock up Mortimers' shed after feeding the chickens earlier. 'Don't tell anyone or I will get into a row from Mr Mortimer,' he urged.

Now this begins to look like an alibi party, because Harold asked not only Ted to accompany him to lock up the shed, but two other friends, Levi Meyrick and Alf Gravenor. 'Come on, Ted,' he said, urging his friend to go into the darkened shed ahead of him. Afraid of the dark? More likely he wanted his friend, once he'd lit a match, to see and remember that there was no body in the shed. If we have the feeling that the little scene is being stage-managed, there is more. Out in the open again, Harold led Ted (the other two boys had left) to the top of a little 'tump' or hill, where his foot in the darkness just happened to hit a rolled-up sack. 'Might be useful for your dad,' he said, handing it to Ted. Mr Clissett was an upholsterer.

Thinking over his little staged drama later, Harold must

have had second thoughts. He recovered the sack from Ted, saying it could have been the one in which Freda's body had been carried, and told his friend Levi, 'Keep the shed [incident] from the police.'

Chief Inspector Helden, understandably, began to lose his Scotland Yard cool trying to sort out the Welsh mist and fairy tales – especially after Greenway, the Jones' lodger, swore that Harold had been in bed the whole of Saturday night, even at a time when his friends said he was performing his little lock-up ritual at Mortimer's shed.

'How would you like a night in the cells?' Helden said, glaring at Ted Clissett as the boy desperately improvised his story.

'I don't mind whether I do or not,' Ted answered impudently.

'Then how would you like to stand in the dock with Harold Jones?' roared the exasperated detective. Heavy-handed police methods would help to swing public opinion in Harold's favour.

Because, make no mistake, by the time Harold was arrested in April and charged with the murder, he was nothing short of a local hero. With the South Wales *Argus* firmly in his corner, Harold was riding a wave of public support, and there was hardly anyone in Abertillery who did not believe he was merely being used as a scapegoat by bumbling London detectives too damned incompetent to find the real killer.

Harold's father, Philip Jones, was a miner, out of work at the time, but the family was not without distinction: Harold's great-grandfather, another Philip, had been a pioneer socialist in the coal valleys in the last century. In no time at all a defence fund was got up for Harold, and four miners who couldn't really afford it pledged to pay for a first-class defence lawyer, a promise that would eventually cost the four a total of £550 – a huge sum in those days.

When Harold appeared in the dock at the Monmouth Assizes in June, it was not hard to see why crowds outside the Shire Hall had cheered his arrival. Radiating confidence, a hearty-looking, solidly built boy in a navy blue serge suit and with, the *Argus* reported, 'a bright and ruddy complexion', he was no one's idea of a pervert and a killer. If there was one moment that crystallized the whole trial it came on the second day when, as Harold was brought into the courtroom, his mother, Nellie, at the back, cried, 'Hullo, son!' The boy swung around and waved: 'Hullo Mam!' It was highly irregular, but it was too late for the judge, Mr Justice Bray, to intervene. There was, it was reported, a lump in many a throat. Not least, perhaps, in those of the jurors, five of whom were women.

The defence counsel, J. B. Matthews, must have suspected that he only had to provide mildly plausible explanations for some of the damaging evidence in order for popular sentiment to vindicate Harold Jones. The handkerchief was a ticklish question: if Harold alone had access to the shed, and Freda had been murdered there, then his guilt was hard to avoid. Matthews' answer: on a visit to the shed with one of the prosecuting counsel, he casually tossed a woman's handkerchief through the window, arguing later that that was exactly what the real murderer had done some time after the murder in order to cast suspicion on Harold. Never mind that evidence showed the window had been boarded up at the time of the murder – only a small seed of doubt was needed.

The sentiments of Mr and Mrs Mortimer and their maid, Dolly, called as Crown witnesses, were clearly with Harold. Was this, asked the prosecutor, C. F. Vachell, showing Henry Mortimer the controversial sack in which the body may have been moved, one of his sacks? 'It's not like the ones we use – it's not strong enough to hold corn,' replied the corn merchant.

'It would hold chaff, though?'

'I don't know, sir.'

But young Frankie Mortimer, the last to see Freda alive, reported a curious incident. When he had gone with Harold to the shed to get bags of potatoes later that morning, Harold had insisted that Frankie wait outside while he, Harold, went to get them. His excuse was that boys might steal their handcart. It had never been a concern before.

Matthews' best stroke was putting Harold in the witness box. Perfectly self-assured, the boy answered every question promptly and with every sign of sincerity. How had he come to leave the shed unlocked that Saturday? He had forgotten to feed the chickens earlier, went to feed them at about four o'clock, and, thinking he heard some boys calling for him, had left the shed open, leaving the key inside.

'You need not laugh,' he told Vachell several times when his answers inspired raised eyebrows. 'I am telling you the truth.'

But Harold didn't mind inspiring a laugh now and then. 'Someone,' said Vachell, referring to the sounds Harold made overhead in the shop, 'said you walked like an elephant.'

'No,' smiled Harold, 'like a carthorse. I had nailed boots.'

It was Harold's unflappable equanimity, Matthews said in his summing-up, that indicated a clear conscience.

No, argued the prosecutor, 'It indicates a heartless callousness.' The prosecution theory was that Jones had told Freda to go to the shed where bags of grit were kept, had followed her, and had been attempting to rape her when she screamed. He had stifled her cries with her wrap then struck her with an axe handle found in the shed. Then, believing he had killed her, he returned to the shop showing 'a wonderful unconcern'. It was after he left Clissett's that evening, in the darkness and with the streets empty, theorized Vachell, that Harold had carried Freda's body in a sack across the street and dumped it in the lane.

If the jury were troubled by inconsistencies in Harold's story, the judge gave them an out. 'In considering the boy's evidence, you are entitled to make allowances,' he told them. 'Even innocent people will sometimes tell lies to avoid some things coming out. You should not reject his evidence merely because he told lies on certain points.'

The jury needed no further encouragement. 'Not guilty!' announced the foreman, Tom Morgan, after they'd pondered their verdict for eighty minutes. Judge Bray threatened to lock up anyone who cheered in the courtroom, but once outside, Harold was mobbed by jubilant crowds. Taken to a nearby hotel, the enthusiasm on the street was so great he finally had to come out on the balcony and cry, 'I thank you all.'

Harold's journey home in a hired charabanc was a triumph, with frequent stops so that he could receive the congratulations from well-wishers. When the bus finally lurched into Abertillery, the streets were hung with bunting and locals put on a grand dinner for him and his parents at a local hotel. And so Harold Jones came home to 10 Darran Road, the little terraced house high above the town, and back to the thing, he told everyone, he had missed the most during his long months in prison: soon, passers-by heard once again the strains of 'There is a Green Hill Far Away' coming from Harold's harmonium. He was also, he said, planning to write his life story in order to help defray the defence costs. The story, though, was far from over.

It is a glorious evening just two weeks later, a blessed coolness creeping up the mountain after a sweltering day. At 4 Darran Road, eleven-year-old Florence Little, whom everyone calls Florrie, is finishing her supper. 'Can I go out to play, Mam?' she asks.

'Fair play, you've studied hard, love,' says Elsie Little. Elsie and her husband, Arthur, a miner, have high hopes that Florrie, the oldest of their four children, will win a county school scholarship. 'But don't stay out long, mind, it will be dark soon.' It's just after nine as Florrie, a pretty little girl with fair hair, goes out to toss her ball and to play hopscotch on the road with Flossie Jones, Harold's young sister.

At the Jones house, three doors up, it's all quiet. Philip and Nellie have gone out shopping and visiting relatives. Earlier, a friend, William Wearfield, had found Harold playing the organ; they were soon joined by Ted Clissett. Harold had sent Flossie to buy them two packets of Woodbine cigarettes, then, as his friends left at about nine, had said, 'I think I'll turn in.'

At nine twenty he tells Flossie: 'Ask Florrie to come here, will you?'

The two girls climb the short flight of steps together and are rewarded with a few pence to buy a bottle of pop. When they return from the shop, Flossie stays only a moment before leaving by the front door on her way to find her parents at her aunt's. Florrie goes out of the back door and up the steep slope of the garden to the lane behind. 'Have you got those scissors?' a neighbour hears Harold asking her. Mrs Little had borrowed his mother's scissors a day or two earlier and hadn't returned them. 'Yes, I do,' she replies. Then Florrie disappears. It was, one of the newspapers would say, 'as if the earth swallowed her up'.

Arthur Little, Florrie's father, had waved to his daughter in the street a little earlier, but when Elsie checked at nine fifty, there was no sign of her. 'Where's our Florrie?' she asked Lil, a younger daughter.

'She went into the Joneses with Flossie,' replied the girl.

Elsie was startled to find the Joneses' door locked. It was almost unheard of to lock the door in the daytime. She knocked – and got no reply. She knocked again. She would estimate it was two minutes before the door opened and Harold stood there wearing a pair of blue trousers, his braces tied around the waist. He was naked from the waist up and carried a military-style wire hairbrush.

'Sorry, I was having a bath,' he said.

'Have you seen Florrie?' asked Elsie.

'No, she's not here,' he replied. 'She did come in, but she went out through the back door.'

'Perhaps she's home by now,' Elsie said, turning to leave.

'Oh, how's the little boy, Mrs Little?' Harold asked. The Littles' six-year-old son was in bed with concussion after falling over the steps of a soup kitchen to which he'd gone for food – surely the ultimate hard-luck tale.

'He's getting better, slowly,' she answered.

At half past ten, Harold's parents, his sister Flossie and the lodger, William Greenway, all arrived home at the same time. They too were surprised to find the front door locked, and Greenway had to knock before Harold, still bare-chested, let them in.

'My shirt fell in the tub, Mam,' he explained.

Nellie was in a jovial mood. 'Well, if you want a clean one, my boy, you'll have to have one of mine!' she said.

'Come on, Mam, let me have a clean shirt,' he pleaded.

'All right then,' she said, giving in. 'But you'll have to have an old one because I want to keep the other one for Sunday. Fell in the tub! I never heard such nonsense.'

At that moment Elsie Little arrived at the door. 'Our Florrie's missing. I don't know what's happened to her,' she said.

It was Freda Burnell all over again. The men scattered over the darkening mountain, their little safety lamps bobbing among the bracken. Harold was a confident presence among them all. 'We'd better tell the police,' he said. 'Bloodhounds are what we need.'

Alongside his father, he scoured the mountainside until, at 3.30 a.m., they returned home bone-tired, had some food and went to bed. Not for one moment during that long night, Philip Jones would say, did he think his son was involved.

Someone else made a quicker connection. Informed at 11.50 p.m. that the little girl was missing, Police Superintendent Henry Lewis, who had taken a leading part in the Freda Burnell case, at 2 a.m. ordered an officer to keep a continuous watch on the Jones house.

It was at quarter past eight that morning that Superintendent Lewis arrived with Constable Wilfred Cox and told Philip Jones that they wished to search the house. 'Come in,' said Jones. 'We have nothing to hide.' The idea that a little girl, dead or alive, could be hidden in a small terraced house occupied by five people seemed, on the face of it, ludicrous.

Heavy police boots tramped from room to tiny room, and then up the narrow stairs. It took only moments to check the wardrobes, and under the beds. The two policemen, accompanied by Philip Jones, were just coming downstairs again when Lewis exclaimed, 'What's that?' He was pointing to the ceiling above the landing. It was quite certain – there were smears, perhaps blood stains, around the tiny trapdoor leading to the attic. 'We must search up there,' said Lewis.

A fragile-looking rush-seat chair was fetched from one of the bedrooms, and Cox climbed up gingerly, steadying himself on the banister. 'Looks as if the wall up here has just been washed,' said the constable. With Lewis holding him, he drew himself up through the small aperture. In a moment he called down, 'I've found the body.'

Florrie Little was lying on her side on the rafters, her right arm extended like a tiny Statue of Liberty. The upper part of her body and her head were covered with an old army shirt, the sleeves of which had been tied around her neck. She was still wearing the blue dress with a white bodice, the black shoes and three-quarter-length socks in which she'd gone out to play. A long ribbon had been tied around her body under the arms.

'I got up on the chair,' Lewis would say, 'and the body

107

was lowered into my arms. I placed it on the floor. It was in a terrible state, covered with blood. And I observed that the throat had been cut.'

If the two policemen were horrified, Jones felt his whole life slip away. Out of the emptiness inside him, he said gruffly, 'I'll fetch my boy.'

He found Harold playing down the road with some friends. 'Sonny, come here,' he called.

'What's up, Dad?'

'They have found a body in our house.'

Harold showed no surprise. He looked at his father with his usual frank expression. 'I never done it, Dad,' he said.

The time for pretence was past. There was anger in his father's voice now. 'You or me will have the blame for this, boy. Now come up to the house and face it.'

As Harold came into the kitchen, his mother fought to control her tears. 'Be brave, my son,' she said, then repeated unnecessarily, 'They have found a body in the house.'

Some kind soul had rushed to the Little house and blurted out the news that Florrie had been found with her throat cut. Elsie had fainted.

But the main sympathy, amazingly, was with Harold. 'Let him alone!' and 'Let him go!' people cried as Lewis and his men left with the boy. There was a scuffle as several men made a move to release him. Shouting crowds surrounded the police station and made the dizzying ascent to Darran Road to view the scene and express their outrage that Harold Jones had been arrested once more. Children sold glasses of water to the perspiring protesters, but nothing could cool their anger.

Finally, Superintendent Lewis returned to make a plea

for understanding before the crowd got out of hand. 'I have found the body of the child at Harold Jones' home, foully murdered,' he shouted. 'And I have arrested Harold Jones.' Boos and whistles. 'I think that is all I can tell you and I think you will help us best by dispersing to your homes.'

'We have only your word for it,' a voice yelled from the crowd, 'Can you give us proof? Show us the body.'

'My word as superintendent is proof,' said Lewis, on his dignity. 'And you will know more later.'

A contemporary photograph shows the covered stretcher holding the body of Florrie Little being lifted over the heads of a crowd packed outside the iron railings of number ten. And then the Jones family moved temporarily to stay with relatives while the real search of the house began.

It was Constable Cox who noticed bloodstains on the kitchen door knob. The wall next to the trapdoor had been rubbed with whiting to conceal the stains. When the police took the cloth off a long, narrow table in Harold's bedroom they found the top covered with suspicious stains that turned out to be blood. The table, lifted over the heads of the crowd outside as it was taken to a police van, aroused murmurs of speculation. Hanging up on the wall in the back yard alongside a bathtub was a rolled-up sack. Could Harold have put it there ready to carry the body away later, just as police believed he had done in the Freda Burnell murder?

In the back kitchen, the officers made two grisly discoveries: in a drawer was a clasp knife with a five-inch blade which would be described as 'reeking of blood'.

'I only sharpened it last week to kill a chicken,' Philip Jones told them. The blood, when tested, proved to be human. Under the kitchen sink, the second discovery – an egg saucepan which, placed beneath a leak in the waste pipe, now contained a soup of human blood.

A girl's handkerchief found in Harold's pocket was stained with blood. Was it Florrie's handkerchief? Possibly not. Because, curiously, the police also found in Harold's pockets seven women's handkerchiefs along with a number of love letters written to him by girls who had fallen in love with him following his triumphant return from the Monmouth Assizes.

Three doors away, ignoring the sceptical crowd, a woman dressed in black slipped almost unnoticed into the Littles' place. Susan Burnell, Freda's mother, had come to express her sorrow and sympathy. The two mothers wept together.

On Monday morning, on the way to the magistrates' court, Harold was his usual jaunty self. 'They have got me for nothing again!' he shouted to the crowd gathered outside, as lightly as if he'd been caught scrumping apples. But by the time the inquest on Florrie opened two weeks later, he had lost his smile. Even in appearance he was not the same, the smart blue suit replaced by a brown sports jacket, open shirt and mud-stained trousers. And as a procession of little girls took their places in the witness stand in pretty dresses and trimmed summer hats to tell their part of what happened on Darran Road that fatal evening, Harold twitched his fingers and trembled. His sister, Flossie, 'a little mite of nine years', refused to appear at all until the coroner, W. R. Dauncey, told her father there could be dire consequences. Then, weeping bitterly, and wearing a pink dress with pink streamers on her hat, she allowed her father to lead her to the front of the courtroom.

'It's all right, little girl,' the coroner told her, 'we are not going to hurt you.'

After Flossie had told of going into the house with Florrie, and not seeing her again, her father led her out once again, giving Harold a smile of encouragement. The boy burst into tears.

In an uncanny replay of the Freda Burnell case, time again was the important element. Harold Jones, said the coroner, summing up, had not been seen between 9.30 and 9.50 p.m. when he had answered the door, smiling and apparently relaxed, to Mrs Little. He had been on his own in the house again until half past ten, when the rest of the family arrived home.

The jury did not need to have pictures drawn for them: they quickly recorded a verdict of 'wilful murder against Harold Jones'. His mother shrieked; little Flossie cried in her father's arms.

There was no talk this time of a defence fund for Harold Jones. Speed was everything now. On 11 January he would be sixteen years old and liable, if convicted, to be executed. On 1 November he appeared once again at the Monmouth Assizes, and there were no crowds this time to cheer.

On 17 September he had confessed. His statement, read in court, begins, 'I, Harold Jones, do confess that I wilfully and deliberately murdered Florrie Little on 8 July, causing her to die without preparation to meet her God, the reason being a desire to kill.' But the flat words of the confession convey little of the horror of the crime that occurred on Darran Road, and seem designed to avoid causing Florrie's family additional suffering. The scene must be imagined.

* * *

He watches her from behind his mother's lace curtains in the front room, her blue dress flying up as she skips from square to chalked square, and the familiar feeling creeps over him. 'Flossie,' he calls from the front steps, 'tell Florrie I want her.'

'You girls want a pop?' he asks, offering them the money when they return together. 'Come back after, Florrie, there's something I want to ask you.'

When she returns: 'I need the scissors your mam borrowed the other day. You can go out the back way through the garden if you like. Flossie, why don't you go down to Auntie's to meet Mam and Dad? They should be coming home soon.'

'All right then,' Flossie quickly agrees, and Harold turns the key firmly in the front door lock behind her.

How Florrie gets the scissors without her mother knowing I am not clear. I do know that when Florrie returns to the back kitchen, Harold is waiting for her, smiling no doubt, his hand behind his back. He has learned his lesson from the Freda Burnell episode. This time there will be no scream. Florrie's eyes barely have time to register surprise as Harold's hand comes out from behind his back and he strikes her on the forehead above the right eye with the broken iron lid of a boiler. She falls without a sound, and he is on her immediately, making the rip they would find in her knickers, struggling to penetrate the unconscious girl and then, failing, staining his own clothing with his semen.

And then, consequences. He is left with an unconscious little girl whose eyes will open any moment and who, seconds later, will be running home screaming to her parents.

He knows the drawer where his father keeps the sharp knife used to kill chickens. He opens the blade, tests its sharpness, then slips his arm beneath Florrie, lifts her and leans her over the sink. The cut, Dr Lloyd, the police surgeon, would say, was three and a quarter inches long, beside the right ear, and the knife blade severed the jugular vein. It would have taken fifteen minutes for her to die, Dr Lloyd estimated. By then there would have been perhaps two tablespoons of blood left in her body.

Harold leaves the body hanging over the sink, and hurries into the front room, glancing at the clock in the kitchen. He has perhaps forty-five minutes before his parents are likely to get home. Rummaging in a box, he finds an old army shirt of his father's, returns to the kitchen and wraps it around Florrie's head. He knows now what he will do, and he doesn't want to leave a trail of blood.

He lifts her in his arms and, panting, carries her up the stairs, resting her on the floor. The attic trapdoor, now he comes to look at it, seems impossibly small and high. He carries the narrow table from his bedroom, places Florrie on it, then scrambles up, pushing open the trapdoor. But no matter how hard he tries to thrust her body through, it comes flopping back on top of him.

Leaving the body on the table, he goes down to the back yard and returns with a rope. Somewhere he finds a ribbon, ties it under her arms, secures it to the rope, then climbs up into the attic. The rope is tantalizingly too short. Down he comes again, ties his handkerchief on the end of the rope, and it is just long enough. From below an observer would see little Florrie rising towards the ceiling, the feet the last part of her to disappear through the trapdoor.

Harold, back on the landing, looks down and sees blood on his shirt, on the table, on the walls. The minutes are passing. He hurries down, gets the bathtub from the back yard, takes some water and a cloth and the jar of whiting up to clean off the landing. Not well enough, it transpires.

Downstairs, with no time to heat water, he fills the tub, pulls off his clothes, cuts up his white shirt (the blood-stained sleeves will be found later in the front room), then sets about washing himself. He is using the wire-bristle hairbrush to get the blood off his hands when there's a knock at the front door. His parents? Home already? Quickly he pulls on his trousers and goes to the door. The smile on his face is one of relief when he sees it is Mrs Little.

'Have you seen Florrie?'

Closing the door and locking it again behind her, Harold leans his back against the cool paint of the door and takes a deep breath. Now he can finish washing and cleaning up.

'Words are not wanted, and I think they are useless in this case,' Mr Justice Roche observed after the facts of the case were outlined. A prison doctor who had examined Harold had found 'no signs of derangement', and the judge speedily ordered the boy detained during His Majesty's pleasure, meaning he could remain in prison indefinitely.

There was one more piece of unfinished business. C. F. Vachell, the prosecutor who had seen Harold Jones go free at the Freda Burnell trial, rose to say that, to reassure Abertillery parents that there was not still a murderer loose in their midst, he wished to read the following statement: 'I, Harold Jones, wilfully and deliberately murdered Freda Burnell in Mr Mortimer's warehouse on the fifth of February.'

Philip Jones, interviewed as he left the courtroom, was full of despair. 'I am down and out,' he said, referring to the costs incurred in the two trials. He felt particularly badly for the four men who had guaranteed the defence costs in the first trial and who could ill afford to pay.

'How is Harold bearing it?' the reporter asked.

'Champion. He is like a brick.' And then a look of bewilderment: 'I cannot understand it at all.'

Neither, of course, can we. Examining a studio photograph taken of Harold just a few days before he committed the second murder, we see a casual, confident figure, leaning on a cane, a smirk on his face. It's not surprising that Mr Justice Roche, before sentencing Harold, observed that, in the first trial, he had been made 'a sort of hero'. He added: 'Among the motives which contributed to the second crime was an overwheening vanity and desire to be in the public eye.' But to kill for attention and adulation? It would have to be a first. Perhaps other explanations were still to be found in Abertillery.

The graves of Freda Burnell and Florrie Little are still easily found, not thirty yards apart, in the town's hillside cemetery. Freda's is marked by a touching statue of a little girl in high boots and a dress with a yoke collar, raised, it says, by public subscription. Someone – perhaps one of Florrie's two sisters who still live in the area – had placed silk flowers on the grave, and a red rose was lovingly twined in the hands of the statue. At her funeral, I remembered, they had sung her favourite hymn: 'Sing, sing for gladness'.

Ted Clissett had died only a few months before, his son told me; of the Jones family there seems no sign. But I met seventy-seven-year-old Alf Parry, a retired bricklayer who knew many of Harold's friends. 'The one thing they said about him,' recalled Alf as he made me a cup of tea, 'was that he was very cruel. When they went bird-nesting as boys, Harold would pull the wings off the little baby birds.'

Alf told me he was only five at the time of the murders, but from his parents' home he had a clear view up Darran Road, and remembered one hot summer's day seeing the huge crowd outside number four for Florrie's funeral. The houses were still there but, said Alf's wife, 'You can't drive up there. It's too steep.'

Driving his wife to visit a friend in town, Alf showed me the now remodelled corn shop where Harold once worked. A woman was leaning on the wall, chatting to a neighbour, at the spot in the lane where Freda's body had been found.

'Now mind you don't try and drive up there,' were his wife's parting words, shaking her finger at him when he dropped her off. 'You got stuck last time.'

I thought Alf was looking for a spot to park, but suddenly I noticed a determined thrust to his jaw, and he seemed to be gripping the wheel tighter. We turned a corner and I thought we were going into a wall. I have never seen a steeper hill. It felt as if the car might roll over on its back like a beetle. But Alf had a special gleam in his eye. The engine faltered, but we made it, and pulled up outside the pebbled front of number ten.

Philip Jones, Alf was telling me, afterwards worked on the garbage trucks. As for Harold, he had remained in jail until the Second World War when, like other prisoners, he had been allowed to volunteer, in his case for the commandos. After the war he even came back to Abertillery for a visit, and was recognized in a pub. According to Alf, he died in the mid-1980s in hospital in Abergavenny, about ten miles from Abertillery.

No one was in at number ten. The middle room where Harold once played the organ has been opened up and is part of the lounge. The back kitchen is still there, though a modern stainless steel sink has replaced the porcelain sink where Harold slit Florrie's throat.

A few days later, in Abertillery again doing research, I was stopped by a young policeman with a rugby forward's build and asked for documentation on my car. I fished the papers out of my briefcase and handed them to him. But as he read, his attention seemed to wander. He thrust them back into my hand with hardly a word. I was turning to get back in the car when I heard a stentorian roar: 'I'll kick your arse, I will!' Not a nice way to treat a stranger in town, I thought, turning in alarm. It was the bad boys of Abertillery at it again. I hadn't noticed that I'd stopped in front of a school. Several of the rascals were crowded in an upstairs window, yelling abuse at the policeman and making obscene gestures.

'All right then!' he yelled, when they paid no attention at all to his first threat. And he charged at the school gate, struggling to open it while the boys laughed all the harder. Harold would have been shocked, I'm sure, at their wickedness.

TWO DUTIFUL
DAUGHTERS

She could not bring herself to use the actual word, so she used instead the Bronx pronunciation she'd heard in Edward G. Robinson gangster movies. 'Deborah dear,' she whispered, her arm around her friend's waist, 'there's only one answer: we must moider Mother.'

The early winter rain rattled against the tall bedroom windows. 'How will that help?' her friend asked finally.

Pauline jumped to her feet. 'Imagine the scene!' she cried. 'Poor Mummy dead! And dearest daughter Pauline absolutely devastated! How to console the poor girl? "Oh, Daddy,"' she sobbed, playing herself in the imagined scene, '"I don't think I can ever get over losing dear Mummy. Unless ... unless I went with Deborah and her father to South Africa. That might help me to forget – just a little bit."' She grabbed the taller girl and danced her around the room, laughing hysterically. 'Oh, Deborah!' she said, using her secret name for her friend, Juliet, 'Just a little bit! I could forget just a little bit, couldn't I?'

They were both laughing now. Until Pauline, out of breath and stumbling a little from her troublesome leg, stopped and, holding Juliet by the shoulders, turned her until they were standing beside each other in front of the dressing table mirror. Pauline's dark brown eyes that some thought flat and distant were afire now as she gazed fiercely into Juliet's cool grey pupils. 'Darling,' said Pauline, 'I adore you.'

'But how?' asked her friend. 'How would we do it?'

On the surface, Pauline Rieper and Juliet Hulme (pronounced Hume) seemed to have little in common. Classmates at Christchurch Girls' High School wondered what Juliet, the slim, attractive, long-legged daughter of Dr Henry Rainsford Hulme, the rector of Canterbury University College, saw in dumpy Pauline, the introverted and often morose daughter of – ugh – a fishmonger!

The relationship should not surprise us: it's not so uncommon for an attractive girl like Juliet, the younger of the two at fifteen, to enjoy the friendship and flattery of a plainer friend who offers no competition in the beauty stakes. But Juliet and sixteen-year-old Pauline recognized in each other something deeper and far more significant: both had been sickly as children, spending long months in bed and acquiring the special emotional intensity and sensitivity of the invalid child.

Juliet's early years had been especially traumatic: born in England in 1938, she was only a toddler when the blast from an exploding bomb dropped in an air raid left her in shock and gave her nightmares for weeks after. Her father, a top mathematician, was engaged on vital, top-secret research work developing a demagnetizing device that would make British ships safe from magnetic mines being dropped in sea lanes by German U-boats.

Then, a second blow: doctors told Hulme and his wife,

This is the disturbing video image which made all who saw it
helpless witnesses to the abduction of two-year-old Jamie
Bulger by two young boys (*Popperfoto*)

Jamie Bulger
(*Syndication
International*)

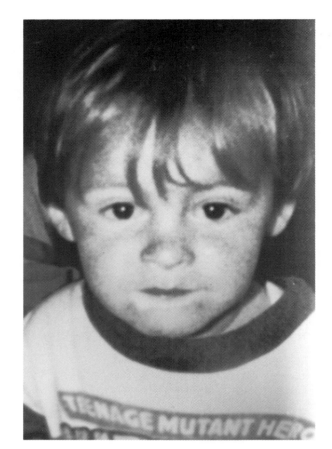

Mourners gather by
the carpet of flowers
laid near the spot
where Jamie died
(*Syndication
International*)

Harold Jones arriving at Usk prison (*Syndication International*)

Marlene Olive. She convinced her boyfriend she was a witch and, once under her spell, he helped to kill her parents (*UPI/Bettmann/Hulton Picture Company*)

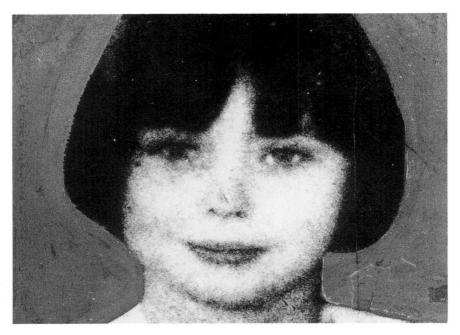

Mary Bell, the little girl who murdered four-year-old Martin Brown and three-year-old Brian Howe (*Syndication International*)

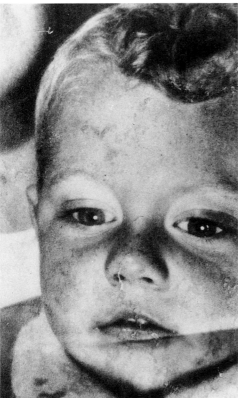

Martin Brown (*Syndication International*)

The Tin Lizzie, where Brian Howe's body was found (*Syndication International*)

Mary Bell, aged twenty, at the time of her escape from prison in 1977 (*Associated Press/Topham*)

Steven Truscott. At the age of fourteen, he was sentenced to hang for the rape and murder of twelve-year-old Lynne Harper (*UPI/Bettmann/Hulton Picture Company*)

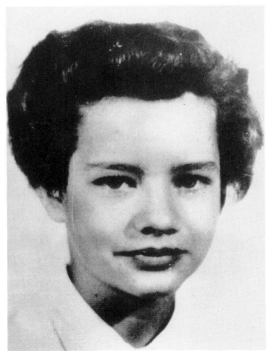

Lynne Harper (*UPI/Bettmann/Hulton Picture Company*)

Steven Truscott, after giving evidence at the review of his trial by the Supreme Court of Canada (*UPI/Bettmann/Hulton Picture Company*)

Pauline Parker (*left*) and Juliet Hulme leave Christchurch magistrates' court. Their obsession with each other was so great, they had been prepared to kill for it (*UPI/Bettmann/Hulton Picture Company*)

Cheryl Pierson and her boyfriend, Rob Cuccio, celebrate her release from jail after three and a half months (*UPI/Bettmann/Hulton Picture Company*)

Just seven hours after meeting for the first time, Shirley Wolf (*left*) and Cindy Collier brutally murdered 85-year-old Anna Brackett (*David Strick/Onyx*)

Hilda, that, with weakened lungs, Juliet was quite likely to contract active tuberculosis. She must leave London as soon as possible, ideally for the purer air of 'the Colonies'.

The war ended and Dr Hulme was being urged to join Britain's atomic research effort where he would have a bright future. To his credit, he put his daughter's health first. He accepted a £2,200-a-year position as rector of Canterbury University College in Christchurch on New Zealand's South Island, a post that carried with it membership of the Senate of New Zealand University. While her parents tied up loose ends in Britain, Juliet was sent ahead on her own, and was there to meet them and her brother, Jonathan, five years her junior, when their ship docked in New Zealand in 1948.

When Juliet's lung problems returned almost immediately and she was confined to a sanatorium for four months, it seemed that the sacrifice of moving to New Zealand had simply not been worthwhile. But there were consolations: soon the family was settled in a sixteen-room mansion called Ilam. And Christchurch, with its gentle, smog-free climate, its gothic cathedral and lush gardens, proved to be an idealized version of England.

At school, Juliet showed herself to have an artistic temperament, learning to recite the classic poets by the page, modelling in clay quite outstandingly, and writing stories in her spare time. Everything was going so well for her by 1953 that her parents felt it was safe to take an overseas trip during the New Zealand winter, leaving her at home. It was during those rather lonely months that Juliet developed a close friendship with Pauline Rieper.

On their return, her parents were pleased at first about the friendship. Juliet, as a result of her weak chest, still

121

had to rest in bed a good deal, and Pauline seemed happy just to sit with her, reading and chatting. The friendship too would help to draw out their somewhat shy daughter, the Hulmes thought. But as friendship developed into crush and crush became all-consuming passion, leaving little time for anything else in their lives, both Juliet's and Pauline's parents started to worry.

Pauline's home life was on an altogether humbler scale than her friend's. Her father, Herbert Rieper, mild and pipe-smoking, ran a modest wholesale fish business, and they lived in the ground-floor flat of a white-painted house not far from Ilam. Her parents had been living together for twenty-five years although, unknown to Pauline, they were not married. Her mother Honora's real last name, it would emerge at the trial, was Parker. It was as Pauline Parker, a name quite unfamiliar to her, that the girl would make her mark in the annals of New Zealand crime.

The couple had known their share of tragedy: of the four children born to them, one was retarded and in an institution, and a second was born a blue baby, with a heart defect, and died soon after. Wendy, their eldest, aged eighteen at this time, was healthy, with a sunny, outgoing personality, but Pauline at the age of five developed osteomyelitis. This infectious inflammatory disease of the bone necessitated a series of operations and long periods in bed. Perhaps as a consequence Pauline had become an especially difficult teenager, refusing to talk to her parents unless she wanted something, cutting them out of her life as much as possible.

And then her new friend, Juliet, came calling – on her pony, Snowball. A pony! As the little horse nuzzled her cheek, Pauline could see clearly what owning a horse

would mean. Instead of being an outsider, unable to play
tennis or take part in sports at school, she'd be in the
saddle, where a horrid old limp didn't matter. She could
join the Horse and Pony Club, like Juliet, and meet all
sorts of interesting people.

'Can I?' she pleaded with her mother after Juliet had
left. 'Can I please, please have a pony, Mummy?'

'I don't know what you're thinking of!' snapped her
mother. 'We're not made of money, you know.' A few
moments later the windows rattled as Pauline slammed
the door of her room.

Like Cinderella at the palace gate, Pauline was profoundly envious of the lifestyle she observed at Ilam, with
the bookish Dr Hulme, his socialite wife, the large,
luxuriously furnished rooms, and the extensive grounds.
Wanting to forget her own meaner background and her
'hateful' parents as much as possible, she stayed with
Juliet at Ilam nearly every weekend, testing the Hulmes'
hospitality to the limit.

Not that the girls were underfoot. In fine weather they
sprawled on the lawns, talking endlessly about their
favourite film stars, about poetry and about the books
they would write together; in foul weather they kept to
Juliet's room, writing historical romances in a steadily
mounting stack of exercise books. After a little, the
stories became almost more real to them than their
everyday lives, and they started writing letters to each
other, assuming the characters from their novels. Juliet
was Charles II, Emperor of Borovnia; then she became
Deborah, the Emperor's mistress by whom she has a son,
Diablo. Pauline assumed the cloak of Lancelot Trelawney,
soldier of fortune, who marries the Empress of Bolumnia.
Soon, even in conversation, they were calling each other

Deborah and, for some reason, Gina.

Their English teacher would have been thrilled at such signs of creativity. Except that, according to Juliet's mother, who later saw the correspondence, the subject matter soon turned to suicide and murder, with buckets of blood and violence unrestrained.

At night, sharing a bed, they talked endlessly about how they could one day be on their own together. 'We could earn money being prostitutes,' Pauline said one day. 'They earn lots.'

'How much?'

'Oh, at least twenty pounds a night. Think of all the clothes we could buy with that!'

'But could you really . . . I mean, with a stranger?'

'Why not! You don't have to kiss them or anything. You just close your eyes and think it's somebody you're really keen on.'

'How do you know?'

'Well, you would, wouldn't you?'

Pauline hadn't told Juliet about Nicholas, the boy who had come to stay at her home for a while the year before. On several nights she had crept along the landing and got into his bed. Mostly they'd messed around, but one night he'd actually done it. She couldn't say it was wonderful. Then, the following night, her father caught them in bed together and made an awful fuss. Nicholas was sent away.

But the fumbling sex she'd had with Nicholas wasn't nearly as much fun as the games she played with Juliet. 'Let's pretend I'm Mario Lanza,' Juliet whispered one night, naming one of their favourite film stars. 'This is how I'd do it.' She deepened her voice and sang one of the tenor's standards, 'Because you come to me, with nought save love . . .'

'Oh, darling Mario,' sighed Pauline. And a little later: 'Now I'll be Rock Hudson.' They invented a whole galaxy of 'saints', all based on their favourite stars.

Sometimes they'd laugh so much Juliet would have a coughing fit that went on for minutes.

'You poor, poor dear,' Pauline would console her, stroking her hair. Once, after a particularly severe bout, she said, 'I wish I had it too. You know, TB.'

'Don't say that!'

'Darling Deborah, I want to share everything with you. Do you think I could catch it from kissing?'

But another day, sitting at the edge of a field looking down on the city, Pauline was in a darker mood. 'It's no good,' she told Juliet, lying on the grass beside her. 'We're wasting our lives.'

'What do you mean?'

'This is just a bloody backwater. We'll never make names for ourselves in this awful country. Who ever heard of a famous New Zealand writer?'

'What about Katherine Mansfield?'

'Exactly. She never made a name for herself until she went to England. If we don't do something, Juliet, it'll be too late. Do you know, there's a French girl called Françoise Sagan who is on the best-seller list. And she's only fifteen. Fifteen!'

'I think we should go to America,' said Juliet suddenly. 'That's where they pay the big money.'

'I know, I know,' replied Pauline. 'But money, how do we get enough money for the fare?'

'I'll sell Snowball! That'll be a good start. Mr Perry has been looking for a little horse. He'll buy her, I bet.'

Walter Perry was to be an important element in the unfolding tragedy. He had arrived in Christchurch in

125

1953, a rugged and charming English engineer on an extended business trip. The Hulmes, very much part of the city's social scene, soon ran into him and found they shared an interest in sociology and social issues. Ironically, in view of what was to follow, they talked of working together to start a marriage guidance bureau.

'You know, Walter is looking for a place to live,' Hilda Hulme told her husband one evening on the way to a faculty dinner. 'We have the maid's apartment that we're not using. Why don't we let him stay there?'

'Good idea,' said her husband.

So at Christmas 1953, bluff Walter Perry came to live at Ilam and became to a surprising degree a member of the Hulme family.

Juliet's parents were surprised when she announced she wanted to sell the horse that she had, only a short time before, doted on. But a few days later Juliet was all excitement meeting Pauline in the playground before school went in. 'I did it,' she said. 'I sold Snowball. Mr Perry gave me fifty pounds for her. He's given the money to my father for safekeeping, but that's all right. I can always get it when I need it.' She was surprised to see no sign of elation on her friend's face. 'What's the matter, Pauline?'

'Mummy's being absolutely beastly,' she replied, close to tears. 'She thinks going to America is a silly idea. She says she won't stand for it.'

'What about your father?'

'I think I could get him to agree – if it wasn't for Mummy. She's such a . . . bitch,' she said vehemently.

The girls' parents had become worried about the relationship to the point where Dr Hulme had even been to see the Riepers at their home. 'I don't know what's got into them,' Honora Rieper said. 'Pauline's marks have been awful this term. We're thinking of taking her to Dr Bennett to see if there's anything wrong with her.'

'Do whatever they ask you to,' Juliet warned when she heard of the impending visit to Dr Francis O. Bennett, the Riepers' family doctor. 'The last thing we want is for them to send you away.'

The doctor, of course, found nothing physically wrong with Pauline. He kept to himself his suspicion that the girls had an active lesbian relationship going on, but advised that perhaps Pauline should be sent to a different school. Her parents, expecting a terrible scene, were quite taken aback when she meekly agreed to the suggestion that she should transfer at the end of the school year.

'Perhaps she was looking for an excuse to bring it to an end anyway,' said Herbert Rieper.

'I hope so,' said his wife.

They would not have felt quite so reassured if they had read the entry in Pauline's diary for 13 February: 'Why could not Mother die? Dozens of people, thousands of people are dying every day. So why not Mother, and Father too? Life is very hard.'

With her newly co-operative attitude, Pauline encountered less resistance at home the next time she told her parents she was spending the weekend at Ilam.

'It'll be over soon enough,' Herbert told Honora. 'Not to worry.'

Juliet too was encountering difficulties at home. 'Mother is being perfectly beastly,' she told Pauline as they sat on a log one glowing autumn day watching members of a riding club go by. 'All I did was borrow a silly old gramophone record from Mr Perry's room. You'd think I'd stolen the

Crown Jewels, the way she carried on! He didn't seem to mind. I hate her, I hate her!'

'Look at that fat thing on the black pony,' said Pauline to distract her friend. 'Hey, Porky! You should be wearing the saddle!' she shouted. 'And look at Miss Nose-in-the-Air! Watch out!' yelled Pauline. 'There's a rip in your bum.'

When Pauline arrived the following weekend, Juliet could hardly wait to get her up to her bedroom to tell her the latest. 'It's too awful!' she cried. 'I don't know what Daddy's going to do!'

'What, for goodness' sake? What's happened?'

'I wasn't trying to be quiet or anything. I mean, I had just got home from school. I'd got a piece of cake from the kitchen. I went into the living room, and there they were!'

'Who? I wish you'd tell me what you're talking about!'

'Mummy and Mr Perry, of course. He was sitting in the armchair and she was sprawled all over him. Oh, Pauline, it was awful. Her skirt was up around here, and they were kissing.'

'My Gawd! What did you say?'

'I couldn't say anything. I just stood there, dumb.'

'Did they know you were there?'

'That's the worst of it. Mr Perry looked up and saw me. They were terribly flustered. Mummy started to say something, but I just ran out of the room. I've been keeping out of the way since.'

'How frightful!' But Pauline, lying back on the bed, her hands behind her head, did not sound as alarmed as her words suggested. 'You know,' she said thoughtfully, 'this could be helpful.'

'What on earth do you mean? It's terrible.'

'But it could help us, don't you see? Why don't you ask Mr Perry if you can borrow some money from him. Say a hundred pounds.'

'A hundred pounds! That's ridiculous. Why would he lend me a hundred pounds?'

'So that you don't snitch on him to your father, silly.'

But before the girls could put their amateurish black-mail plan into operation, events overtook them. On 24 April Dr Hulme told Juliet sadly that he and her mother would probably part.

'Deborah and I are sticking to one thing,' Pauline wrote in her diary next day. 'We sink or swim together.'

A few days later, she was writing: 'Anger against Mother boiled up inside me. It is she who is one of the main obstacles in my path. Suddenly a means of ridding myself of the obstacle occurred to me. If she were to die!'

By 29 April: 'I did not tell Deborah of my plans for removing Mother. The last fate I would wish to meet is one in Borstal [the approved school for young offenders]. I am trying to think of some other way. I want it to appear either a natural or an accidental death.'

In May, to raise money for their voyage, the pair started shoplifting, selling items like lipsticks and powder to girls at school. On 27 May, Pauline got up in the early hours of the morning and walked the considerable distance to her father's business with the intention of robbing the till. Only the sight of a policeman on patrol frightened her off.

And then, suddenly, Pauline's plans for her mother took on a desperate urgency. Dr Hulme came calling to tell her parents that they needn't remove their daughter from the Girls' High School after all. His marriage was at an end; he had resigned his position as rector, and on 3

July he was returning to England to join an atomic research team headed by Sir William Penney.

'I'm taking Jonathan with me,' he told them. 'Juliet will come as far as South Africa with us. We have friends there she can stay with before returning to Christchurch. Basically, though, I think she's better off staying in New Zealand with her mother. I don't think her lungs could stand the English damp and cold.' The South African trip would separate the girls and allow their obsession with each other to cool, he said. He didn't add that it would also remove Juliet from the scene while Hilda sorted out her relationship with Walter Perry.

To Pauline's parents, it couldn't have been better news. To Juliet and Pauline, it was disaster.

'I won't go unless Pauline comes with me!' insisted Juliet.

'It's out of the question, I'm afraid, dear,' replied her father. 'Her parents, I'm sure, wouldn't let her go.'

He was right. Even when Juliet and Pauline together asked the Riepers if Pauline could go, the answer was still no. 'Put it out of your mind,' Honora told Pauline.

That was when Pauline told Juliet that they should 'moider' her mother. 'But how would we do it?' asked Juliet, appalled, yet intrigued at the same time.

'There's lots of ways. I've been thinking about it for a long time.' That night Pauline wrote in her diary: 'We are both mad. We are both stark, staring, raving mad. There is definitely no doubt about it and we are thrilled by the thought.'

On 12 June: 'Eventually we enacted how each [film star] saint would make love in bed. We felt exhausted, but very satisfied.'

On 19 June: 'We practically finished our books today.'

Their main subject for discussion, she wrote, had been how to 'moider' Mother. 'We have worked it out carefully and are both thrilled by the idea. Naturally we feel a trifle nervous, but the pleasure of anticipation is great.'

On 21 June: 'I rose late and helped Mother vigorously this morning. Deborah rang and ... we discussed the moider fully. I feel very keyed up, as if I was planning a surprise party. Mother has fallen in with everything beautifully and the happy event is to take place tomorrow afternoon. So next time I write in this diary Mother will be dead. How odd – yet how pleasing! I washed my hair and came to bed at quarter to nine.'

She could not resist a further entry in the diary the following morning, heading it: 'The Day of the Happy Event'. She wrote: 'I am writing a little of this up on the morning before the death. I felt very excited and "morning-before-Christmasish" last night. I didn't have pleasant dreams though.'

Honora was once again surprised at her difficult daughter's rapid mood changes. Pauline had been all thunderclouds after the South African refusal. Now, unaccountably, she was putting herself out to be agreeable, and even – something unheard of – helping around the house.

'Mums,' she'd said affectionately a few days before, 'why don't we have Juliet over for a farewell lunch on Monday, and then the three of us can go for a walk in Victoria Park afterwards. With all the packing and everything, she won't have much time later.'

'That would be nice,' said Honora. 'I'd like that.'

On the Monday, Juliet joined Mr and Mrs Rieper and Pauline for lunch at the flat. The girls seemed in high spirits, laughing and joking, and Herbert Rieper was surprised at their hilarity considering Juliet was leaving in two weeks.

'Not a very nice day,' said Honora, closing the front door behind her as they left for the park later. 'I do hate winter.'

'We'll be warm enough, Mrs Rieper, once we're walking,' said Juliet.

Victoria Park, one of the many open spaces that dot Christchurch, is in the Cashmere Hills area above the city. On this overcast, chilly day, there were few people around as Honora and the two girls stopped at the refreshment kiosk for teas. The girls in their navy gaberdine school coats, Honora in her winter coat, they walked briskly along the labyrinthine paths winding through groves of laurels and rhododendrons to keep warm. They were on their way back towards the park gates when, with Juliet ahead and almost out of sight, Pauline returned to the old, familiar topic.

'Mummy,' she said, 'have you thought any more about me going with Juliet?'

Honora stopped and turned towards her daughter. 'Now please, we've said everything there is to say about that matter, Pauline. Let's not spoil a pleasant occasion by bringing it up again.'

'But I can't live without Juliet, don't you understand?'

'Don't be ridiculous,' snapped her mother, walking on. 'You do exaggerate so.'

'Mummy, I'm telling you for the last time, I have to go with Juliet.'

'And I'm telling you . . .' Her mother's voice was rising now, 'to put it out of your mind once and for all. Come to your senses, girl.'

Pauline bit her lower lip, holding back whatever it was

132

she meant to say. Juliet had crossed the rustic bridge ahead of them and was almost out of sight around a bend. 'What's that?' she said to her mother.

Honora stopped. 'How pretty!' she said, stooping to pick up the pink pebble that had caught her eye.

Pauline's hand came out of her coat pocket. Wound around it was the top of a woman's stocking, a weight in the toe. Bracing herself, legs apart, she swung the stocking with all her strength and brought it down on the back of her mother's head. With a groan, Honora pitched forward on the path. Birds twittered in the trees, a cool wind shook the leaves. But there was no one, no strange eyes anyway, to see the strange tableau in this peaceful spot of a schoolgirl in her navy school uniform coat, swinging the stocking and smashing it down time and again on the head and face of the twitching, writhing figure on the path.

'Here, give it to me!' said Juliet, running up. The foot of the stocking was soaked in blood. The half-brick inside was visible through the fraying material. Juliet brought back her arm and brought it down with all her strength on the shaking, slobbering object on the path. 'Why won't she die!' she screamed, striking again and again. 'Hold her, won't you.'

Pauline was on her knees now. She grabbed her mother by the throat, felt the convulsive movements beneath her fingers. Then the brick landed again with a soft thud on the back of Honora's head. And again. And again.

Pauline got to her feet, panting. Juliet let the stocking and the brick drop to the ground. They looked at each other. They hadn't bargained on the blood that was now splattered on their faces and smeared on their hands. They hadn't counted on Honora taking so many blows to kill. They had thought one would do it. But there was nothing for it: they had to carry through with their plan.

Agnes Ritchie was washing the cups in the back of the refreshment kiosk when the two girls ran up, screaming. 'It's Mummy!' cried Pauline. 'She's terribly hurt. Please come.'

'She's all covered with blood,' added Juliet, as if to confirm. 'It's terrible.'

Mrs Ritchie stared at them, noticing that they too were covered in blood.

'We tried to lift her,' said Pauline, reading the thought in her eyes. 'She was too heavy.'

'What happened?'

'She fell and hit her head on a plank,' said Pauline. 'And then she kept falling and banging her head.'

'I'll never forget it,' said Juliet, trying to add credence to the unlikely-sounding tale. 'The way her head kept banging.'

'Don't make us go down there again,' pleaded Pauline.

'Come in here. I'll fetch my husband.' As she went to get him, leaving the pair to wash their hands, Agnes Ritchie was quite certain she heard the girls laughing. She put it down to hysteria.

When Ken Ritchie found her, lying on a bed of pine needles beneath a tall evergreen, Honora Rieper was, of course, quite, quite dead. Looking at the terribly damaged face and skull, it was obvious to him that this was no accidental fall. The brick in the bloodstained stocking nearby confirmed his suspicions. The pathologist's final count would be forty-five blows landed on poor Honora, many of the later ones leaving traces of brick dust.

The girls' stories of the 'accident' were simply unbelievable. In quite a short time Pauline found herself at the police station talking to Senior Detective Macdonald Brown.

'We don't believe your friend, Juliet, was present when it happened,' he told her. She looked surprised. 'You're the one we suspect of murdering your mother. Do you want to make a statement?'

She shook her head almost imperceptibly. 'No. Ask me questions,' she said.

'Okay. Who assaulted your mother?'

'I did.'

'Why?'

'If you don't mind, I won't answer that question.'

'When did you make up your mind to kill your mother?'

'A few days ago.'

'Did you tell anyone you were going to do it?'

'No. My friend did not know anything about it. She was out of sight at the time. She had gone on ahead.'

'What did you use?'

'A half-brick inside the foot of a stocking. I had the brick in my shoulder bag.'

Over and over, Pauline repeated that Juliet was not involved.

'Why did she tell the same story to the lady at the tea kiosk then?' asked the detective.

'I think she simply copied what I said,' said the girl quickly.

Pauline was sitting on a bench in the police station shortly afterwards when Brown noticed her trying to conceal a piece of paper. He grabbed it from her. On it was written: 'I am taking the blame for everything.'

Juliet, like Pauline, insisted at first that Mrs Rieper had slipped and fallen. The following day she apologized to the policeman and said she had misled him. She had brought the half-brick, wrapped in newspaper, from Ilam by prearrangement. They had talked originally of using a bag of sand, but had settled on the brick as being more sure. Juliet had also found the pretty pink pebble the day before the murder, and it was her job to drop it on the path where Mrs Rieper would notice it.

'I heard noises behind me,' she said. 'It was a loud conversation and anger. I saw Mrs Rieper in a sort of squatting position. I saw Pauline hit Mrs Rieper with the brick in the stocking. I took the stocking and hit her too. I was terrified. I thought that one of them had to die. I wanted to help Pauline. It was terrible. Mrs Rieper moved convulsively. We both held her.'

Juliet's version was that, when they went to the park, she thought the brick might convince Mrs Rieper to change her mind. 'But after the first blow was struck, I knew it would be necessary for us to kill her.'

By the time the trial opened in Christchurch's grey stone courthouse two months later, Dr Hulme had left for England with Jonathan. Sitting beside Hilda Hulme was Walter Perry, whose last name she would soon acquire by deed poll. Herbert Rieper was a forlorn figure, supported now only by his elder daughter, Wendy.

The two girls, sitting in the dock with a wardress between them, never gave evidence, but the jury was able to form quite an accurate picture of their unusual personalities. There was Pauline's bound diary for one thing, and the fourteen exercise books also seized from her bedroom and containing the girls' 'novels'; there was the testimony of several psychiatrists who had interviewed them, and, not least, their behaviour in court.

Dr Reginald Medlicott, a psychiatrist, complained that Pauline had called him an irritating fool, and ugly to boot.

Juliet, forced to submit to a medical examination by the doctor, screamed, 'I hope you break your flaming neck.'

The girls, he said, showed 'a gross reversal of moral sense. They admired those things which are evil and condemned those things the community considers good.'

They had lived in what they called 'the Fourth World', a dimension only they could perceive. A diary entry from 1953 explains: 'Today Juliet and I found a being of the Fourth World. We saw a gateway through the clouds. We sat at the edge of a field and looked down the hill and over the bay. The island looked beautiful, the sea was blue and everything was full of peace and bliss. We then realized we had the key. We have an extra part to the brain which can appreciate the Fourth World.'

Her daughter, testified Hilda wonderingly, had always been 'full of fantasy'.

The jury heard that the girls had bathed together, slept together, dressed in costume and danced on the lawns of Ilam by moonlight, that they had set out to break all ten commandments. But one example of their dubious behaviour must especially have brought gasps from the citizens of patriotic 1950s Christchurch: Pauline and Juliet had actually refused to join the cheering throngs that met the Queen on her first official visit to the city.

The girls found it difficult to maintain a serious demeanour in court. Juliet passed the time trying to outstare first one and then another of the reporters in the press box. And when one doctor was asked if they had understood the consequences of murder, before he could reply, she ran her finger gleefully across her throat.

The pathologist's evidence of the forty-five head wounds, and of Honora's lacerated hand where she had

137

tried to ward off the blows, passed Juliet by. Only once did she become agitated. That was when Dr Medlicott confirmed that Pauline had on one occasion had sexual intercourse with Nicholas, the boy who had stayed at the Rieper house. Juliet, suddenly aware of what had been said, contorted her face in fury, leaned across the wardress, and whispered angrily. Pauline sat impassively, ignoring the outburst.

Their attitude towards the woman whose life they'd stolen seemed only to bear out the contention of the prosecutor, A. W. Brown, that this was 'a callously planned and premeditated murder, committed by two highly intelligent and perfectly sane, but precocious and dirty-minded girls.'

We might, in this day of greater sexual enlightenment, balk at 'dirty-minded', but callousness just about hit the mark.

Juliet told one of the doctors that she fully believed that Mrs Rieper, on the day of the murder, knew what was going to happen. 'And she did not bear any grudge.'

Pauline told one doctor impatiently, 'I knew it was wrong to murder and I knew at the time I was murdering somebody. You would have to be an absolute moron not to know murder was against the law.'

'I don't wish to place myself above the law,' was how Juliet explained it. 'I'm apart from it.' You see, she told the bumbling medic, 'we do believe we're geniuses.'

The defence was one of insanity. The girls were paranoics, said Dr Medlicott, and they had reinforced each other in their insanity – a condition known as folie à deux. Dr Bennett, the family physician who had known the girls best, agreed with the diagnosis. 'They had delusions of grandeur, formed a society of their own and lived in it,' said the doctor. 'In this society they were no longer under the censure and nagging of their mothers.

'There came the threat of separation,' he testified. 'Anything that threatens the paranoic makes him dangerous. They thought that by removing Pauline's mother the way would be clear. The idea was stupid, but they have steadily maintained it was justified. Neither will admit contrition or regret. Pauline told me she would still feel justified today in killing her mother if she was a threat to their being together. Juliet Hulme was more outspoken. She not only considers the murder justified, but also that other murders might be justified if there was a threat to the association of the two accused.'

There was only one hint that either of the girls was the least bit haunted by what they had done: Pauline told Dr Medlicott that she now tried to sleep on her left side. When she slept on her right, 'Mother seems to come back.'

The murder might have been 'stupid', but a prosecution witness, Dr Kenneth Stallworthy, reminded the court, 'These two girls were very, very fond of each other. The most important thing in the world was for them to be together. There have been other great loves in the world where one person would stick at nothing to be with the other.' He had no doubt that they had enjoyed a physical homosexual relationship.

Stallworthy, of the Avondale Mental Hospital, disagreed with the diagnosis of paranoia. The girls were aware of the nature of their crime and showed no sign of the delusions that go with paranoia. In his opinion, 'the accused had some justification for conceit'. Juliet had displayed a shrewdness in answering difficult questions far beyond her years, and Pauline was 'well above average in intelligence'.

The arrogance and conceit were there for all to hear in a muddy poem written by Pauline and entitled 'The Ones That I Worship', which was read out in court:

> There are living amongst two dutiful daughters
> Of a man who possesses two beautiful daughters.
> The most glorious beings in creation,
> They'd be the pride and joy of any nation.
> You cannot know nor try to guess
> The sweet soothingness of their caress.
> The outstanding genius of this pair
> Is understood by few, they are so rare . . .
>
> Both sets of eyes, though different far, hold many
> mysteries strange.
> Impassively they watch the race of man decay and
> change,
> Hatred burning bright in the brown eyes with
> enemies for fuel.
> Icy scorn glitters in the grey eyes, contemptuous and
> cruel.
> Why are men such fools they will not realize
> The wisdom that is hidden behind these strange eyes?
> And these wonderful people are you and I.

'They are not incurably insane,' the prosecutor said on the sixth and final day of the trial. 'They are incurably bad.' The girls did nothing to counter that impression. As they entered the courtroom to hear the jury's verdict, they were laughing and joking. Inevitably, they were found guilty of murder. They said nothing before the judge sentenced them to be detained during Her Majesty's pleasure – a sentence that meant they could remain in prison indefinitely. As they left the courtroom, Pauline still looked sullen and defiant. Juliet for once looked worried and unhappy.

The penal system did what their parents had never managed to do; it separated them. The fate that, according to Pauline's diary, she had most wanted to avoid overtook her: she was sent to Arohata Borstal, near Wellington, New Zealand's capital. Juliet, a year older, was locked up at Mount Eden, a grim prison near Auckland.

The authorities, though, took the humane view. Because of their youth and possibly because of Juliet's medical condition, both were released in 1958, after only four years' detention. Neither of them had arrived at their twenty-first birthdays; they had whole lives yet to live.

My New Zealand contacts tell me that, at that point, their names simply disappear from the public records, leaving us with many unanswered questions. Did Juliet Hulme survive her early chest complaint? Had their love, as I suspect, long burned itself out by the time the two emerged from prison? I imagine them both assuming new names and, after a while, moving, perhaps to Australia, perhaps to England, where, if they did not actually achieve their original ambitions to be writers, they may have become English teachers.

As I write this, they would be in their mid-fifties, two women still harbouring a very old secret. I see them at their desks, watching with careful eyes the all-consuming passions that flare up so easily between girls at a certain stage. Friendships that, as they know so well, can become obsessions leading, in the most extreme cases, to murder. I see them watching – and gently warning.

A TERRIBLE COLDNESS
INSIDE ME

She cried the day she had to part with Graham. 'He was nearly three years old, and he was really a lovely boy,' Winnie Jouvenat told me. 'It was me that fetched him from the hospital when he was only three weeks old. He was blue, and so tiny, but he was always a nice baby.'

That was in September 1947. Graham's mother had pleurisy at the time of his birth in the Honeypot Lane Maternity Hospital in Neasden, a London suburb. It developed into tuberculosis, and two days before Christmas she died. Everyone was desperately sorry for her husband, Fred Young, a machine setter, left with an eight-year-old daughter, Winifred, and the new baby to care for. The decision on baby Graham was easy: he was already being looked after by Fred's sister, Winnie, and her bus-driver husband, Jack. Winnie was only too happy to keep him – perhaps for good. Winifred, it was decided, would be brought up by her gran, who lived on nearby Links Road in Neasden.

'You don't bring up a baby without loving it,' said Winnie, who was eighty-three when I talked to her. 'He loved me and I loved him, and that was it.' Even after the terrible things that happened later, she said, 'To me he was always my boy. I could see no wrong in him.'

For those precious three years, life at the little terraced house at 768 North Circular Road seems to have been an idyll of love. Winnie's own daughter, Sandra, five when Graham arrived, loved him from the start. 'She was wonderful with him,' said Winnie. Sandra and Graham's sister, Winifred, would spend happy hours playing with him at the Welsh Harp, an oddly named green space surrounding a reservoir in Neasden.

'My husband absolutely idolized him,' said Winnie. As the little boy grew, Jack on his days off would take him for rides on the buses and tube trains. Graham especially loved the escalators. 'He called him Daddy Jack,' recalled Winnie. 'But I never let him call me Mum. I was always Aunty Panty.'

Different? She thought about my question. No, he was just an ordinary little boy, a happy, chubby boy whose nickname was 'Pudding'. Except, she added, 'that he would shake in his cot. All night he'd do it. We used to call it the dig-digs.'

Then a shadow fell over the little house on the North Circular. Graham's father was seeing a girl named Molly. No one has a bad word to say about Molly. She was a good soul. But when Fred announced they were to be married, Winnie and Jack felt torn. Making a new life was exactly what Fred needed to do. But losing Graham would leave an awful gap in Winnie and Jack's lives.

'His father wanted him back again,' Winnie told me, a catch in her voice. 'He said, "He's my son, I want him. I want my family together." I would have liked to have kept him.'

Fred and his new bride would be moving into the North Circular house while Jack and Winnie would take over Gran's house on Links Road. Winnie doesn't like to talk about the day of the move, when they had to leave Graham behind. 'We got out of there as quick as we could,' she said. And she did her crying later.

Psychiatrists, Winnie told me, said later that 'taking him away from me, that was what more or less unsettled him'. Today childhood experts might say too that those first three weeks of his life, when he was in a hospital nursery and without the chance to bond with his desperately ill mother, could also have been damaging.

In his new family setting, Graham apparently found Molly an easy person to love. Soon he was calling her Mummy, and following her around everywhere. But he never forgot Aunty Panty and Daddy Jack. He was at their house nearly every day and when he started school, he would always go to his aunty's for tea.

And, of course, they would do anything for him. Even when, later on, he was in Broadmoor Hospital for the criminally insane and wrote asking them to get him a copy of Hitler's *Mein Kampf*. They dutifully went to a bookshop and ordered it sent to him. By then, of course, Graham had achieved the first phase of his singular plan to become one of the world's great poisoners.

When he was released from Broadmoor, Winnie said, Graham would visit her and Jack at their new home in Sheerness, in Kent, 'and never without a big bunch of roses'. It was what he didn't do that spoke loudest for Graham's affection for his aunt and uncle and his cousin Sandra: of all his close relatives and friends, they seem to be the only ones he didn't try to poison.

145

* * *

My sister-in-law, who was in the same class as Graham in his final year at Braintcroft Junior School in Neasden, writes to me from Australia that, by then, he was 'a likeable chap, though somewhat odd. He liked playing practical jokes and he always seemed to have a pill for you if you had any aches and pains. He was not a popular boy. Other boys took the mickey out of him, but he didn't seem to mind.' He was still chubby, and it was his weight that exposed him to ridicule. His special friend, she reports, was a boy named Chris Williams, who shared Graham's interest in chemistry. It was a friendship that would almost cost Chris his life.

It was when they had both moved on to John Kelly Secondary School that Graham, by then aged thirteen, became jealous one day of Chris' friendship with another boy, and challenged Chris to a fight. He was smaller than Chris, and soon found himself pinned to the ground. 'I'll kill you for that,' he hissed. It's the sort of thing kids say, but a week later Chris felt bilious and started throwing up at school.

His bouts of sickness lasted for a year, causing him cramps in the legs and chest and bringing on excruciating headaches. There was that Saturday trip he made with Graham to London Zoo. And ended up doubled over after Graham thoughtfully shared his lunch with him. Every time he became ill, Graham was always full of solicitude and medical advice. And not for a moment did Chris connect his attacks with the sandwiches Graham brought from home for him.

By then Graham Young's strange obsession was firmly established. It had begun, Winnie told me, with experiments using various substances to kill caterpillars and beetles at the Welsh Harp when he was perhaps nine. Nearly empty perfume and nail varnish bottles would disappear from his stepmother's and his aunt's dressing tables, and one day, after noticing a hole in his jacket, Molly found a bottle containing acid in his pocket.

'Where did you get this?' she demanded when he got home from school.

'I found it,' he mumbled.

'Found it where?' Finally he admitted he'd been rooting in dustbins behind a chemist's shop. The next day Molly called at the shop and warned them to be more careful how they disposed of dangerous substances. For good measure, she called at the library too and asked the librarian to be circumspect in the books they allowed Graham to borrow.

'Don't worry,' she was told. 'It's quite normal for boys his age to want to read about murder and morbid things like that.'

Graham's interest went rather beyond the normal: while other boys worshipped football and cricket stars, Graham, never keen on sports but always an avid reader, studied books about famous poisoners. He admired Dr Crippen, who murdered his wife in 1910 then fled to Canada, taking with him his mistress disguised as a boy. But his special hero was Dr William Palmer, the nineteenth-century physician and racing enthusiast, who pioneered the use of antimony as a poison in disposing of some sixteen inconvenient family members, business associates and unwanted children, but who wasn't averse to using any other poison that came to hand.

Graham's school friends, of course, laughed when he told them of his ambition to be a great poisoner. Old Graham was just joking too when he'd comb his dark hair to one side, hold a comb under his nose and goose-step around pretending to be one of his other heroes, Adolf Hitler.

But even before the Chris Williams episode, Graham's weird obsession had taken a sinister turn at home. On the face of it he was still polite and reasonably affectionate towards Molly, but beneath the surface resentments simmered. She would lock him out of the house while his father was at work, he'd say, and once broke his model aeroplanes. He claimed to friends that he sometimes cried himself to sleep thinking what life would have been like with his own mother. I doubt it. If he had a 'real' mother, it was Winnie. More likely Molly, who can't tell us now, was exposed to an uglier side of Graham's nature and found herself repelled by this strange child.

The turning point may have come the day he brought home the dead mouse. By now he had the run of the school lab to conduct his experiments, killing mice with various substances. 'Throw the horrid thing away!' Molly screamed when she found the animal.

'I'm going to conduct a post-mortem on it,' he insisted.

'If you don't get rid of it this minute, I will,' she cried.

After he'd left for school the following morning, she discovered a sheet of paper on which he'd drawn a gravestone surrounded by figures of snakes and spiders. The inscription: 'In hateful memory of Molly Young. RIP.'

One day in April 1961, Geoffrey Reis, who had his chemist shop on Neasden High Street, looked up to see a schoolboy with a mop of dark hair and a long, narrow face standing behind the counter. 'Twenty-five grams of antimony, please,' he said as casually as if he'd been buying throat lozenges.

Reis gave the boy a careful look. 'How old are you?'

'Seventeen,' said the thirteen-year-old Graham.

'And what do you need it for? It's on the poison list, you know.'

As the pharmacist listened, impressed, Graham gave a convincing account of a series of experiments for which he needed the antimony. A short time later he left the chemist's, after signing the poison register as 'M. E. Evans', with a small bottle in his pocket and a satisfied smile on his face.

His satisfaction changed to fury when, some time later, the astute Molly found the little bottle of antimony in his bedroom. She couldn't know exactly what it was, but the poison symbol was clear enough, and when Fred heard about it, he hit the ceiling. There'd be no more of that nonsense, he shouted, and next day Molly went along to ask Reis not to sell Graham any more poisons. From then on, Graham, putting on his eager young researcher act, used his pocket money to buy poisons instead from another Neasden chemist, Edgar Davis, again signing the register as 'M. E. Evans', and giving a false address.

In the summer of 1961, his sister Winifred had met Dennis Shannon, the man she would eventually marry. One evening, on the way to meet him to go to the cinema, she suddenly felt weak and dizzy just outside Neasden underground station. In an instant, all dignity gone, she found herself retching on the pavement until there was nothing left but bile. It was only the first of many such mysterious attacks Winifred experienced in the following months. She never connected her illness with Graham – until the belladonna affair.

Winifred was often late leaving for work. On a certain morning, behind time as usual, she grabbed the cup of tea

Molly had brought to her in her bedroom.

'Ew!' she said after one mouthful. 'It's horrible.'

'Throw it away then,' said Molly. Thinking about it after Winnie had left, Molly wondered if the cup had been used inadvertently for shampoo, and broke it and threw it away.

Winifred, on the train to work, was experiencing the strangest sensations – as if her eyes had gone out of control, making things appear as if they were rushing towards her one moment and retreating the next. At work, her boss insisted on sending her to the Middlesex Hospital where, to her astonishment, a doctor took her to a mirror, showed her her enormously enlarged pupils, and told her she had been poisoned with belladonna, the product of deadly nightshade. Could she account for it?

'It must be my little brother,' she said. 'He's always messing about with chemicals. He must have used one of the cups by mistake,' she added, remembering the bitter tea.

Confronted by his father that evening, Graham denied indignantly that he'd been experimenting at home and went off crying to his room. A search produced no evidence of poisons, and Winifred found herself apologizing to him for having suspected him unjustly.

Nausea, bilious attacks and headaches were now the norm in the Young household. Fred was often home from work ill, but his sufferings were minor compared with Molly's. Day after day she would be stretched in agony on the couch. The attractive woman of twenty-seven whom he had married a decade earlier was becoming an old woman before their eyes, her skin papery, her back bent over in agony, struggling pathetically to conceal her pain from her husband.

Perhaps after all, Winifred suggested, her symptoms were connected with Graham's well-known fascination with poisons. But Molly wouldn't hear of it.

'It must have something to do with the crash,' she insisted. In the summer of 1961 Molly had been involved in a bus accident when she was thrown out of her seat and hit her head violently on the roof of the bus. 'That's the only thing it could be.'

As the stepmother, she didn't want to drive a wedge between Graham and his dad – a move that could backfire on her. Besides, how could she suspect Graham, who was always so solicitous of her in her pain, who fetched her glasses of water, picked up her medicine from the chemist's, and who was for ever asking how she felt?

Finally persuaded to go to Willesden General Hospital for tests, she was told there was no obvious reason for her illness and sent home. But on Easter Saturday 1962, Molly's illness took on a new dimension. When she woke, in addition to her usual pains, her hands and feet felt numb as if from pins and needles, and her neck was stiff. She still insisted, though, on going out to do her weekend shopping.

'You coming?' Fred asked Graham as usual as he set off for his Saturday noon pint at the local. Graham usually went along and, too young to go in, sat outside with his dad on the wall. Fred would realize later that it was probably when he went for a pee that Graham would lace his beer with the poison that made his father's weekends agony.

'No thanks, Dad,' said Graham on this occasion. 'I've got some things to do.'

When he came home for his dinner, Fred found his son standing at the kitchen window, staring out. Looking past him, he saw Molly writhing in pain on the lawn at the back.

'Love, love, you've got to go to the doctor's,' he insisted, helping her into the house a moment later.

'You'd better take her to Willesden Hospital. I can't tell what's causing the trouble,' the family doctor told Fred after examining her. At the hospital she joked with the nurses as she was put to bed, 'I can't stay long. I've got to get my husband's dinner!'

'Well, well,' said an affable doctor, looking at her chart, 'with a name like Young you should live for ever.' With that, Molly's head dropped. She was dead.

Following a post-mortem, the pathologist gave as the cause of death a prolapsed bone at the top of the spinal column – confirmation that her death was connected with the bus crash.

'You're not going to have her buried, are you, Dad?' said Graham on the way home from the hospital. 'It's so old-fashioned. Cremation is the way they do it today. And it's cheaper.' He kept on about it and Fred, not the strongest character, finally gave in: Molly's body was cremated at the Golders Green crematorium the following Thursday, with the ashes to be scattered later.

It must have been difficult for Graham as they left the crematorium to keep from grinning. He was fourteen, he had committed his first perfect murder, and at that very moment the evidence of his crime was being consumed in the flames. Back home, as relatives commiserated with the boy who had now lost two mothers, Graham allowed himself one small indulgence. He slipped a little antimony into his Uncle John's ham sandwich, causing the poor man to be violently sick.

Graham would never be charged with Molly's murder.

He did tell the police later that he had been adding antimony to her food for months. 'When he was in Broadmoor,' Winnie told me, 'he told Jack and me one day that he had sprinkled thallium on some trifle. Molly ate it the night before she died.'

Thallium? Even the doctors would be puzzled. It is a poison, sometimes used in lens manufacture, that is tasteless, odourless and difficult to detect. One small spoonful is enough to cause an excruciating death preceded by intense abdominal pain, brain disorders, and other distressing symptoms. It was even used as a poison by the ancient Egyptians but, surprisingly, Graham Young would be the first person ever charged in Britain with using it to cause death.

If most doctors had never heard of it, Agatha Christie, who once worked in a hospital dispensary, certainly had. The previous year, 1961, the prolific mystery writer had published *The Pale Horse*, a thriller in which a woman uses thallium to poison seven people. The symptoms and the advantages of thallium are described in detail in the book. Graham always claimed he had not read it, but perhaps pride made him prevaricate: a master poisoner might not want to admit he got his scientific knowledge from a mystery novel.

The day following the funeral Fred, struggling to absorb a repeat of the tragedy that had hit the family a dozen years earlier, asked Winifred and Graham to sit down.

'I don't know how we're going to carry on without Molly,' he said. 'She did everything round here.'

'We'll pitch in, Daddy,' said Winifred. 'Don't worry now.'

'It's so rotten unfair,' said Fred. 'See, we scrimped and

153

saved all these years to get the house paid off so we wouldn't have to worry. And we just got it paid up. Free and clear.'

'It's all right, Daddy,' said Winifred, putting her arms around him. 'It's all right.'

'I just wanted you both to know,' he said, unable to hold the tears back now. 'The house will go to the two of you, you know, if anything should happen.'

'Don't think about it, Dad,' said Graham. 'We've just got to get on as best we can.'

A few days later, Fred's attacks returned with increased violence. 'See that Daddy gets something to eat,' Winifred told Graham. 'If he won't eat anything else, give him some Bengers food [for invalids]. He's got to take something.' She had no way of knowing that Graham was adding antimony to the Bengers. At the doctor's one day, Fred collapsed and was taken to Willesden Hospital by ambulance.

Graham was an assiduous visitor. He seemed to be in his element, discussing his father's illness with any medical people who came by. And he listened eagerly one evening when the doctor took him, his Aunt Winnie and his sister aside and told them it was simply inexplicable – the tests showed that Fred had been poisoned with either arsenic or antimony. Was he perhaps trying to kill himself out of grief from losing Molly?

On the way home Graham had only derision for the doctors. 'What a bunch of incompetents! They can't even tell the difference between arsenic and antimony poisoning. They don't know anything. If it was arsenic, he'd be . . .' and he reeled off the distinct symptoms caused by the two poisons. For the first time, listening to him, his sister knew that Graham was somehow connected with the sicknesses that had afflicted them.

Aunt Winnie had had her suspicions earlier, but had confided them only to her husband. One day she'd confronted the boy: 'Look here, Graham. Be straight with me now. Are you the one doing this?'

He'd looked her straight in the eye and, with patent honesty, assured her, 'No, Aunty, honestly I'm not.'

But nobody did anything. Finally, even Fred, conscious of Graham sitting beside his hospital bed every evening, studying him with those cold, emotionless eyes, perceived dimly that Graham was somehow connected with what was happening to him. 'Don't bring Graham with you next time,' he told Winnie when the boy was out of the room.

Fred had by now been told that the cause of his illness was antimony poisoning. One more dose would have killed him, he learned. The doctors could save his life, but his liver would be permanently damaged.

Graham was a mildly disturbing boy in normal times, solitary, given to strange, disconnected statements. Now his behaviour became downright alarming. More and more his family would catch him staring at them in a frightening fashion, and, arriving at Aunt Winnie's house, where he was staying while his dad was in hospital, he'd scare his cousin Sandra silly by standing right up against the door so that when she opened it she'd find herself staring right into his face. He'd taken to sniffing ether – his aunt could smell it on his breath. No, he assured her, not ether, Victory V lozenges. He loved Victory V's. She became so worried she started searching his pockets, and now she didn't leave any food around when Graham was there.

How long this state of affairs might have continued is

anybody's guess. Fortunately, the suspicions of Geoffrey Hughes, Graham's science master, had also been aroused. Although Graham's performance at school was mediocre in most subjects, and downright hopeless in maths, Hughes had spotted the boy's aptitude for chemistry from the start, and had put him in the science A-stream. He was a frustrating student, though, often neglecting work assignments in favour of his own experiments.

Wondering what Graham was up to, Hughes one night opened the boy's desk, and discovered a notebook he hadn't seen before. He turned the pages with increasing alarm. They contained poems and essays about famous poisoners and horrific drawings of people dying. Hughes suddenly remembered the unexplained attacks Graham's friend, Chris Williams, had experienced. Next morning he took his concerns to the headmaster.

As teachers, though, they couldn't simply call the police and tell them that one of the boys had been acting a bit peculiar. It wasn't on. Their first step was to speak to the Youngs' family physician. Funny thing, said the doctor, the family had been dogged by strange illnesses, just like Chris Williams'. Next day Graham was told that a man from child guidance would like a word with him. In fact, he was a school psychiatrist.

'You're a pretty bright young chap,' the doctor told him encouragingly. 'It says here you're doing some very good work in science. You'll have to brush up a lot in maths, though. That is if you plan on taking a science degree.'

'A degree?'

'Oh, yes. A lad of your abilities. I would say a university scholarship isn't out of the question. Tell me about your interests, Graham.'

It was too good a chance to miss. Flattered, Graham

went on and on about his knowledge of poisons, dazzling the guidance man with his remarkable technical know-how.

'He says I could have a really good career ahead of me,' Graham told his uncle and aunt excitedly that night. 'I could even get a university scholarship.'

The psychiatrist, meanwhile, was reporting his concerns to the police. When Graham arrived home at his aunt and uncle's from school the following afternoon, a police car was parked outside the house. He made no attempt to run away; in fact, entering the house he seemed as relaxed as he ever was. He was, after all, walking towards his destiny. Soon his name would be ranked alongside Palmer and Crippen and the rest. And at the age of fourteen!

He emptied his pockets when Detective Inspector Edward Crabbe told him to. Nothing there except a schoolboy's oddments.

'Now your shoes and socks, son.' Graham dutifully took them off. Nothing there either. It was only when he was taking off his shirt that his 'little friend' – a small bottle of antimony, kept, he'd told his friends, as a last expedient – fell out on the floor. 'What's that?'

'I don't know,' he told the inspector blandly. And he didn't know either what was in the other two bottles found in his shirt pocket.

'Then we'll find out, won't we?' said the inspector, ordering him to get dressed. For the inspector it was no mere fishing trip. He'd already been to the house on the North Circular and found in Graham's bedroom, in addition to books on poisons and poisoners, bottles of antimony, thallium, atropine, digitalis, ionine, and barium chloride.

All evening Graham stonewalled the officers questioning him at Harlesden police station. His father, terribly weak in hospital and in danger of dying, heard the news of Graham's arrest from Winifred and Aunt Winnie. There is no word of his reaction.

Winifred had told the police of her nasty little encounter with belladonna, and by morning the game was up: Graham made a full confession in a curiously dispassionate tone that sounds like a prize student's English essay on 'What I did in my summer holidays'.

'I have been interested in poisons, their properties and effects, since I was about eleven,' it begins. 'I tried out one of them on my friend, Williams... After that I started experimenting at home by putting sometimes one and sometimes three grains of poison on prepared foods which my mother, father and sister would eat.'

By the previous September, poisoning, he said, had become an obsession. 'One morning at the end of November I was getting ready to go to school when I saw my sister's cup of tea on the dresser. I put one-tenth of a grain of belladonna in the milk, and left for school. That night my mother told me my sister had been ill during the day ... I knew it was the effect of the belladonna. I gave some of the remainder to Williams.

'On occasion,' the confession went on, 'I have also put antimony tartrate solution and powder on foods at home which my mother and father have taken. My mother lost weight all the time through it, and I stopped giving it to her about February of this year [1962]. After my mother died on 21 April I started putting poisons at home in milk and water and on food. As a result, my father became ill and was taken to hospital. I then realized how ill he was ... I knew that the doses I was giving were not fatal, but I knew I was doing wrong. It grew on me – like a drug habit, except it was not me who was taking the drugs. I realize how stupid I have been with these poisons. I knew this all along, but I could not stop it.'

We can take Graham's conventional expressions of remorse with a pinch of ... well, poison. 'I miss my antimony,' he told Dr Christopher Fysh, the psychiatrist at the Ashford remand centre, as he awaited trial. 'I miss the power it gives me.' And when Aunt Winnie and his sister visited him, the one thing he wanted to know was what press coverage his case was getting.

On 6 July, Graham, wearing his navy school blazer and grey flannels, appeared at the Old Bailey – just as many of his heroes had done. Where any other youngster of fourteen might have felt terror in those intimidating surroundings, Graham appeared relaxed, sitting cross-legged, taking an eager interest in the proceedings – just as if his class was on a school outing to the courts.

The most ticklish question the prosecutors had faced was whether to charge him with Molly's murder. The answer in the end had to be no. In spite of Graham's implied admission, the post-mortem carried out immediately after her death had produced no evidence of poison. And, thanks to Graham's insistence on cremation, there was no possibility of going back to take a second look. Graham at that point had not told anyone about giving Molly thallium. So, in the dock, Graham pleaded guilty only to three charges of poisoning involving his sister, his father and Chris Williams.

We can only admire the prescience of the doctors who testified in court that day about Graham's condition. They didn't mince words, and events would show they'd got it exactly right.

Dr Fysh said Graham was not mentally ill, but was suffering from a psychopathic disorder – in other words he was a psychopath. His prognosis was bad.

'Does that mean that this behaviour is likely to be repeated?' asked Mr Justice Melford Stevenson.

'I think it is extremely likely,' replied the doctor.

Dr Donald Blair, another psychiatrist who had examined Graham at Ashford, found him 'highly intelligent, but his emotional responses are slow and he has never exhibited the slightest distress in relating the instances of poisoning. Indeed, he seemed to experience emotional satisfaction in doing so, and particularly in revealing his intimate knowledge of the toxicology of the various drugs concerned.'

Dr Blair's conclusion: 'There is no doubt in my mind that this youth is at present a very serious danger to other people. His intense obsession and almost exclusive interest in drugs and their poisoning effect is not likely to change, and he could well repeat his cool, calm, calculating administrations of these poisons at any time.'

Graham Young, the judge ordered, would be detained in Broadmoor, the psychiatric hospital for the criminally insane, for fifteen years, and could not be released earlier without the express authority of the Home Secretary.

It was all over quite briefly, and only gradually did it dawn on Graham that he had made a mistake in pleading guilty. With no witnesses required to give evidence, he had cheated himself of maximum press exposure, and now – the thought pained him more than the sufferings of his victims ever had – he would be a mere footnote in the history of the great poisoners. Well, he'd know better next time – if there was a next time.

* * *

In its one hundred years of existence, Broadmoor, thirty miles from London in the Berkshire countryside, had entertained younger guests – although Graham was one of the three youngest patients this century. His youth made him something of a pet with the nurses and they tended to feel protective towards the serious lad detained for his own safety in a small room in the reception area.

But his unswerving interest in poisons made him as dangerous as he was endearing. Soon nurses were telling difficult patients with a wink, 'If you don't behave yourself, I'll ask Graham to make your coffee.'

A month after Graham's arrival, a patient named John Berridge collapsed in convulsions and died. To their amazement, the hospital authorities learned he had died of cyanide poisoning. It was unheard of – there was no cyanide stored at Broadmoor. Finally it was realized that a thick hedge of laurels surrounding the hospital provided a ready source of cyanide for anyone skilled enough to distil the poison from the laurel leaves. It was never determined whether Berridge's death was a case of suicide or murder. But Graham, studying his medical books in the little room decorated now with Nazi memorabilia, was regarded with respect, not to say fear, from then on. And the laurels were cut down.

Nothing could distract him from his one obsessive interest. He labelled the tea and sugar he was allowed to keep in his room, 'strychnine' and 'potassium cyanide'.

'This coffee tastes funny,' one of the nurses observed one day after Graham had brewed a pot in the staff room. 'So does mine,' said another. Graham finally admitted he'd added Harpic, a toilet cleaner, to the pot.

Turned down for release when he applied after three

years (Fred Young made a special trip to the hospital to argue that his son should never be let out again), Graham turned resentful. Shortly afterwards a whole packet of Mangers sugar soap, used to clean paintwork, went missing and ended up in the tea urn. It wasn't funny any more. Graham was put into solitary confinement – the cooler. He emerged a changed young man. Now he talked less and less about poisons, and became co-operative to the point where other patients started to refer to him as the doctors' blue-eyed boy. He had realized, in fact, that if he wanted to get out he had to put on a show of being 'cured'.

He still had his little quirks: he treasured the brick from Hitler's mountaintop home, Berchtesgaden, brought back from Austria for him by a sympathetic retired social worker; he sent away for membership of the fascist National Front, and he pronounced himself surprised and disappointed when his application for a job at the police forensic lab was turned down.

But, as the years passed, Dr Edgar Udwin, the senior resident psychiatrist, felt increasingly confident that Graham had outgrown his homicidal tendencies and his passion for poisons. The warnings given at his trial were forgotten. A preliminary report leading up to an application for release went to the Home Secretary, the cabinet minister who could authorize his release, in June 1970. 'He is no longer a danger to others,' Dr Udwin wrote.

'The pot is now almost boiling,' Graham wrote to his sister the same month. 'Just think, Win, another few months and your friendly neighbourhood Frankenstein will be at liberty once again!!!'

His father still regarded Graham with the deepest suspicion. Winifred, who was by now married with a baby, was also worried, but after a trip to Broadmoor to talk to Dr Udwin, her fears were put to rest. In November, in a freedom try-out, Graham, now aged twenty-three, spent a wholly successful week with Winifred and Dennis at their home in Hemel Hempstead, happily playing with the baby, taking Rupert, the dog, for walks and – having missed out on the experimental adolescent years – downing pint after pint at the local pub. Home again with his sister and brother-in-law for Christmas, he bought everyone modest presents and, after so many dismal holidays spent in Broadmoor, became positively maudlin over the whole business.

On 4 February 1971, carrying with him his doctor's good wishes, Graham Young walked out of Broadmoor for the last time. The nurses were less sanguine about his release. They knew better than anyone that he still harboured ambitions to be one of the great poisoners. 'When I get out,' he told one nurse, 'I'm going to kill one person for every year I've spent in this place.' Why didn't they tell the doctors? Call it a breakdown in communications – a fatal breakdown.

Just a few days later thirty-four-year-old Trevor Sparkes, a keen footballer, was stricken in the middle of a game. His legs went wobbly, and knife-like pains shot through his abdomen. The trouble kept recurring. He never connected it with the odd glass of wine he had with the new chap who had recently checked into the hostel in Chippenham, near Slough, where Sparkes was staying. Chap by the name of Graham Young, who was taking a training course to be a storekeeper. Sparkes survived, but his system was permanently damaged: he never played football again.

In April, his course almost completed at the Slough training centre, Graham applied for a job as storekeeper at John Hadland Ltd, a lens manufacturer in the village of Bovingdon, Hertfordshire, close to where his sister lived in Hemel Hempstead. How to explain never having worked before? The Slough authorities forwarded a report from Dr Udwin, explaining that Graham had had a breakdown that had kept him in hospital during his adolescent years, but was now 'entirely fit for discharge'. He was, the report went on, 'of above average intelligence and capable of sustained effort. He would fit in well and not draw attention to himself in any community.' The letter made no mention of Broadmoor.

Certain that he would get the job, Graham made his preparations. He informed the pharmacist at John Bell and Croyden, a fine old chemist's firm on Wigmore Street in central London, that he required twenty-five grams of antimony. When his usual explanations about 'experiments' didn't work, he returned to the shop a few days later with a forged authorization and this time was able to make his purchase. In an act of bravado, he signed the poison register 'M. E. Evans' – just like the old days.

Graham's new colleagues at Hadland's, where he began work on 10 May, knew nothing of his 'breakdown', but they seemed to sense that the moody new storekeeper – talkative one moment, morose the next – needed drawing out. They befriended him, kidded him, and even indulged him when he got on to his favourite topic, Hitler. Graham too made the effort to be friendly; he was always offering to fetch the tea from the trolley that came around twice a day.

At Hadland's, 1971 was the year of what the employees

were soon calling 'the Bovingdon bug'. One after another, people were falling ill with mysterious symptoms, including dire stomach upsets, hallucinations, loss of hair, impotency and even stinking feet. By 19 November, the day a second employee, sixty-year-old Fred Biggs, died, the staff were in a state close to panic. The first to go had been Bob Egle, the popular fifty-nine-year-old storeroom manager, who had died in the St Albans City Hospital on 7 July and who, like Biggs, had suffered the same mysterious Bovingdon bug symptoms. With employees threatening to resign *en masse*, the firm's owner, John Hadland, asked Dr Iain Anderson, a general practitioner who acted as the company's medical officer, to reassure the staff.

It was a worried and subdued group of employees that gathered in the cafeteria that afternoon to hear Dr Anderson. There were, the doctor said, three possible causes for the illnesses: radioactive contamination from an old airfield nearby, heavy metal poisoning from thallium, which is used in certain types of lens manufacture, or some as-yet-unidentified virus. The airfield had been checked out, thallium was not used at Hadland's, so that only left the virus, and urgent efforts were being made to identify it, he assured them.

'Any questions?' John Hadland asked when Anderson sat down.

Why, asked a complaining voice from the back, had they been so quick to dismiss heavy metal poisoning? And then the questioner – it was, of course, Graham Young – launched into a detailed comparison of the employees' symptoms with those experienced in cases of heavy metal poisoning. Anderson, disconcerted because he personally suspected poisoning, tried to shrug off Young's persistent

165

questions, and Hadland called a hasty end to the meeting.

'You made some rather good points in there.' Graham, back in the storeroom a few minutes later, turned to find Dr Anderson regarding him curiously. 'I really must compliment you on your knowledge of poisons. Wherever did you learn so much?'

'Oh,' Graham replied offhandedly, 'it's a bit of a hobby of mine. You know, reading about some of the famous cases.'

'I don't recall thallium ever being used in those cases. Do you suppose it would be effective?'

Anderson had touched the trigger. For the next ten minutes Graham rattled off the properties of thallium, showing off unabashedly and citing the many advantages of thallium as a poison that was deadly in its effects and difficult to detect.

When the doctor drove away, he and John Hadland had agreed to let matters rest for the time being, to keep an eye on Graham Young and see what happened. But, pacing his office, Hadland knew that wasn't good enough. He put in a call to his solicitor to make sure what he was doing was correct, and then he called the police.

Detective Chief Inspector John Kirkpatrick's first move was to check the Hadland employment records. Yes, he confirmed, the onset of the strange attacks coincided with the date six months earlier when Graham had first started work with the firm. Graham's name was flashed to Scotland Yard for a check. That was when it was discovered that he had only that year been released from Broadmoor.

It was Fred Young who answered the impatient knock of the police on his sister Winnie's door in Sheerness that night. 'Is Graham Young here?' one of the officers asked.

Fred stood aside and indicated his son – on a visit to his aunt – who was in the kitchen making a sandwich.

'Oh, Graham,' entreated his aunt as they handcuffed him, 'what have you done now?'

'I don't know what they're talking about, Aunty,' he replied.

Meanwhile, two other officers, sent to check the £4-a-week bedsitter Graham rented from a Pakistani family, walked in on Graham Young's own little chamber of horrors. The walls were decorated with pictures of Hitler, swastikas were everywhere, and strewn around were grotesque drawings of dying men, some with their hair falling out, clutching their throats, of tombstones, giant syringes and skulls and crossbones. Of more direct interest was the row of little bottles and phials on the windowsill with poison warnings on some of the labels. The most significant find of all: a loose-leaf diary for October and November in which Graham had recorded the poison doses he had administered to various colleagues at work whom he identified in the record by initials. 'I have administered a fatal dose of the special compound to F [Fred Biggs],' he noted on 31 October.

At the police station in Sheerness, Chief Inspector Kirkpatrick was finding Graham Young an arch and evasive suspect who in turn lectured him on his legal rights and teased him with scraps of information. 'I can't tell you everything,' he said with a superior air, 'but some things I will. I seemed to be a misfit when I was young. Not like other children. I used to withdraw a lot within myself. I read a lot, and I became obsessed with the macabre. Toxicology always fascinated me. My father married again,' he added enigmatically, 'and I began to experiment.'

Kirkpatrick wanted facts, not psychological analysis. What had he given two of his fellow employees whose condition was at that moment deteriorating? he demanded.

'I won't tell you the agent I used,' said Graham carefully. 'But I will tell you what the hospital should give as an antidote.'

You can sense the policemen's perplexity in the questions they asked that night: 'None of these people were your enemies. Why did you do it?'

'I suppose,' mused Graham, 'that I had ceased to see them as people . . . They became guinea pigs.'

Was there a hint of remorse, or was he revelling in his notoriety when, after delivering another lecture on the effects of the poisons he'd used, he told one of the officers, 'You must feel revulsion for me.'

'Do you know what the things you have described mean in human terms?' the officer inquired.

'No,' was the surprising answer. 'I have never seen death.'

With Detective Chief Superintendent Ronald Harvey looking on anxiously and an expert on thallium poisoning on hand, an urgent post-mortem was performed on the body of Fred Biggs. At the end, even after microscopic examination of the organs, the doctors had bad news: no cause of death could be established. Harvey took a gamble: the following day he charged Graham with Biggs' murder. It would be ten days before a thorough analysis of the organs at the forensic lab would reveal the presence of thallium. By then an analysis of the ashes of Bob Egle, who had been cremated, had produced a similar result.

When Graham Young appeared in the dock at the St Albans Crown Court on 19 June 1972, charged with two counts of murder, two of attempted murder, and four of malicious poisoning, he did not make the same mistake he had at the Old Bailey a decade earlier. This time he pleaded not guilty to all charges. He wanted his day in court.

'The diary of death', as the tabloids called it, provided all the sensation newspaper readers could wish for. 'Di [Diana Smart, who also worked in the storeroom] irritated me intensely yesterday,' Graham had recorded. 'So I packed her off home with an attack of illness. I only gave her something to shake her up. I now regret I didn't give her a larger dose capable of laying her up for a few days.'

The diary, he claimed blithely from the witness box, was simply a practice exercise for a work of fiction he was planning. 'I am interested in developing my somewhat stilted style as a narrative writer,' he claimed.

During two days in the witness box, Graham, relaxed with his left hand in his trouser pocket, seemed always in command, even when pressed by the prosecutor, John Leonard QC. His confession to the police? It was a fake, he argued, coerced out of him by the police who had promised him, in return for food, clothing to wear instead of the blankets he was draped in, and a chance to sleep. Citing a quotation from the diary, Leonard asked dryly if Graham had intended to be flippant in this otherwise serious work of 'fiction'.

'Since when, Mr Leonard, have poisoners been noted for their absence of humour?' Graham inquired mischievously.

'I don't know, Mr Young. I've never met any.'

'Thank you, Mr Leonard,' Graham said, with a bow in the direction of the embarrassed counsel.

The haughty performance may not have scored points with the jury, but then Graham Young was really playing to a gallery beyond the courtroom – to posterity. The verdict – guilty on two counts of murder, two of attempted murder, and two of administering poison – was arrived at after only an hour's consideration by the jury and was no surprise. His counsel was on his feet immediately to say that, given a choice between another stretch in Broadmoor and a prison sentence, his client rather preferred prison. Request granted. Mr Justice Eveleigh sentenced him to life imprisonment.

Graham had smiled at the sentence. In the room below immediately afterwards he finally dropped the mask; as Aunt Winnie dabbed at her tears he seemed, his cousin Sandra would say, 'genuinely moved'.

'Graham, why did you do it?' his aunt asked.

He was silent. How could he tell her, of all people? Finally, inadequately, he mumbled, 'I'm terribly sorry for the trouble I've caused you all.' He sent his regards to Rupert, his sister Winifred's dog.

Winifred later wrote a very perceptive book about her brother entitled *Obsessive Poisoner*. What distinguished her brother from the other notorious poisoners of history, she pointed out, was that his crimes had no apparent motive. Most poisoners kill either for gain or, like Crippen, to remove a spouse. 'Graham had absolutely no motives of this nature,' wrote Winifred. 'And we have never been able to discover if he actually hated any of us.'

Wouldn't it be terrible, someone had once said to her, if Graham had walked into a restaurant and poisoned the food of all the people there? It would never happen, was her reply, because he would have no chance of observing the aftereffects on his victims. 'His real reason for poisoning people,' she wrote, 'was that he wanted to study the effects; to watch how the poison worked, as though he were merely carrying through a clinical experiment.' At times, she wrote, Graham seemed to understand the emotional deficiency that made him act the way he did. 'You see,' he told her once, 'there's a terrible coldness inside me.'

Winifred, the mother of two young children, died of cancer at the age of forty-three, and her father, Fred, whose liver was permanently damaged from the poison episode, died a couple of years later. Who is to say whether their deaths were hastened by the poison Graham gave them?

For as long as she could, his Aunt Winnie, with her daughter, Sandra, would visit Graham at Parkhurst Prison on the Isle of Wight. In August 1990 a letter dropped through her letterbox in Sheerness from the prison, informing her that Graham had one morning been found dead in his cell from a heart attack. In spite of the heartbreak and tragedy he had brought the family, Aunt Winnie could still mourn.

'I paid for the funeral, although I couldn't go,' she told me. 'It was a wonderful funeral, I hear. He was cremated, and the ashes were scattered.'

Graham died knowing that the one ambition he had often talked of had been achieved: today a wax figure of him stands in the Chamber of Horrors in Madame Tussaud's in London, along with those of other famous poisoners. There is nothing of 'your friendly neighbourhood Frankenstein' about the figure. Instead, with the thin, drawn lips, the long, narrow nose and piercing dark eyes beneath a protruding forehead crowned by a receding cap of dark hair, there is more than a hint of Count Dracula. He would not be displeased, I think, by the effect.

SHIRLEY AND CINDY'S FUN DAY

The sun rose full of promise into a cloudless blue California sky on the morning of 14 June 1983, but Anna Brackett, tiny, delicate and eighty-five years old, felt a twinge of sadness as she opened the curtains in her apartment. Her best and truest lover was dying.

No one could remember how long Anna and Jim Wedgeworth had been together – fifteen, maybe twenty years? It seemed as if they had always been there, a fixture at every dance in Auburn, a foothills town thirty-three miles north-east of Sacramento, Anna impeccably dressed, always wearing a skirt rather than slacks, an ash-blonde wig holding back the years, Jim, the perfect gentleman, always holding ladies' chairs for them, fetching their drinks, complimenting them. It was when they took to the dance floor that you saw the perfection of the partnership – they danced divinely, as if they were meant for each other.

Now Jim was in the Hillside Convalescent Hospital, just up the road from the pleasant four-unit building in Auburn Greens where the unmarried couple had lived together, calling themselves for the form of things Mr and Mrs Wedgeworth. And, seeing his wasted, pain-racked

173

frame, Anna could not deceive herself. Death would be a mercy now.

At least, she consoled herself, she would not be alone. Her son, Carl, and his wife, Geri, who lived a twenty-minute drive away in a village called Meadow Vista, were so kind, taking her to visit Jim, driving her to the bingo games which, since she'd given up dancing, had become her main source of entertainment. If he had time, Carl had said he'd take her to a game that evening.

And so, with thoughts sweet and melancholy, Anna passed her day, dusting where there was no dust, tidying nonexistent mess, making herself a light lunch. Until, just before five, there was a knock at the door.

'Hi,' said the taller of the two girls she found standing on the doorstep. 'Ma'am,' she said, looking over her shoulder, 'would you mind if I used your phone to call my mum to come and pick us up. There's a couple of creepy guys following us. We're kinda like scared.'

Anna hesitated for only a moment. Both the girls had their hair dyed a bizarre burgundy tinge, their running shoes were ragged, their jeans none too clean. But wasn't that the way young girls dressed these days? They didn't seem to take any pride in themselves any more. It was shocking, but what could you do? The one who'd spoken had the rugged build of a football player, looked as if she could handle any fellow. But, Anna thought, who was she to judge? 'Yes, come in,' she said.

'And could we please have a glass of water?' the taller girl asked as Anna brought them into the living room. 'It's that hot out there!'

'The phone's over there.' Anna nodded towards the counter between the kitchen and the dining area.

'Ma'am, you sure do have a nice little place here,' said the talkative one, while the slimmer girl with the lively, impish features took a seat. 'Do you live here all alone?

Anna had plonked ice cubes into two glasses and was filling them from the tap. 'Well, right now I do,' she said wistfully.

'No answer. I guess she's out,' said the girl, putting down the phone. 'Mm-mm, that feels good,' she said, drinking from the glass Anna had handed her. 'What do you mean, "right now"? Do you have a husband?'

'Yes, I do, but the fact is... What did you say your name is?'

'Cindy, and this is Shirley.'

'Melissa,' said the other one, speaking for the first time.

'She means Shirley Melissa,' said Cindy with a laugh. 'You were saying about your husband?'

'Yes, he's in the hospital, and I'm afraid he's pretty bad.'

'Gee, that's a shame. I hope he gets better.' Cindy was looking around the apartment appraisingly. 'It must be hard for you to get around. Do you drive?'

'Not so much these days, although we still have our car.'

'Where do you keep it?' If Shirley's question was odd, Anna seemed not to notice.

'Over there in the carport with the others, see. It's the old brown Dodge.'

The phone's ring interrupted them. 'Hello, dear,' said Anna Brackett after listening for a moment. 'What? Yes ... oh, that would be very nice.' Then, after a moment,

'Oh, hi, Geri, nice to hear you too. Yes, I'll be ready. See you soon.'

'My son and his wife,' she explained after putting down the receiver. 'They're coming to pick me up.'

The girls exchanged a glance. 'When will they be here?' asked Shirley.

'Oh, they don't live far away. Twenty minutes, I guess. Can I get you girls some more water?' But when she turned towards them, they weren't looking at her at all.

Cindy, the bigger girl, was standing over her friend. 'It's time,' she said between her teeth.

'What?' Shirley looked startled.

'We got to do it now. Now!'

It seemed to Shirley that the voice was coming from a thousand miles away. Perhaps from back in her childhood. 'Now!' She pulled herself to her feet from the leatherette couch. 'Now!' It was the command she had been waiting to hear for so long.

Anna Brackett knew something terrible was about to happen. Her blue eyes widened in terror as Shirley grabbed her by the shoulders and spun her around. Then she felt the girl's powerful arm tighten around her throat from behind. She knew she only had seconds before she'd lose consciousness. She had to hold on, hold on. She tried to scream, but no sound came. She tried to grab Shirley's hair, but the girl jerked back her head. Ragged fingernails scored the back of her neck, blows rained down on her head, her bottom denture shot out and together she and Shirley crashed to the floor.

From a guttural grunt, Shirley had now begun almost a chant: 'I'm gonna kill you, gonna kill you, gonna kill you . . .'

176

Cindy had ripped the phone off the wall and was rummaging in the kitchen drawers. 'Here!' she said triumphantly, dropping a paring knife into Shirley's outstretched hand. 'Do it!' she cried, and even with the woman's face pressed into the rug, they could hear the scream of pain as Shirley plunged the knife into her back. But instead of dying, she was getting stronger. She struggled. She writhed. She broke loose from Shirley's grip and came blubbering and sobbing to her knees.

Cindy grabbed up a heavy brush from a chair. 'Sorry, lady,' she said, a grin on her face, and brought the brush down time and again with calculated force on the side of Anna's face. The woman collapsed to the ground and Shirley resumed stabbing her in the back. 'Die, you bitch, die,' she groaned.

Instead Anna Brackett turned her head like some ancient old tortoise. 'You won't get away with this,' she muttered.

Cindy was running through the apartment, looking for a gun. Instead, she came back with a blue nylon nightdress. 'Stuff this in her mouth,' she said. 'We don't want her waking up the whole neighbourhood.'

Shirley wrenched open the woman's mouth and pushed as much of the nightdress inside as she could. The eyes continued to stare at her. She swung the knife again, then looked in puzzlement at the bent blade.

'It's fucking broke,' she yelled to Cindy. 'Get me another one.'

This time Cindy brought a mean-looking carving knife with a much longer blade. Stabbing wasn't doing it. Shirley slashed at the side of the old woman's exposed throat. A few moments later blood trickled from her

177

mouth and nose, and Shirley was sure she was dead.

'No, look, she's still breathing,' said Cindy, grabbing the knife. She hacked several times at the throat, then paused to gauge the effect. Finally she stopped and both of them knelt looking down at the old lady. Blood was congealing on the pretty blue and white floral top Anna had put on for bingo. The girls were smiling.

'Let's get the fuck out of here!' said Cindy. She reached for Anna's white handbag, emptied the contents on a chair and picked out a ring of keys and a wallet.

After checking to see that no one was around, Cindy slipped out of the front door. Shirley, holding something close to her, followed a second later. Dropping any pretence of caution, they ran towards the brown 1970 Dodge. Shit, the passenger door was locked. No room to go around, they jumped up on the bonnet and down the other 'side, scrambling over each other to get inside. Shirley grabbed up a rag, wiped her hands and the handle of the carving knife, which she'd brought with her, then shoved them both under the seat. No way she wanted them to find her prints on that! She didn't stop to think that their prints were on the door, the phone, the glasses, the other knife and probably elsewhere in the apartment.

No time to think because the key wouldn't go into the ignition. 'Oh, Jesus, we can't start it,' said Cindy, panicking and flinging the keys angrily towards Shirley.

'Hey, wait for me!' Shirley called as Cindy took off down the lane. Stopping only to grab the keys and shove them in her pocket, she hurried after her new friend. Yes, new, because Shirley Wolf, just fourteen, had only met Cindy Collier, two months past her fifteenth birthday, for the first time seven hours earlier. But they'd hit it off right away. They were on the same wavelength.

Carl Brackett was turning into Auburn Greens with his wife moments later to pick up his mother when he noticed two girls hitchhiking beside the main road. 'Stupid kids!' he told Geri. 'That's the way they get in trouble.'

Pulling up in front of his mother's building, he was surprised not to see her waiting outside for him. She was nearly always outside the front door when they arrived. Geri walked up to the door, knocked and turned the handle. Locked. That was unlike her too. Even if she wasn't outside she'd have left the door open for them. Carl, who had joined his wife, stepped into the flowerbed and peered through the window.

His mother was lying face down on the floor, her head turned to one side. That was all he took in. 'We need an ambulance!' he yelled to his wife, then ran to a next-door unit and phoned.

Back at his mother's apartment, he smashed at the door with his fist and shoulder. It wouldn't budge. He had to help her! Finally he broke the window and, ignoring the shards of glass, climbed in. Oh my God! The blood! It was everywhere. He touched his mother's face gently. It had to be her face, but it was so battered and mutilated he had to somehow make sure. Her neck, her back were a mass of blood where she had not so much been stabbed as gored. Carl was on the point of passing out when someone banged on the door. 'Ambulance company!' a voice called. He opened the door and stood back.

Who? Why? The questions pounded in his head as the medics went through the motions of attaching a heart monitor to his mother. A deranged patient from a nearby mental hospital? That was his first thought. The scene seemed somehow familiar. And then it came to him: *Psycho*. It was as if he'd walked in on the famous knifing scene in the shower in Hitchcock's movie.

'I'm sorry, sir,' the attendant was saying. 'She seems to be dead.' He nodded.

Homicide Deputy George Coelho of the Placer County sheriff's department was equally struck by the savagery of the attack after inspecting the body a few minutes later. Some sort of sex maniac? Robbery seemed too petty a motive for a man to kill so brutally. It didn't enter his head that the murderer wasn't a man.

So he listened with a hint of scepticism as two neighbours of Anna's, Pete and Mabel Fredericks, tried to explain to him something odd that had happened late that afternoon. 'Two teenage girls,' said Mabel, 'they came to my door about five o'clock. One of them asked if she could use my phone to call her mother. Said a fellow was following them. I let them in. Who wouldn't? And the other one asked for a glass of water.

'Well, sir, the first one finishes phoning – said there wasn't no answer – when my husband walks in. At that, they thank me, and off they go.' A description? The Fredericks could agree on little, except that one of the girls was wearing a dark halter top while the other had on a pink satin jacket with writing on the back. Something like 'Rock and Roll'. Perhaps they could raise some prints from the glasses the girls had used, or the telephone? Not a chance. The couple had been so disturbed by the two girls, they'd immediately washed the glasses and cleaned the telephone receiver with alcohol.

Coelho, an easy-going man of Portuguese background,

had cut his teeth working in an investigations unit in steamy Newport Beach in southern California. He'd moved north to Auburn to get his family, which would eventually number eight children, away from that high-crime area. In a quiet place like Auburn, murder was comparatively rare. And when it did happen it was not the sort of crime where you looked for a female perpetrator, let alone young girls. Still ... he had noticed two water glasses on the counter in the Brackett apartment. And the phone receiver had been ripped from the wall ...

Thank you kindly, ma'am. Anything else? Sure, said Mabel. Half an hour later she'd been eating her supper when, looking out of the window, she'd seen the same two girls running towards the carport.

Other neighbours reported two girls coming to the door with the same story. Within an hour the local radio station was broadcasting descriptions of the pair. By 10.30 p.m. a teenage girl named Donna was describing to Sheriff Donald Nunes seeing two girls at one of the Auburn Greens swimming pools that afternoon who matched the descriptions. The girl in the halter top she didn't know, the other one with the satin jacket, she said, was Cindy Collier.

It was 2.30 a.m. when a posse of four officers moved in quietly on a run-down house with an overgrown garden in one of Auburn's canyon neighbourhoods. Cindy Collier, they'd discovered, was on probation for drug offences, which meant the police could enter and search her mother's home at any time without the need for a warrant. Coelho, covering the side of the house, flashed his torch through the basement windows. Even today the image stays with him: the two girls were asleep in a set of rustic knotty pine bunk beds, Cindy in the top

181

one, Shirley below, their faces in repose a picture of peace and innocence. Babes in the wood.

Well, he thought, he never had given much credence to the idea that two teenage girls had murdered Anna Brackett. It didn't make sense. Now he knew for sure that they were wasting their time. Just going through the motions. And waking people up in the middle of the night for no good reason. He shivered in the desert-dry night air.

Sergeant Ray Mahlberg was knocking at the front door. 'Police!' he called when a light went on in the hall. Betty, Cindy's mother, woke up fast when he explained that they were investigating a homicide and wanted to speak to Cindy. 'Oh my God!' she cried. Was Cindy home? Yes, replied Betty, she was asleep downstairs with her friend Melissa. But what was going on? Mahlberg told her there had been a homicide earlier in the evening at Auburn Greens, and several people had spotted Cindy in the area. It was just a question of following up all leads, a matter of routine, he said. What time, for instance, had the two girls arrived home?

'Around nine. They said there'd been a murder at the Greens,' she offered. 'And that the place was crawling with cops.'

Downstairs in the panelled basement bedroom Cindy didn't want to wake up. She pulled the covers over her face as Mahlberg called her name. Finally she lifted herself on one elbow and looked at the officers through the slits of half-asleep eyes. 'Can you understand what I'm telling you, Miss Collier?'

'Yeah, yeah, yeah,' she muttered. They wanted to search her belongings, he'd said. 'Go ahead,' she muttered.

Shirley, by now awake and sitting up, agreed to accompany Coelho and another officer into the next room for questioning. No, her name wasn't Melissa, she told him first. It was Shirley Katherine Wolf. 'Shirley,' said Coelho, after mentioning that they knew the girls had been in the Auburn Greens area when the murder took place, 'would you be willing to give us a hand in clearing this thing up?' It was the standard approach for the friendly, balding cop with the soft brown eyes. Be a pal. No heavy-handed stuff.

'Sure I'll help. You know, we thought about turning ourselves in.'

Was he hearing right? 'It blew me away,' Coelho said when I spoke to him recently. 'I wasn't expecting that answer. After seeing them asleep like that ... well, it just didn't dawn on me that someone could sleep after doing something like that.'

'So what happened, Shirley? Take your time.'

'Well, we did it,' she said. 'We killed her.' And then she told the cops about her whole wonderful day.

'Can you tell me what you were wearing?' he asked when she finally stopped talking.

'I was wearing my bathing suit with my old blue Jordache cords on over top. Oh, and my pink Roller Disco jacket.' So that was it, 'Roller Disco,' not 'Rock and Roll'.

'Where are your clothes now?'

'In the bedroom. There's something else in there too. It's my journal. You wanna see it?'

Returning to the other room, Coelho gathered up the clothes. Something jangled. In the pocket of the cords he found a set of keys. They would be identified as belonging to Anna Brackett. The journal, with the sort of

183

floral-patterned cover young girls favour, was lying on the bedside table. Coelho picked it up and opened it. Shirley's signature was inside the cover. Flipping to the last entry he saw, penned in a childish scrawl, the most chilling murder confession he had ever read: 'Today Cindy and I ran away and killed an old woman. It was lots of fun.' And then, as if the thought had surprised her: 'I am becoming meaner.'

Why did they do it? When children murder, society is often left without answers. But in Shirley Wolf's case, and perhaps in Cindy Collier's, answers were not hard to find. Shirley's childhood, from the time she could remember, was haunted by monsters. One monster, in fact. Her father.

Placerville, another foothills town, twenty-eight miles from Auburn, is as good a place as any to begin Shirley Wolf's unhappy story. Her family lived for a while in a ratty-looking house standing on its own on a street named, ironically, Grand View Drive. You can get a view of the back yard from the picture window in the Carver family's house nearby. From here young David Carver one day saw Lou Wolf beating his daughter, Shirley, and her younger brother, LJ, with an electrical cord, whipping them until they screamed.

Then Lou, a big, heavy-set man, over six feet tall, who sometimes used a wheelchair and sometimes walked with a cane, had a better idea. David, peering through the picture window, couldn't figure out what Lou and a friend of his were building. It sure didn't look like a swing seat. It was a sort of board with holes in it on a stand. A real puzzle. Until, one hot summer's day, young Carver was out playing and saw – and heard – LJ getting another beating. Right away he realized what the device was: stocks. LJ's head and wrists were fastened in the holes, his trousers had been pulled down, and Lou was pitching into him with the electric cord. He whipped the boy until his arm got tired. A few days later David saw Shirley get the same treatment. After that Lou Wolf got a lot of use out of those stocks.

Why didn't the neighbours interfere? You don't mess with a guy who goes out looking for his children with a sub-machine-gun strapped across his chest, and who keeps them in line with an electric cattle prod.

Even when Lou, in his own mind, was having fun with his four children, there was always a sadistic edge to his games. Like the time the family had just acquired a motorless go-cart. Shirley was eager to try it on the Grand View hill. Hey, Lou suggested, wouldn't it be even more fun if he pulled her behind the station wagon? She wasn't so sure, but a few minutes later the cart was roped behind the car and Lou was putting his foot on the gas. His wife, Katherine, in the car, yelled to him that Shirley had tipped over. A funny thing, though, Lou didn't seem to hear. It was a few minutes before he touched the brake. By then Shirley, who hadn't had the wit to let go, was lying in the street all blood and bruises and with a compound fracture of her arm.

The Lou the neighbours saw was bad enough; inside the walls of his own home he was even worse. And it went a long way back to the time when they lived in Brooklyn, New York.

Katherine remembered a night when Lou had woken her out of a deep sleep. 'Kathy, you won't believe this.' As she cleared the sleep from her eyes she saw an odd look on his face, kind of sheepish. 'See, I was sleeping,

185

and I was having this dream like you was giving me a blow job. And I'm kind of half awake, see . . .'

'Yeah?'

'And it ain't you. It's little Shirley. Honest to God, I dunno how she got in here.'

'Lou, what are you saying? Lou, for Chrissake!'

'It ain't my fault. What am I s'posed to do? I was asleep. I couldn't help myself, could I! She crawled right in on top of me. Baby, I think maybe you should go clean her up, okay?'

Katherine got out of the bed as if she was in a trance. A little girl, only three years old! Why? Why? That's what she couldn't get her mind around. What was going on that she didn't understand? Maybe it hadn't happened after all. Maybe the dumb bastard was imagining it. Him and his wet dreams!

She opened the door to Shirley's bedroom, letting in the light from the hall. Shirley turned her face towards the wall. 'Honey? You okay?' She didn't say anything, only stared. Katherine pulled the bedding back. A large damp patch covered the crotch of Shirley's pyjamas. She didn't need to touch it to know – the sharp, rancid smell told her. 'Come on, honey, let's give you some dry ones.' The little girl's panties were wet too. What sort of blow job was that?

From the day Shirley started kindergarten in September 1975, her teacher knew something wasn't right in the little girl's life. She had no time for other children; she just wanted to ingratiate herself with adults, clinging fiercely, seeking affection wherever she could get it. One minute she'd seem happy enough, the next she'd be in deep despondency. The teacher called her parents but, she'd say later, they didn't seem to hear what she was saying. They said they'd seek professional help for Shirley, but never did.

In October 1975 they called Katherine to tell her Lou had had an accident at his construction job and was in hospital. He'd fallen off a ledge while installing windows, and plunged through fifteen sheets of plate glass stacked against the wall below. There would be different opinions about the degree to which Lou eventually recovered. Certainly right after the accident he was in a lot of pain and couldn't walk. Later on, people saw him walking often enough – except when it was time to go to one government office or another to make disability claims. Then he needed his wheelchair.

About one result there was no argument: if Lou had been hard to live with before, he was worse now. The children, Shirley especially, went in dread of his unpredictable blows, his apparent sweet-tempered interludes that would suddenly be replaced by blind rages when he would throw them against the wall. To Katherine, the oddest thing was that the more Lou abused Shirley, the more she seemed to worship him. When he wasn't angry with her, they would share little secrets, and by the time she was seven she was becoming Lou's 'little wife.'

In 1978, when Shirley was nine, Lou had had enough of their seedy Brooklyn neighbourhood. He was remembering his days with his first wife when they'd lived in Placerville, in California. Katherine didn't have much say. The family jammed into the car, with a friend along to help Lou with the driving, and drove westward day and night. Shirley's earliest memories of California would not be the best: her father raped her.

It happened on one of the first days they were there,

187

when she was holding the screws for him while he fixed a heater in the bathroom of the crummy house they'd rented. 'I'll be needing a part before I can finish the job,' he said. 'Kathy!' A few minutes later Katherine left in the car for the hardware store on the other side of town. 'You guys,' said Lou, coming into the living room where Shirley's three younger brothers were playing, 'out! Come on, you don't need to be inside.'

With the boys gone, he put his arm around Shirley's shoulders. 'Come on, princess,' he said, taking her back into the bathroom. Every second of the next few minutes is etched on her mind. It runs like one of those little videos you see in museums, over and over again. She sees him washing his hands, all the while talking about how he loves her and how special she is and how they're going to have this special, secret thing between them that will be just theirs.

'Do you really love me, baby?' he asked. She nodded, feeling sick inside. 'Take your clothes off, baby, come on,' he said, softly. When her jeans and top and underwear were on the floor, he lifted her, a skinny waif, all bones, with dark hair hanging down into her frightened eyes, and sat her on the countertop. And in the horror that followed, as she felt herself torn apart and saw the blood running down her legs, her daddy seemed to be miles away. When she looked in his face, he had this faraway look, as if she wasn't even there for him.

But when they'd finished, and she was pulling on her clothes and trying to ignore the pain, it was her own father again, telling her in a cold, hard voice, 'Okay, get outta here.'

After that, according to Shirley, her father would have

sex with her at every chance he got, eventually as much as three times a day. If Katherine suspected, she wasn't letting on. A lank, thin woman, she was completely submissive to her husband although often violent towards the children.

At school Shirley was the despair of her teachers. She'd arrive dressed like a tart in sexy, revealing tops, but no one wanted to sit next to her because she smelt. She'd get in fights, yell in class for no reason, and didn't have a single friend. Until an older girl, Tina Beaulieu, befriended her as part of the Cross-Age programme which was intended to provide any younger kid experiencing problems with an older friend to confide in.

Tina genuinely liked Shirley. Looking past the rough exterior, the acting-up, she saw a girl with ambitions and plans. 'Come in and meet my folks,' Shirley said one day when the two were going out swimming. Katherine nodded to Tina and then disappeared. In the living room, Lou, sitting smoking in his wheelchair, told Shirley to get lost. NOW! Tina jumped at his loud voice. When they were alone he started telling her about his accident and his tough life, She felt more and more uncomfortable, especially when, a couple of times, he looked her up and down suggestively. She made her escape as fast as possible. A counsellor told her later that Lou had called to complain that Tina was dressed too provocatively, that her shorts were too short, that she'd given him a hard-on. She didn't have to defend herself to the counsellor. It was just a warning that, with a crazy guy like Lou, the best thing was to steer clear.

At the start of the eighth grade, Shirley finally found friends among a small group of girls, none of them over thirteen, most with problems, some of them with a history

189

of being sexually abused at home. In the school cafeteria one day she finally found the courage to tell the others about her life with Lou. By now her father was becoming wilder all the time, making scenes at the school, boasting to the principal one day that he'd put his little girl on birth control pills because he knew she was sexually active, waving his .357 Magnum in the grocery store, threatening people and lashing out at home with ever-increasing fury.

On a day not so unlike many others, when her mother had run into her bedroom to try to escape another beating, Shirley tapped on the door. 'Mom,' she said, 'if dad did something real bad, would they take him away?' She had something to tell her, said Shirley. Something that might remove him from their lives for good.

By that night, after Shirley and Katherine had spoken to a sympathetic Placerville police officer, the family had been removed to a motel for their own safety. Lou gave the police one stormy interview in which he denied everything, failed to turn up for a polygraph test he'd promised to take, and took off in his van, a warrant hanging over his head for committing 'lewd and lascivious acts' with a child under fourteen. The all-points bulletin described him as thirty-nine years old, six foot one and a half, nearly seventeen stone, his arms tattooed, and warned, 'Suspect armed with numerous weapons and has stated he will not be taken into custody.' Next day Katherine flew with her children to New York to stay with her mother.

It wasn't far enough. Lou quickly found them. He even persuaded them to return to Placerville with him, where he gave himself up to the police. He wasn't that stupid. He pleaded guilty to a reduced charge of child molesting and served only a hundred days in jail. 'They told me if I pleaded innocent [and was convicted], guaranteed I'd get from one to fifty years,' he said later. 'I'd rather serve a couple of months than risk fifty years. I'd rather be with my family.'

It was the end for Shirley. While Lou's case was pending and he was still at home, she was put in a foster home. So it wasn't her father who had been kicked out for incest, it was her. At school the other children shunned her: all she wanted to talk about was what her father had done to her – in graphic detail. Finally she saw there was only one way to be part of her family again: by denying the incest. 'Today I plan to go home by saying I lied about my father molesting me,' she wrote in the diary she was now keeping. Before that could happen, Shirley's constant running away from foster homes and her violence towards other children finally exhausted the patience of the authorities: she was placed in a group home in Sacramento. She had lived a lifetime of trouble; she was still only thirteen.

Attending school during the day, she was rarely out of trouble. A month after her fourteenth birthday she ran away, heading home towards Placerville. But there really was no home to run to. After spending several miserable nights in the open, she gave herself up to the police and was returned to the group home. School was ending one day in June when a husky-looking stranger came into the room Shirley shared with a girl named Jana Jarvis.

'Cindy!' screamed Jana, embracing the girl. 'Shit! It's good to see ya.'

Cindy Collier, who faced the world with a scowl of contempt, had just absconded from a work programme in Auburn and hitchhiked down to see her old friend. 'Come on, Jana, let's take off,' she said. Jana looked doubtful. 'No, sorry, Cindy. Things are going real good for me right now. But, hey, maybe Shirley would.' Shirley smiled shyly.

Cindy Collier was born on 18 April 1968 in Auburn, and the signs were not auspicious. Her mother, Betty, had gone through one marriage that had produced two sons, and was now living with David Collier, a roughneck drifter who had been in and out of trouble with the law. Born with misaligned hip sockets, Cindy spent her first two years in a heavy brace, and hearing and bronchial problems dogged her childhood. When she was five, and Betty had had another baby boy, her father disappeared to be replaced by a succession of men who came and went unpredictably during the remainder of her growing-up years.

Home life was a round of booze, drugs and violence. 'I've been beaten since I was born, and raped a few times,' she would say. 'I have tried to kill myself before and all it did was bring frustrations. So I take it out on others. I don't like them because they probably think they're better than I am. I don't want them around. I want them to pay.'

At school, Cindy, like Shirley, was soon getting into fights. With her rugged build, serious fights. The familiar pattern began: shoplifting, thievery at school, stays in juvenile hall, punctuated by running-away episodes. Once she disappeared for a whole month after stealing her mother's car and was brought back from Monterey, two hundred miles away, dirty, ragged, much thinner than when she'd left, and suffering from gonorrhoea. She'd acquired it, she said, from her stepbrother, who had been molesting her at home since she was seven.

Cindy had finished her most recent spell in juvenile hall on Monday, 13 June. Next morning, when Betty went to wake Cindy up in her basement bedroom, her daughter was groaning. 'It's the cramps again, Mum,' she said. 'They get worse all the time.'

'We got to go,' said her mother. At nine o'clock that morning Cindy was due to start 150 hours of court-ordered community service at the local work project office. 'You don't want more trouble.'

Cindy dragged herself out of bed, complaining, and her mother drove her to the project office, getting there just in time. Cindy, in her dirty jeans and halter top, stood in the hot morning sun, watching as her mother drove off. Then she headed for the main road.

Hitchhiking back to Auburn, sitting on the grass beside the road in between lifts, the two absconding girls talked about all the rotten things that had happened to them in their lives. And, hey, it was as if they were both talking about the same life. And they were, really. 'Shirley's exactly like me,' Cindy would say. 'She had the same childhood.'

Something clicked between them. On this one special day they were free to be themselves, without pretence. To be what circumstance had made them. Out with all that old shit!

The best place to begin their new lives, they decided when they got to Auburn, was at the hair-colouring shelf in the drugstore. They bought – or maybe stole – two bottles of Miss Clairol Loving Care hair colouring. In Red Ginger. The sinks in the women's toilets at the Auburn Greens swimming pool were stained a vivid red by the time they'd finished applying the stuff. 'I want a car, that's what I want,' said Cindy as they walked away from the pool.

'Me too,' said Shirley. 'Then we'd be outta here.'

'I know how,' said Cindy, lighting a cigarette. 'See, we just knock on some old lady's door an' take her keys away from her. There's lots of old ladies live in the apartments.'

'She'd scream the place down.'

'So we kill her.'

'You mean, commit murder?'

'Yeah. That's right.'

'Because why?'

'Because I'm not about to have her open her mouth. See, even if we tie her up she'll still be able to identify us. Dead, what can she do?'

'Yeah, okay. But don't forget, anybody we talk to, my name's Melissa. Melissa Brown.' Shirley had started writing a book about her life. The title: *Melissa's Choices*.

After it all happened, after they stabbed the old lady and when they were on the highway thumbing a lift away from Auburn Greens, they couldn't stop laughing. It had been so easy. 'To honestly tell you the truth,' Cindy would tell Deputy Coelho, 'we didn't feel any badness. We felt good inside. We wanted to go out and celebrate. We were full of laughter, and we were . . . like, it was fun. Like afterwards we wanted to do another one. We just wanted to kill someone.'

Full of laughter. They were exactly the words used by Mary Bell a continent away in Newcastle in describing how she felt the day she killed little Brian Howe.

Several drivers who gave them lifts that evening never realized the danger they were in from the two giggling girls. The pair hitchhiked to Roseville, a small town where

194

Cindy used to live, and where she threw her bloodstained shoes out of the window of one of the cars before they hitched lifts back to Auburn.

Betty, Cindy's mother, would wonder the next day why her carving knife was on the stove instead of in its usual drawer – and then remembered Shirley coming into the room at one point that evening with something concealed behind her back, her eyes shining.

'It was just a crazy game,' Shirley would say of the day's events. 'I wonder how it happened?'

And of course, it was the day that changed their lives. They were celebrities now, bigshots on the local television news as they were led shackled to and from court, featured in a spread in *People* magazine, the subjects eventually of a powerful book by Joan Merriam, the founding director of the Placer County Child Abuse Prevention Council. Both their fathers, perhaps envying them the limelight, came back into their lives. Lou complained bitterly about how hard his life had been and tried to sell his daughter's story to the TV networks; David Collier attended court regularly until, one day, extra security was laid on because he'd threatened to shoot Cindy. After that he left town.

One night in juvenile hall Shirley woke screaming from a nightmare in which Anna Brackett appeared to her (Anna's body, meanwhile, had been flown to Meridian, Mississippi, where she was buried alongside Jim Wedgeworth, who had died the day after her murder). But both girls were as brash and aggressive as ever, revelling in their new notoriety.

As one psychiatrist's report on Shirley put it: 'All the evidence points towards the most unpleasant and quite inescapable conclusion that Shirley Wolf is, at the age of fourteen, thoroughly comfortable with her role as a cold-blooded killer.'

Judge J. Richard Couzens, giving Cindy the maximum sentence available to him, incarceration until she reached the age of twenty-seven, recognized the girls' celebrity status. 'However, I hope at some time after all the cameras are gone,' he said, 'that there will be a quiet moment when ... I hope it will creep into your consciousness what you have done, and the staggering consequences of taking another's life.'

That realization was a long time coming. Both girls continued to be violent and destructive, although Cindy eventually obtained a junior college degree while in detention, and studied law before being released on parole in August 1992. But Shirley's demons continued to torment her. Her violent temper was always getting her into trouble. In December 1989, making an escape attempt, she drove off in a prison fire truck in which someone had carelessly left the keys. Like so much of Shirley's life, what she did made no sense. The truck careened across the prison grounds, destroying a parked car and a shed, and sending a guard leaping for safety. Alarms screamed as again and again she drove the truck into the unyielding prison fence and then hit an oak tree, causing the truck to burst into flames.

That escapade earned her 540 days in solitary confinement, an awful lot of time to think. 'You know,' she would tell Joan Merriam later, 'when I murdered Mrs Brackett, I didn't just murder one person. There were lots of victims of what I did ... so many victims.'

'You're a victim, too, Shirley,' her visitor reminded her.

Shirley remains in the Central California Women's

Facility near Chowchilla. She's had no contact with her family, who now live in the Pacific Northwest, since 1988. She is due for release in 1994.

'It's a strange thing to say,' said Coelho, when I caught up with him on duty at the county jail, 'but I ended up liking both girls. I thought Wolf was a likeable little girl, and so was Collier.' Coelho, a grandfather now, added, 'That case was a new experience for me. It opened my eyes to the fact that anybody is capable of anything.'

DID YOU KILL
LYNNE HARPER?

It was the kind of golden evening we all remember – or imagine we can remember – from our childhoods. At the end of a sweltering day, with the temperature still in the eighties, boys fished from the bridge over the Bayfield River while others splashed and screamed in the swimming hole. Back up the road at the Royal Canadian Air Force base, a boy stood leaning on his green English racing bicycle in the school playground, watching little girls in the Brownie pack running excitedly from one hiding spot to another on their scavenger hunt.

'Hi, Lynne,' he called to a slightly older girl who was helping the Brownie leader. 'Whatcha doin' later?'

She scuffed the earth shyly with her running shoes as she came over to talk to him. 'Oh, I dunno.'

'Going swimming?'

Lynne's face flushed. 'No. My parents are being really mean. I can't go.'

'Why not?'

'Well, you know, because I'm only twelve I can't get a swimming pass if they don't go with me. And they won't go. It's not fair!'

'Have you seen the newborn calves over at Lawson's farm?'

'No. Are they cute?'

'You wouldn't believe it. Want me to show you?'

'Sure,' Lynne felt flattered. Although they were in the same class at school, he was two years older than her, handsome, with warm, lively eyes and a wide mouth that broke easily into a grin. He had also just been named the school's best all-round athlete of the year, and was to receive a trophy. Until that moment he had never paid any attention to Lynne Harper.

They walked across the grass, pushing the bike between them. 'I'll ride you,' he offered when they came to the paved county road. As she climbed on to the crossbar in her shorts and sleeveless blouse, he was acutely aware of the smoothness of her brown arms and the smell of her sun-bleached hair a few inches from his face.

'Hey, isn't that the turn for the farm?' she said a few minutes later.

'Yes,' he replied. 'But Bob Lawson doesn't like a lot of kids around the place. We'll go in the back way, through the bush.'

As they cycled past Lawson's Bush, a twenty-acre wilderness of young ash, elm, maple and basswood trees, twelve-year-old Richard Gellatly, riding home from the river to get his swimming trunks, waved to them.

'Here we are,' said the boy, stopping and helping her down. 'We'll take the tractor road.' Within a few moments of starting down the lane bordering the edge of the woods, they were out of sight of the road. Eleven-year-old Philip Burns, walking home from the swimming hole just a few minutes behind the Gellatly boy, didn't see them.

A short time later, Jocelyne Goddette, aged thirteen, came riding down the road on her bicycle and got off by Lawson's Bush. She waited a few moments, looking up and down the road. A few minutes later she walked her bicycle down the tractor road a little way and stopped, listening. 'Steven,' she called. 'Steven.' There was no reply.

His full name is Steven Murray Truscott. And although I have described the sequence of events leading up to the rape and murder of Lynne Harper on Monday, 9 June 1959, just the way I believe it happened, millions of people believe otherwise. And for several rather good reasons.

People around the world can remember exactly what they were doing when they heard that President John F. Kennedy had been shot. Similarly, many Canadians – and a good number of people elsewhere – can place the exact moment when, on 30 September 1959, they read a particularly shocking headline: BOY, 14, SENTENCED TO HANG.

Even apart from the horror of Steven Truscott's sentence, this was the first really big case in the post-war period of a minor convicted of murder. It was a watershed and there would be many far more gruesome cases to come. But at that particular moment, at the end of a relatively innocent decade, people simply didn't want to believe that a nice-looking, normal-seeming kid would rape and murder a young girl.

Steven's sentence was soon commuted to one of life imprisonment. But the public's feeling of rancour and guilt over the original sentence lingered, and when, seven years later, a writer named Isabel LeBourdais produced a well-meant but gravely misleading account of the case

201

arguing the boy's innocence, people were ready to listen.

One Canadian Member of Parliament, John Byrne, after reading proofs of the LeBourdais book (dispatched cannily by the publisher to all Members of Parliament before publication), staked his seat in the Commons on Truscott being exonerated if a royal commission was appointed.

Wrote Walter Raeburn, a commissioner at the Old Bailey, in a review published in the *Sunday Telegraph*: 'The elaborate system of criminal justice had plainly broken down. A mere child, now grown to a bleak and barren manhood, has been made and is being made to suffer the misery of a blighted life for a hideous crime committed by someone unknown.'

Ludovic Kennedy, a crime writer who had fought his own battles on behalf of wrongly convicted murderers, commented: 'An almost certainly innocent person is convicted on the flimsiest of evidence.'

Down the years a veritable industry sprang up aimed at clearing the Truscott name. It included several books, including two accounts by Steven himself, radio and television shows and countless articles. As a result, even though the guilty verdict was upheld following a unique and thoroughgoing judicial review, there is still a general impression that an innocent boy was falsely convicted and nearly executed.

What really happened? We need to go back to that calm, cloudless Tuesday evening at the base in Clinton, in the rich farming country of south-west Ontario, to try to sift the facts from the rumours and lies that soon formed an almost impenetrable thicket around the murder of Lynne Harper.

What we know is this: two women in charge of the

Brownies, who had seen Steven talking to Lynne, said the couple left soon after 7 p.m., and certainly not later than quarter past. Steven would claim they had not left until half past. He was back in the schoolyard by 8 p.m., where he chatted with a bunch of friends. 'What did you do with Harper? Feed her to the fishes?' asked one friend who had obviously seen the two of them riding towards the river. 'I dropped her at the highway,' Steven replied.

He was supposed to be home by half past eight to babysit his younger brother and sister, Bill and Barbara, while his parents, Dan and Doris, went out. He arrived with a minute or two to spare.

A few minutes later, when his friend Arnold 'Butch' George dropped in, Steven joined him tossing a ball back and forth outside. 'Where were you?' asked Butch. 'I was looking for you.' Butch, in fact, had seen and spoken to Jocelyne at Lawson's Bush when she was looking for Steven.

'Down at the river,' replied Steven.

Butch grinned: 'I heard you gave Lynne a ride down there.'

'So what! She wanted a lift down to Number Eight Highway.'

'Not what I heard. I heard you were in the bush with her.'

'No way. We were just at the side of the bush looking for a cow and a calf. What business is it of yours anyway?'

'Skip it. Let's play ball.'

When Lynne Harper failed to return home by 9.15 p.m., her mother went looking for her. Lynne had left home in a huff after being told she couldn't go swimming. Was she staying out late deliberately to get her

203

own back? But when they still hadn't found her at half past eleven, her father, Flying Officer Leslie Harper, informed the base police, who, in turn, immediately called in the Ontario Provincial Police. By 11.40 p.m. a description of the missing girl was being broadcast on radio stations in the area.

Next morning, on the Wednesday, Leslie Harper, having learned that Lynne had been seen with Steven, called at the Truscott house. It was a small base, but, as in any military establishment, officers did not generally mix with non-commissioned types, and Harper had never actually met Warrant Officer Dan Truscott or his wife. Doris Truscott called Steven, who was getting ready for school. Had he seen Lynne the night before?

'Yes,' he replied. 'I gave her a lift on my bicycle.'

'Oh, my God!' It seemed, Truscott would say, that any news was good news to the distraught father. 'Try to remember. When did you see her, and where did you take her?'

He'd met her at the school after supper, he said. She'd asked him to take her to Number Eight Highway. He'd left her there and cycled back to the bridge over the Bayfield River. It was from there, he said, that he had seen Lynne hitch a ride on the highway.

Harper's heart missed a beat. 'Are you sure?'

'Yes. I saw her.'

A little geography here: going north along the county road from the base, one comes first to the Lawson farm on the right, followed by Lawson's Bush, a railway crossing and, a mile from the base, the bridge over the river. A quarter of a mile further on, the county road intersects Number Eight Highway, a main east-west road.

It was going to be another ninety-degree scorcher that

day. Steven's history class at AVM Hugh Campbell School dragged by in dull lassitude. Until the principal, after a whispered conference with the teacher, began asking first one boy and then another to come outside. Butch George, sitting behind Steven, was called, and when he returned, Steven heard his name.

The principal escorted him to a Provincial Police car outside. 'This is Steven Truscott,' he said, ushering him into the back seat. One of the two officers in the front turned and stared at him while the one at the wheel asked him: 'Did you see Lynne Harper last night?'

He repeated the story he'd told Leslie Harper.

'Did she say where she was going?'

'Yes. Wait a minute. She said she was going to the little white house on the highway where the man keeps ponies.'

Standing on the bridge and looking back to the highway he had seen her thumbing a ride, and then a car had stopped and picked her up.

That afternoon, called from his classroom again, Steven was surprised to see his father sitting in the back of the police cruiser. 'Over here, Steve,' he called, and explained that the policemen wanted him to show them where exactly he had dropped Lynne. They drove to the intersection and then back to the bridge.

'Any idea what kind of car it was picked her up?' one of the officers asked.

From that distance, he wasn't really expecting an answer. 'It was a 1959 Chevrolet,' Steven answered without hesitation. 'Grey. And I caught a flash of yellow or orange. It could have been the licence plate or maybe a bumper sticker.'

A yellow licence plate in that part of the country would probably have come from the state of Michigan, just a few miles away across the American border.

The policeman looked at Steven sceptically, but said nothing. Much would be made in the investigation and trial of the fact that a policeman standing on the bridge was unable to identify car makes from that distance. That ignored the fact that 1959 Chevrolets, with their fluted fins, were the most distinctive cars on the road, and underestimated the ability of young car-spotters like Steven to identify a make at surprising distances. A more telling question: how could he have seen the licence plate unless the car had actually reversed into the county road?

Later that Wednesday, Steven ran into Butch George.

'They been giving you a real grilling, eh?' said Butch.

'Yeah. And I got a problem. See, I told them you saw me down by the river. But I was wrong – it was Gordie Logan saw me. But how's it going to sound if I go back and say I goofed? Those cops'll jump on me for anything.'

'So?'

'All you got to say is you saw me by the bridge when you was down there looking for me.'

'No sweat.'

That, in fact, was what Butch George did tell the police that day. But the next day, when matters became more serious, he retracted his story.

That evening, on the surface at least, life had returned to normal at the base. The shouts of children could be heard at the swimming hole, and on the bridge several boys stood astride their bicycles, talking. 'The way I heard it,' said one of the boys, Paul Desjardines, 'Steven here had Lynne in the bush.'

'I did not!' said Steven indignantly. 'That's bull. Isn't it, Butch?'

'Sure,' said Butch George. 'He didn't take her in the

bush. He was just at the side of the bush showing her a cow and calf.' It didn't sound very convincing, even to himself.

It was all bustle and activity next morning as 250 airmen from the base, already sweating and uncomfortable in their uniforms, assembled for a search. Buses carried some to start the hunt along Number Eight Highway, while two other search parties were to comb either side of the county road. It looked as if they had a long and uncomfortable job ahead of them, contending in the heat with bush, swamp and mosquitoes, but there were no complaints. It could have been one of their kids.

And as it turned out, it was one of the shortest such searches on record: at 1.45 p.m., men struggling through Lawson's Bush about thirty yards in from the tractor trail caught a glimpse of something white in the undergrowth. It could almost have been a life-size doll. The flies told another story. The body of Lynne Harper lay on its back, legs apart, the left arm lying casually across the abdomen. She was naked except for her vest and her sleeveless blouse which had been ripped open at one side then knotted around her neck in a ligature.

Dr John Penistan, the pathologist in charge of the laboratories at the Stratford General Hospital (the same Ontario Stratford now famous for its annual Shakespearean festival), noticed when he arrived later that afternoon that, in the great heat of the previous days, decomposition had already set in. He had the body turned on its side, and noticed puncture marks in the underside consistent with the girl being pressed into the twigs on the ground by the weight of someone on top of her. Traces of semen would be found in the vagina. A pool of blood lay on the ground from a wound in her back, while a gash in her leg might

207

have been caused by Lynne being dragged through a nearby barbed-wire fence.

Plants around the body had been flattened, as if in a struggle, and several saplings had been bent and broken in an effort to cover and conceal the body. Dr Penistan noted two mounds of earth between her feet that might have been caused by her rapist bracing his feet. The earth showed the pattern of a pair of crêpe-soled shoes.

That evening, conducting the autopsy in a funeral home in Clinton, Dr Penistan came to a conclusion that would have a crucial effect on the case and, ultimately, pit some of the greatest names in forensic medicine against each other.

Lynne Harper's mother obviously believed in hearty meals, even in the hot weather. Before she left home around 6 p.m., Lynne had eaten a supper of turkey, cranberry sauce, peas, potatoes and pineapple upside-down cake. Dr Penistan found the remains of the meal still in the stomach, the contents still identifiable. Although emotional factors can affect the speed of digestion, there was nothing to suggest Lynne had encountered any shock or upset – until the final attack. So Dr Penistan gave it as his opinion that death occurred prior to 7.45 p.m. and perhaps as early as 7.15 p.m., a period of time when, even by his own admission, Steven Truscott had been the only one with her.

Inspector Harold Graham, now in charge of the investigation, had not regarded Steven as a prime suspect, if only because of the boy's age. Now his story of seeing Lynne picked up by the grey car was looking more and more implausible. Who ever heard of a sex killer bringing home his date, as it were, and dumping her body only a few hundred yards from her home? And everything pointed to the rape and murder having occurred where the body was found.

Steven, who sometimes did chores for Bob Lawson in the barn, was walking home from the farm the following evening when a police car pulled up beside him. 'Hey, Truscott,' called the driver. 'Get in.' At the Goderich police station it was Inspector Graham who this time led the interrogation, making Steven go over and over the details of his story of that bicycle ride with Lynne. When his father arrived, Graham told him it was his belief the boy had killed Lynne Harper and asked if he objected to Steven being medically examined.

It was the end of a long day for Dr J. A. Addison, a Clinton general practitioner. He didn't relish giving medical examinations at midnight but, in the presence of Steven's father and a doctor from the base, he asked Steven to strip. The scratch on the shoulder? A football injury, said the boy. A gash on the back of his leg? Could have happened when he fell off his bike the day Lynne disappeared. Then the doctor's interest focused on Steven's well-developed penis. Just below the head and on either side of the shaft he found two lesions or 'brush burns', each the size of a twenty-five-cent piece, both open and discharging. The injuries, Dr Addison ventured, had occurred about sixty or eighty hours earlier and were consistent with a boy of Truscott's size trying to penetrate the vagina of a twelve-year-old girl. As with the evidence of the stomach contents, this finding would create considerable controversy among the medical experts.

At the Truscott home, meanwhile, Steven's mother was surprised by the arrival of police officers with a search warrant. The new red trousers Steven had worn the night Lynn had disappeared were found hanging out to dry in

209

the basement after being laundered. There were grass stains on the knees and a tear in the back corresponding to the gash on his leg.

Inspector Graham believed he had enough: Steven was charged with the murder of Lynne Harper and at three o'clock on Saturday morning he was lodged in a small room with a bed and a table in the Goderich courthouse.

In this rural community the murder of Lynne Harper, quite naturally, had aroused the strongest emotions, and the Crown Prosecutor, H. Glenn Hayes, would press the charges with a terrier-like ferocity. His first move was to get the case shifted from juvenile court to adult court, 'in the interests of the community'. No mention was made at that stage of the fact that conviction would lead to an automatic death sentence on a fourteen-year-old.

The trial of Steven Truscott, which began in Goderich on 16 September 1959, was in two acts: The Children's Hour and The Doctors' Dilemma. To a surprising degree, the case rested on the uncertain, and sometimes contradictory, memories of children, of whom the Crown called no fewer than twenty-one. But it was Jocelyne Goddette who provided a context for what might have happened between Steven and Lynne that evening.

On Sunday, two days before Lynne disappeared, she'd seen a newborn calf in Lawson's barn.

'He's so cute!' she told Steven when she saw him at school on Monday.

'I know where there are two more. You want to see them?' he asked.

'Sure thing.'

'Can you make it tonight?'

'No, I have to go to Guides. But I'll try tomorrow.'

Steven, according to Jocelyne, told her on Tuesday to

meet him by Lawson's Bush at six o'clock, when he would show her the calves. But when he called at her house at ten to six she still hadn't had her supper. She said she'd come later. Leaving the house on her bicycle at close to six thirty, she went first to Lawson's barn to look for Steven. Emerging on the county road again, she saw Philip Burns walking towards home. She rode along the edge of Lawson's Bush, dismounting at the tractor road and calling for Steven. On the county road again, she met Butch George, who was also looking for Steven.

The evidence of several children seemed to pin Steven and Lynne down to Lawson's Bush at the crucial time. But two defence witnesses had a different story. Gordon Logan, thirteen, said he had been at the swimming hole until about half past seven that evening, and he remembered seeing Steven cycle across the bridge carrying Lynne towards the highway, returning alone about five minutes later. In fact, the swimming hole is two hundred yards from the bridge, and Gordon would have been looking into the setting sun.

But Douglas Oates, twelve, said he was right at the bridge, looking for turtles in the water, when he saw Steven go by carrying Lynne on the crossbar. She smiled at him when he waved, he said, although Steven seemed not to see him. The only problem with his evidence: he said he had seen them around seven o'clock, but it could have been half an hour either way. Steven had told the police that, just prior to going to the playground and meeting Lynne, he had cycled to the bridge and back, and several youngsters remembered seeing him riding around in circles opposite Lawson's Bush at that time. What it came down to was, if the jury believed Douglas and Gordon, then Steven was innocent. If they believed

211

Richard Gellatly, the boy on the bike who had seen Steven and Lynne near Lawson's Bush, and Philip Burns, the boy walking a short distance behind, who hadn't, there was a strong suspicion of guilt.

The doctors' evidence was every bit as contradictory. The pathologist, Dr Penistan, insisted that the extent of decomposition, the fact that rigor mortis, which occurs for a fixed period following death, had passed off and, most of all, the state of the stomach contents, established that death had taken place between 7.15 and 7.45 p.m. Dr Penistan had made his finding before Steven had been accused of the murder; it was not a case of bending the medical facts to fit the suspect's known movements. Dr Addison, the family physician, insisted in the witness box that the injuries on Steven's penis were consistent with forced intercourse.

Both prosecution doctors were refuted by Dr Berkeley Brown, an expert on the digestive system who had also, handily, been a military doctor for five years. During that time, he said, he had examined 'many thousands' of penises. 'It is highly unlikely that penetration would produce lesions [of the sort Steven had],' he declared. 'The penis is rarely injured in rape, and when it is, it is a tearing injury confined to the head of the penis.' The injuries, he said, were more consistent with masturbation, which had been Steven's claim.

Putting on his other specialist hat, Dr Brown was just as adamant that, judging by the stomach contents, death had taken place three and a half to four hours after the last meal.

One other piece of evidence never saw the light of day. The Crown claimed to have the canvas and crêpe shoes Steven wore on 9 July but, denied permission on technical grounds to call an expert witness who supposedly would have tried to link them to the footprints found at the death scene, the shoes were not produced.

The prosecutor would be severely criticized for his excesses in the Truscott trial. In his opening remarks, Hayes referred to a statement Steven had given police (not a confession) and which was subsequently not allowed into evidence. That was cause enough for calling a mistrial. In his summing-up, Hayes again went over the line, telling the all-male jury that, if Jocelyne Goddette was late having her supper, 'it was God's blessing to that girl', implying that she was the intended victim. The judge's summing-up too was confusing and misleading, but the trial rolled on to its inevitable climax: a verdict, after only two hours' consideration, of guilty with a recommendation for mercy. Had Steven anything to say, Mr Justice R. I. Ferguson asked, before sentence was passed? He said nothing.

The prisoner turned pale, and several of the jurors turned away as the judge intoned the fearful words: 'The sentence of this court upon you is that you be taken from here to the place from whence you came and there be kept in close confinement until Tuesday, the eighth day of December 1959, and that upon that day and date you be taken to the place of execution and that you there be hanged by the neck until you are dead. And may the Lord have mercy on your soul.'

Because the judge had imposed a ban on publication of evidence, the trial had received little publicity. So the sentence came as a tremendous shock to the Canadian public. 'The most disgraceful episode in a Canadian courtroom in this century,' *Toronto Star* columnist Ron Haggart would call it.

In Britain where, since 1933, the death penalty had not applied to those under eighteen, *The Guardian* declared that the sentence 'outrages every human instinct' and called on the Canadian government to reprieve Steven immediately.

Privately the Truscott family was assured he would be reprieved, and the law, in fact, was changed immediately so that a juvenile could not again receive the death penalty. But forms had to be observed: while his appeal was heard, and rejected, Steven remained in a Goderich death cell for forty-six days before his sentence was changed to one of life imprisonment.

He was sent to the Guelph training school, a juvenile facility, and eventually transferred to an adult penitentiary. His case would have been remembered only as an anomaly, a gruesome reminder of harsh nineteenth-century ideas of justice, if LeBourdais, a Toronto writer, had not taken up Steven's cause.

Originally her concern had been that a fourteen-year-old rapist-killer had been put in jail instead of receiving psychiatric care. But, 'when I read the trial transcript,' Mrs LeBourdais would say, 'I became convinced that this was not a sick boy who needed treatment, but a perfectly normal boy who was innocent. I was filled with a horrible sense of injustice.'

Her book, *The Trial of Steven Truscott*, caused a huge fuss. Because the original trial had received so little publicity and because hardly anyone had time to plough through the 2,500-page transcript, as Mrs LeBourdais had many times, politicians and journalists had only her version of the facts to go on, and cries were heard from all sides for the case to be reopened.

Indeed, according to the LeBourdais version, Steven

had been terribly wronged. Her view was that he had been picked from the start by the police, even before the body was found, as the sole suspect (Inspector Graham had, in fact, interrogated an eighteen-year-old airman who, at one point, was considered more likely to have been the killer). The fact that the search was started so close to the base, rather than further afield in line with Steven's statement that Lynne had been picked up by a motorist, only went to show that they didn't believe him. Presumably, a futile search some miles away would have better met Mrs LeBourdais' ideas of fair play. Her most surprising contention was that Lynne Harper had been murdered elsewhere and that her body was then returned to Lawson's Bush.

She claimed, in the face of photographic evidence to the contrary, that the girl's shorts and shoes and socks were neatly stacked when found beside the body. Mrs LeBourdais also believed that, before leaving, the murderer had deliberately kicked up the earth to create the footprints found between Lynne's feet. Mrs LeBourdais would argue too that, if Steven's story that they left the playground around 7.30 p.m. is accepted, there simply wasn't time for him to rape and strangle Lynne Harper and be back at the playground by eight, showing no sign of dirt, blood or upset.

Mrs LeBourdais used medical textbooks to refute Dr Penistan's estimate of the time of death as well as the prosecution claim that the sores on the penis had been caused by the rape. Given the vagueness of the times mentioned by some of the child witnesses, particularly Jocelyne Goddette, the author had little difficulty casting doubt on the Crown's murder scenario. She had also been

215

able to elicit from members of the Truscott jury prejudicial remarks like: 'That boy is an animal capable of anything', and 'I knew by the third day no one was going to prove that young monster innocent', and 'I guess there wasn't anybody hadn't heard about the boy's guilt before the trial'. It seemed positively morbid when several jurors admitted that they'd got on so well that, a year after the trial, they'd all gathered with their families for a picnic.

It would, of course, have been better if the trial had been moved to another location where feelings about the murder did not run as high. But it's a fact too that most jurors, in spite of the instructions they receive, are not circumspect and do, like the rest of us, feel strong emotions. The amazing thing is that they still more times than not manage to do the right thing.

There was really no one to answer Mrs LeBourdais' accusations. Seeking a way out, the government for the first time in Canadian history asked the Supreme Court of Canada to, in effect, rehear the case. It was a novel experience indeed for the nine robed justices who took their places in the high-ceilinged red chamber in Ottawa on 5 October 1966. It would be the first time in its ninety-one-year history that the Supreme Court had heard direct evidence. Some of the elderly justices, accustomed only to the arcane arguments of lawyers, had not heard a real, live witness in decades. Making it all the more intriguing, Steven was now represented by G. Arthur Martin, perhaps Canada's most outstanding criminal lawyer of the century, while both sides had called an all-star cast of medical experts, including two famous British rivals, neither of whom would escape the engagement with their feathers unruffled.

216

Graham Young, the boy who wanted to be one of the world's great poisoners when he grew up (*Syndication International*)

Graham Young's aunt, Winifred Jouvenat, and his sister, Winifred, in 1972 (*Syndication International*)

Darren Huenemann with his mother, Sharon

Doris Leatherbarrow, Darren's grandmother and his 'best buddy'

David Muir (*right*) and Derik Lord (*below*), the schoolfriends who brutally murdered Darren Huenemann's mother and grandmother at his instigation

Laurie Tackett (*above centre*), Melinda Loveless (*right*), Toni Lawrence (*opposite above*) and Hope Rippey (*opposite below*). Psychologist Eric Erigum said at their trial for the brutal murder of Shanda Sharer that the killing had the characteristics of 'sharks in a feeding frenzy' (*The Madison Courier*)

Shanda Sharer was just twelve years old at the time of her murder (*Associated Press*)

Enfield Lodge, the home of Miss Gwendoline Marshall. Her battered body was discovered in the garden shed (*Kent Messenger Group*)

Peter Luckhurst (*Kent Messenger Group*)

Miss Gwendoline Marshall (*Kent Messenger Group*)

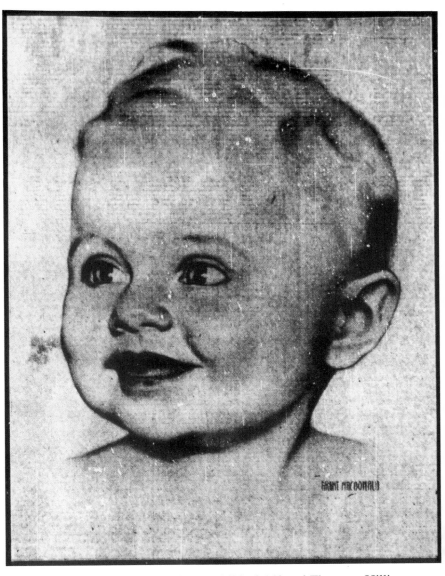

Baby Bunty, the adored only child of Alf and Florence Hillier, who was abducted by two small boys in 1933

For hours the medical controversy raged like a Punch and Judy show, one famous expert affirming the two-hours-after-the-last-meal estimate of the time of death, the next as surely knocking it down. Dr Milton Helpern, New York City's famous medical examiner, was one who believed Lynne had died within two hours of eating. 'What!' he exclaimed when asked if she could have been murdered elsewhere. 'Murdered and then brought back near to her home and put there with her shoes and things scattered around? It just doesn't make sense!'

In arguing that the murder had taken place elsewhere, Mrs LeBourdais had made much of a curious circumstance – a piece of Lynne's ripped blouse had been cut out and was missing at the time of the trial. A forensic scientist, Elgin Brown, using an attractive chemist named Donna Deaken from the Centre of Forensic Sciences in Toronto, gave the justices a startling demonstration of how it might have happened. After Miss Deaken slipped on a pink sleeveless blouse over her own blouse, Brown ripped it up the left seam and then, apologizing for his roughness, tied it under Miss Deaken's chin, just the way Lynne's blouse had been tied. As he released her with a dramatic snip-snip with a pair of scissors, a ragged piece of cloth fell to the floor just like the one missing from Lynne's blouse. Clearly the piece had gone missing when the blouse was cut from her throat at the time of the autopsy. The demonstration was doubly valuable for the newspapers: it provided a titillating headline: 'Blouse Ripped from Blonde'.

The appearance of Dr Francis Camps, one of Britain's leading forensic scientists, provided its own drama. After testifying that death could have occurred up to ten hours after the last meal, Camps added that to have suggested a limit of two hours would have been 'dangerously misleading to the investigating officers'.

The famous doctor could have anticipated little trouble from Donald Scott, a prosecutor from the small city of Welland, as he rose to cross-examine. But Scott came armed. 'I feel bound to ask you,' he began mildly, 'whether you had made up your mind long before you had read the evidence in this case?'

As the great expert began to waffle, Scott waved a sheet of paper. 'I have a copy of a letter...' Camps looked increasingly discomfited as Scott read out the scientist's words addressed to the Lord Chancellor of England. Based on his reading of Isabel LeBourdais' book, wrote Camps, 'I do not think the medical evidence of the prosecution can possibly stand up to scrutiny.' He would be prepared to say so in writing or in court if asked, wrote the doctor.

'I had no idea it [the letter] was to be divulged!' spluttered Camps, and left the courtroom a few minutes later so red and angry he forgot his briefcase. His arch rival, a forensic scientist of even greater eminence, Dr Keith Simpson, was sitting at the prosecution table, and could hardly contain his glee. Camps, he would write, 'had plainly touted for work'. Simpson would shortly enjoy his own moment of discomfiture.

Like Camps, he had reviewed the LeBourdais book. In his autobiography, *Forty Years of Murder*, he would describe it as 'tendentious, irrational and medically ill-informed'. The author, he said, had relied on textbooks that were long out of date. When he eventually read Penistan's post-mortem report, he was filled with admiration: 'I do not remember, in thirty years, having seen a

218

more thorough or painstaking report, or any more impartial deductions.'

Hadn't he, like Camps, formed an opinion of the medical evidence from reading the book? Martin, the defence lawyer, asked. Simpson had to agree that he had. Hadn't Simpson, in one of his books, written about a woman whose stomach contents were entirely like those of Lynne Harper, and yet who had been strangled nine hours after her last meal? 'Yes, but we don't know what the facts were in my case . . .'

'We don't know what the facts were in Lynne Harper's case,' snapped Martin. 'We don't know what duress or fear was working on this girl prior to her death.'

'No,' admitted Simpson, and returned to his place only a little less humbled than Camps.

The moment everyone had waited for came when the double doors opened and Steven Truscott, thin, with dark hair, wearing a brown suit and grown into a man now, walked the length of the red carpet and took his place before the justices. On his lawyer's advice, he had not testified at his trial. Now he would finally have his say.

He described his long-ago, carefree years, going to the cinema with girls, taking part in sports, neglecting his school work and dropping behind a year at school. With his parents anxiously leaning forward to hear his hushed voice, he told the familiar story of giving Lynne Harper a ride to the highway and seeing her picked up by the driver of the grey Chevrolet. He explained too that the blistering on his penis had appeared about six weeks before he was arrested, and since he'd been in prison, he'd been treated by skin specialists for similar outbreaks on other parts of his body.

Certain that Scott would introduce it if he didn't,

219

Martin produced a letter Steven had written to the parole board in 1964 in which he'd written, 'Please grant me one chance to make a success of my life and prove that one dreadful mistake does not mean that I will ever make another.'

Steven explained what every prisoner knows: that parole boards want to hear words of repentance, not outraged denials of guilt. He did not, by his letter, mean to admit to the crime, he insisted.

'Did you kill Lynne Harper?' Martin asked at the end.

'No, I didn't,' he replied quickly,

It was his last good moment. Did he really mean to tell them, Scott asked incredulously, that he had never spoken to his father or anyone else about the sores on his penis, even after his arrest? The little white house with the ponies where Lynne, according to Steven, was headed, was about four hundred yards from the spot where he said he dropped her. 'Do you think anyone would hitchhike three or four hundred yards?' Scott demanded.

'We used to sometimes,' was the feeble answer.

Steven denied ever inviting Jocelyne Goddette to see the calves with him, denied the conversations Butch George said he'd had with him and, most curiously, seemed to have no memory at all of the various witnesses who had testified to his movements with Lynne that fatal evening.

'I am wondering, frankly, Mr Truscott,' said Scott, exasperated, 'bearing in mind the nature of their evidence that I have read to you, why you cannot even recall these people giving evidence?'

'Because I have forgotten.' It was a weak ending. Perhaps he realized as he walked back towards the doors where guards waited to return him to prison that, after waiting so long, he'd done his cause more harm than good that day.

Seven months later, the justices gave their answer. By a majority of eight to one they voted to uphold the conviction. 'There were many incredulities inherent in the evidence given by Truscott before us, and we do not believe his testimony,' said the majority report. The dissenting voice was that of Mr Justice Emmett Hall who, on the grounds of irregularities in the original trial, would have ordered a new trial.

Lynne Harper's parents maintained a dignified silence the day the decision was announced. But we can guess their reaction. Leslie Harper, visiting the editor of a United Church newspaper, had ripped up a review favourable to Isabel LeBourdais' book and thrown it on the floor.

Only a few had held back from the general enthusiasm to free Steven Truscott. One was the Reverend S. G. West, then director of the Anglican Correctional Chaplaincy for the Diocese of Toronto. I met West recently, eighty-three years old, long-retired, yet busy as ever visiting 'the elderly' and writing books about his life.

'Sid West,' he said, giving me a vigorous handshake when I caught up with him at an Anglican seniors' residence. In view of his work in the prisons, he said, he'd been invited by Mrs LeBourdais, prior to the publication of her book, to write an introduction for it. 'I wanted to be clear what I was getting into,' said West, who comes from Brentwood in Essex. So, unlike so many politicians and journalists, he read the transcript of the trial. He also went to see Steven several times. And then he wrote to Mrs LeBourdais to say that he was convinced Steven had done what he was accused of doing. He didn't hear from her again.

This, in his own words, is what West believes happened: 'Steven was going to take this twelve-year-old girl to his hiding place. She was a slim little thing, very undeveloped. Of course, she was just tickled to death to be asked by this boy who was a very good athlete. I expect they started out with you show me yours and I'll show you mine, thất sort of thing, and Steven got horny. That's when he tried to penetrate her.' Like many rapists before and since, her cries must have panicked him, and that was when he ripped open her blouse, knotting it tighter and tighter under her chin. 'After that, he showed amazing originality in coming up with that story,' said West.

What was it about Steven that convinced West he was capable of the crime? 'What struck me was his total lack of emotion,' he said (a psychiatrist, Dr James Hartford, who had examined Steven soon after he entered the Guelph training school, was similarly impressed by the boy's 'marked lack of emotional response. I felt the boy was ill,' he had told the justices). In his time, Sid West told me, he'd met many men in prison with that characteristic.

Steven Truscott was released from jail in the summer of 1969, although he is on lifetime parole. He took a new name and married a woman who had collected petitions to win him a new trial. They have two children.

He still maintains his innocence and whenever the case is revived on radio or television or in print, it is nearly always Steven's version of the facts that is presented. The teenage boy riding the young girl to the highway and dropping her off on that glorious summer's evening and the arrival of the mysterious Chevrolet a few minutes later is now a scene stamped on the Canadian consciousness. People still try to link up Lynne Harper's murder with similar crimes of the period committed by others, and re-peddle old rumours about strangers seen in the Clinton area that night. The case is touted as one of the great unsolved mysteries. It shouldn't be: there's really no mystery about who murdered Lynne Harper.

SWEET
SIXTEEN

The people who were there will never forget Jim Pierson dancing with his daughter, Cheryl, the night of her Sweet Sixteen. Pink balloons festooned the hired hall, pink and white carnations decorated every table, and the spotlights danced on Cheryl's white silk, off-the-shoulder jumpsuit as her father swept her around the darkened dance floor to that anthem of emerging womanhood, 'Sixteen Candles'.

It was a father's as well as a daughter's dream. And other fathers there that night could only be a mite envious that, out of the storms of adolescence, this pretty picture had emerged of father and daughter affection.

Only Jim Pierson knew that the show of affection, on his part, went far beyond what was acceptable or normal.

The Sweet Sixteen dance is a peculiarly North American tradition, a quaint hangover from the days before teenage drugs and promiscuity, when a sixteenth birthday really did mark the end of childhood and initiation for a girl into the grown-up world of make-up and dating and late-night parties. Like the high school prom, with white limos, awkward youths in black tuxedos and blushing girls in their first evening dresses, it's a pretty illusion that's often at odds with the steamy reality of modern teenage life.

But for once image seemed close to reality: Cheryl Pierson, pretty and popular, was the apple of her wealthy father's eye, a girl who, if not tops in academic subjects, was never in trouble, was co-captain of her high school cheerleading team (and author of a favourite football chant, 'Move it up, sock it to 'em'), and dreamed in class about love and gauzy dresses and the grand wedding she'd have some day. And if Cheryl was the sort of girl for whom Sweet Sixteens still had significance, there was too a special poignancy to the affair at the Country Squire restaurant that night: only three months previously, her mother, Cathleen, had died after several distressing years battling kidney disease.

Planning the dance with Cheryl – making up guest lists and talking about the flowers, the place cards and the music – had been the one thing that had distracted Cathleen from her suffering in the final weeks. It was something to live for, only she didn't make it. Cancelling the dance after Cathleen's death would have been unthinkable. The whole night Cheryl imagined her mother up there, watching, enjoying, proud of the way they'd carried through with her plans.

It was the same that Christmas of 1985, the first since Cathleen had died. Everyone felt the weight of it, knowing how difficult it would be to keep up a front. So they tried all the harder. Cheryl and her eight-year-old sister, JoAnn, spent the day with their father at their Aunt Marilyn's. Even Cheryl's nineteen-year-old brother, Jimmy, who hadn't been getting along with his father and who was living away from home, arrived with a shirt as a gift for his father.

Jim Senior, a noisy, roustabout kind of guy, all abuse one moment and tears the next, yelled for his mother, Virginia, who lived with Marilyn, to come on out and see his new car, a shiny oversized boat of a Chrysler. Next minute he was putting the keys in her hand. His little surprise for her. Typical Jim. Just as, typically, he made everyone uncomfortable later, arguing in the kitchen with his sister about how she made the potatoes or some such.

Cheryl didn't want to hear it. She went into the living room and sat down on the couch to talk with her brother, whom she didn't get to see too often. That was when she asked him to find someone to kill their father.

Selden, Long Island, is not the swanky part of Long Island you see on *Homes of the Rich and Famous*. It's just a nondescript strip of neon signs, gas stations, fast-food spots and supermarkets sticking up out of flat terrain east of Manhattan. And the Piersons' bungalow at 293 Magnolia Drive, even though Jim had hollowed out a large underground garage to house his car collection, is definitely not the sort of home to which the word 'estate' is added in gossip column items about Long Island high society.

Magnolia Drive is Everywhere, USA, the kind of suburban street favoured by New York City cops and firemen whose shift work makes the fifty-mile drive to work no hassle at all. As Jim Pierson, a burly man witn a round Irish face, let himself out of the front door on his way to work at 6.20 a.m. on 5 February 1986 he would not even have given the street a glance; the scene was part of the permanent furniture of his mind.

And so he didn't see the gunman who stepped from behind a tree alongside the driveway. Jim was walking

227

towards his pick-up truck, the keys ready in his hand, when the .22 rifle went off – not like the noisy gunfire you hear on television, but more like a taut elastic snapping. As the bullet struck him in the back of the head, he half turned, fell forward, his ankles twisted together, and lay still. The gunman stepped up to the body on the driveway, fired four more shots into it, and then, after waiting a moment to check there was no movement, walked swiftly back along the street. He had to get home because soon it would be time to go to school.

Nobody noticed when murder came to Magnolia Drive. Neighbours slept on; others left for work without seeing the body at number 293. Cheryl had dozed back after hearing the front door slam when her father left, and it was the family poodle, Noel, barking to be let out, who woke her.

Wearing a flowered nightdress and knee socks, she went to the bathroom, then to the front door to let out the toy poodle who was yapping at her heels. Then something unfamiliar, something terribly wrong caught her eye. Through the glass she saw her father lying face down on the driveway. She rushed out to him. 'Dad, are you hurt?' she cried, then, feeling the biting cold air cut through her nightdress, she ran back inside, flung on a tracksuit top and ran across to the neighbours, Alberta and Michael Kosser. After a quick check of the inert figure, Mike Kosser phoned for an ambulance. 'A guy's slipped and fallen on the ice,' he said. 'He's hurt bad.'

Cheryl, concerned that her sister, JoAnn, might wake up and come outside, woke her gently and told her she wouldn't be going to school that day: 'Daddy's slipped and fallen on the ice.'

The two girls stood at the window, their arms around

each other, watching the early-morning drama. They saw a police car, its flashing red light reflected on the snow, and two officers, a man and a woman, jumping out almost before the car had stopped, followed a few moments later by a second car. Two fire department volunteers, one a registered nurse, hurried up the driveway. Half a dozen people were crowded around the body. Someone rolled their father over on to his back. Why weren't they doing something to help him? Then one of the policemen left the group and came up to the door.

Constable Roy Baillard had seen the two girls in the window. The task ahead pained him more than he could tell. 'I've got some bad news for you, girls,' he said. 'Your dad is dead.'

Lieutenant Frank Dunn, head of the Suffolk County homicide squad, took only a cursory look at the corpse stiffening on the driveway before asking to use the Kossers' phone to notify the coroner and the other functionaries involved when any killing occurs. The abundance of blood apparent when the body was rolled over and the spent bullets found nearby in the snow made it immediately obvious that murder was involved.

Later Dunn would recall the oddest thing: as he finished his calls, a teenage girl, one of the group of people sitting at the table glumly drinking coffee, asked him, 'What's that cologne you're wearing?'

'Dunno,' he said, caught off guard.

'Ralph Lauren, I think,' she said.

Strange the things people will say under stress, Dunn told Detective Jim McCready, the officer who would be in charge of the case, when he met him outside a few minutes later. Who was the girl anyway?

229

'She's the daughter,' said McCready, nodding towards the body. 'She was the one that found him.'

Then Dunn had one of his famous inspirations: 'She did it,' he said. 'She stood here in the door like this and shot him.'

Yeah, yeah. Frank Dunn's intuitions often hit the mark. You couldn't discount them. But right then the killing looked like a mob job, and the more McCready learnt about Jim Pierson the more plausible that theory seemed.

The guns to start with. Guns are the norm in the American home. But a .357 Magnum beside the bed? A Uzi sub-machine-gun in the living room and five other guns concealed around the house? Not to mention an elaborate security system that allowed Pierson from his bedroom to monitor the movements of his children or anyone else in any part of the house. This seemed one nervous guy.

Maybe with reason. Jim Pierson, an electrician, earned around fifteen thousand pounds a year as a foreman for a firm repairing traffic lights; on the side he was partner in a little company that fixed TV cable receivers. But none of this seemed enough to explain the three vintage cars and five motorcycles in the huge basement garage and Jim's lavish generosity when it came to giving gifts. When McCready learned too that Pierson had kept large sums of money around the house which he loaned out freely – whether at exorbitant interest rates is not known – it seemed possible that plenty of people would have had their reasons for killing him.

The murder could easily have remained unsolved, one of those puzzling affairs familiar to every big-city homicide squad and involving twilight characters, murky motives and a frustrating absence of suspects. Could have, except for the loquaciousness of some of those nearest to Jim Pierson.

McCready's first jolt came when he questioned Cheryl. She described finding her father and running to the neighbours. 'Is my father going to be okay?' she asked him. He studied her carefully.

'I thought the officer told you your father was dead.'

'Dead! My father dead?' She was crying her heart out. It had to be the shock. Did odd things to people.

And then the police learned about Jim Junior, the son who'd had violent arguments with his father for years and whom, they would discover, Jim Senior was about to cut out of his will.

Young Jim didn't hear about the murder until late afternoon, and then made a typically outrageous entrance. Earrings dangling, long orange hair flying, he gave his grandma sitting on the couch a breezy greeting, grabbed a jam doughnut and told the assembled friends and relatives, 'Okay everyone, time to leave.'

McCready, ordered out too by Jim, listened in surprise to the shouts, banging doors, and furious arguments as Virginia Pierson stoutly refused to leave her two grand-daughters to sleep unguarded in the house while the murderer was still at large.

It was Cheryl, sitting in the living room with her boyfriend, Rob Cuccio, and trying to ignore the rumpus, who finally brought peace: nearly everyone, including Rob, left, and Jim retreated to the study to watch television.

For Cheryl and her brother the next few days, leading up to the funeral, were a daze of meeting relatives at the airport, setting up fold-up beds and arranging meals. The day before the funeral, Cheryl took JoAnn, who would not be attending the ceremony, to the funeral home for her last farewell. The little girl leant over the coffin and pinned on his lapel the badge she had given her father on Father's Day. 'The World's Best Dad', it said.

Jim Pierson had been a braggart and a bore at times, but he could not be ignored, and the chapel was jammed next day. There was no doubt at all what people remembered as they left afterwards. It was a tribute written by Cheryl to 'Our Dad' read out by the priest. 'He did a great job as mother and father this past year,' it concluded. 'And we all knew he tried his hardest to comfort us through everything. He was our best friend as well as our dad. We believe that one day we will see him again.' Tears flowed freely throughout the room.

After five days, McCready hadn't a single lead. There was no sign of the murder weapon, no clue to the motive and all he had was the whisperings of friends that young Jim had to be involved somehow. Maybe if he leaned on him . . . So that was how, one evening as he left the beauty school where he'd been taking hairdressing classes since January, Jim heard the cop's familiar growl of greeting.

'We been finding out some stuff and I'd like to check it out with you,' McCready said. 'Would you mind coming to headquarters?'

'You got any idea who it is?' Jim asked as they drove off.

'Yeah,' McCready replied, pausing for effect. 'You.'

'No way.'

'That's what we're hearing.'

'Then you're hearing wrong.'

'If not you, then who?'

'My sister.' If McCready had thought to shock Jim with

his accusation, the tables had been turned on him.

'Your sister! What are you telling me?'

'On Christmas Day. We were over at my aunt's place. She said she wanted me to find someone to kill him.'

'Why, for Chrissake?'

'She didn't say.'

'Come on!'

'She said he wouldn't let her go out New Year's Eve.'

'For that she wanted him killed?'

'She said she couldn't take any more of his abuse. And she wasn't about to leave because then JoAnn would get it. I told her I went through it. Hang in there.'

At the police station, with the door shut, McCready laid into the boy, loudly accusing him of lying. He stuck to his story.

'So what did you do when she asked you?'

'I told her, okay, I'd find someone. But I didn't mean it.'

'Did she ask you again?'

'Yeah, she called me a couple of times. I said I'd found a guy, but the cops were watching him. Then her boyfriend, Rob Cuccio, he came over and asked me if I'd found somebody to do the job.'

If you believed Jim, Cheryl was going around town canvassing for a killer as casually as she'd ask for change for a dollar. And McCready was inclined to believe Jim, because he'd already checked and discovered that the boy had been at a factory job during the vital hours.

Cheryl's affair with Rob Cuccio had begun with an act of sympathy. She'd known him in a casual way at Newfield High School, but the week following her mother's death in February 1985, he'd put his arm around her shoulder and told her how sorry he felt for her. Their

233

first real date was her Sweet Sixteen.

As they danced the final dance of the evening – again, inevitably, 'Sixteen Candles' – Rob asked her to be his steady girlfriend. Their relationship sputtered off and on all year, partly because, with her mother's death, Cheryl had become the mother at home, cooking and cleaning after school, and partly because her father had decidedly old-fashioned ideas about young girls dating. Finally Rob resigned himself to sitting uncomfortably in the Pierson living room most evenings watching television with Cheryl and her father and sister. It wasn't much fun but it was the one way he could be sure of seeing her. And by May or June, Rob, the son of a retired New York policeman who operated a coffee truck, knew Cheryl needed his support in a special way: she had told him she wanted her father killed.

Later on the night of his interview with young Jim, McCready returned to the Pierson house. It was after midnight, but Virginia Pierson, who had moved in to look after her grandchildren, was still up. She and McCready had struck up a good working relationship: 'Call me Mum,' she'd told him, and he'd made her a solemn promise he would find out who killed her son. Now, he told her as she led him into the living room, he could tell her. Jimmy? He shook his head. 'Cheryl.'

She held on to the back of the couch. 'But why?'

He didn't know, admitted McCready. That was why he needed her to wake Cheryl so they could take her down to the police station to question her. A few minutes later Cheryl came out of her room, stretching and bleary-eyed.

It was worth a try, thought McCready. 'I think you've got something to tell your grandmother,' he said.

'What about?'

'About who killed your father.' Cheryl did not take the bait. Perhaps it was too much to expect a confession that easily. McCready had a back-up plan. He made a signal at the window. A moment later another detective walked in holding Rob, who had been arrested shortly before, by the arm.

'Tell her, Rob,' said McCready.

Rob Cuccio, slim, with a tentative moustache and nervous, darting eyes, looked at the floor. 'I'm arrested,' he said. 'They know.'

The effective date was 7 November 1985. If you check the local papers for that day you'll find an account of a forty-year-old Long Island waitress arrested for hiring two men to kill her husband who, she afterwards claimed, had beaten and raped her. In the short homeroom period before class, some of the kids in room 226 at Newfield High School were talking about the case.

'You're joking! Who'd do something like that, kill someone for money?' exclaimed Cheryl.

A boy named Sean Pica, a sixteen-year-old who sat next to Cheryl simply because his last name came before hers in the alphabetic sequence, said, 'I dunno, I guess anybody would do it. If the money was right.'

'Come on,' said Cheryl. 'How much would you need to do something like that?'

'Oh,' said Sean, a skinny little guy with braces on his teeth, flattered that the prettiest girl in class was finally paying attention to him, 'a thousand bucks.'

'A hundred thousand bucks!'

'No, a thousand.'

'I know someone who'd pay that to have a guy knocked off.'

'Yeah?'

'Yeah.'

And that was it. Just idle talk. Then a few days later she told him she was the one willing to pay. Was he serious? Sure he was. And she kept on at him. Could he do it tonight? Because her dad was beating her, had even thrown her out of the car when it was still moving. Okay, I'll do it tonight. Then, next day, What happened? I couldn't get out of the house. Sean, things are getting kind of worse . . . Sean, please.

To outsiders it would seem ludicrous, unbelievable, that three well-scrubbed teenagers who never gave any trouble were planning a murder. But then this was the hermetically sealed teenage world where the rules are different, where loyalty is everything and consequences don't count.

Nothing about Cheryl Pierson, Rob Cuccio or Sean Pica predisposed them to murder. It would be hard to imagine, on the face of it, a more unlikely hit man than Sean Pica, a keen Boy Scout who was working for his Eagle badge, and who, a few weeks later, was to represent his school in a statewide carpentry contest. He was a quiet, polite youngster, known for his kindness, and he showed no apparent emotional scars from the fact that his mother, who had three boys still at home, had been twice divorced.

The first murder attempt was a fiasco. Sean was supposed to throw a brick through the window of a house Jim Pierson owned across the street from 293 Magnolia Drive, setting off the alarm. When Pierson came storming out, Sean was supposed to stab him. Who would have ended up the worse – runty little Sean or burly six-foot-two Jim – is a moot question. Sean threw his brick but, luckily for him, Jim didn't come out. Sean went home, no doubt relieved.

One lunch hour Rob and Cheryl drove Sean over to the Piersons' house. A gun fancier, Rob was fascinated by Jim Pierson's large arsenal. They even arranged to leave the Uzi sub-machine-gun in a dustbin for Sean to use in the killing, but later changed that plan because they feared the gun could be traced back to the family. Sean would have to get his own gun.

On 4 February, at a game at school, Sean told Cheryl he would do it the next day. For sure. He's said that before, Rob told her when he heard.

Next morning Sean opened his eyes at 5 a.m. with the certainty that today he'd act. His mother, an intensive-care nurse, was out doing an overnight shift of private nursing – a necessity forced on her by the financial needs of her family. He slipped out of his room, shutting the family dog, Butterscotch, in the kitchen so he wouldn't wake Sean's thirteen-year-old brother, Vincent, who was sleeping upstairs.

In the dark outside he opened the door of his Pinto – temporarily out of action since he'd skidded on an ice patch and bent the wheels – and reached inside for the .22 pump rifle that he was keeping for a friend. The gun had been stolen during a burglary. By the light of the car's interior roof lamp, he slid five bullets into place. That should be enough. Then he set off down the street, the snow crunching beneath his running shoes.

A few hours after the murder, with Rob standing guard at the door, Cheryl climbed on a chair and, reaching into the light fixture, found the piece of paper on which her father had written down the combination of his wall safe.

Opening the safe, she cleared out the cash. The next day, during carpentry class, she and Rob gave Sean the initial $400 of his $1,000 fee. 'Nice shot,' Rob complimented him. After school Sean took his girlfriend to a shopping mall and put down $150 on a pair of gold bracelets costing $1,100.

That, Detective McCready now knew, was how Jim Pierson was murdered. After his talk with Rob, he thought he knew why.

'I know what was going on between you and your father,' he said in a kindly tone to Cheryl, whose eyes were still red from crying. 'Is it true?'

Finally she nodded. She could talk about it, he told her. Cops heard a lot of things. She didn't have to feel uncomfortable. When had it started?

'When I was eleven.' It began with wrestling around. Then he would grab her. Where? Eyes down, she pointed at her breasts and her crotch. For three-quarters of an hour McCready and another detective listened to Cheryl's story.

'Until my mother got sick he never really bothered me. He always did stuff with my brother. Little League and stuff, and I always stayed with my mother. When she got sick, my mother wasn't around and I felt no one was paying attention to me. And my father started paying attention to me. At first I was really happy that he did it because before he hadn't known I existed. Then it got out of hand, I guess.'

Her mother would be sleeping on the couch in the living room, said Cheryl, and her father would call her into the bedroom to watch TV. At first she'd be under the blanket with her clothes on.

'With the touching stuff, I don't think I realized it.

Then, like, it was to the point where it wasn't with clothes any more. That's when I think I realized it.'

'Did he have intercourse with you?' She didn't answer for a moment. Then she nodded. How old was she when it happened? Thirteen.

Jim Pierson had been lover and stern father at the same time. Driving to the hospital to see his wife, he'd warn her that guys were after just one thing and that she wasn't to do it until she was married. 'If I catch you, I'll kill you.' What she did with him, that was different. Because he loved her.

It was after her mother died and when his demands became more and more insistent that she began thinking about other alternatives. She was out of the house more – to cheerleading practice, occasionally to the movies with Rob. Now he'd wrestle around with JoAnn – just the way he'd started with her. And when she'd come home she'd find JoAnn in his bed.

Why didn't she tell someone? 'I didn't think anyone would believe me.'

McCready had spent half his life listening to people's stories, sifting for the truth. He figured he knew enough to know Cheryl Pierson was telling the truth.

There was only one hitch. As Dena Kleiman, a writer for *The New York Times* who followed the case for two years, told me when I spoke to her in Paris where she now lives: 'Cheryl was a pathological liar.'

Sean was arrested on the way to school. His mother only learnt of his arrest when she contacted the school after a friend had told her she had seen Sean being abducted on the street by two men in a grey car.

No three accused ever looked more clean-cut and less criminal than the three conspirators who appeared in

Suffolk Criminal Court for a bail hearing on 13 February. Sean, with his braces, could have passed for thirteen, while Cheryl was the brightest sight in the sombre courtroom, wearing her red Newfield High School jacket with '87' on the sleeve and the Wolverines basketball team crest on the back.

'Cheryl is more a victim here than a defendant,' her lawyer, Paul Gianelli, argued. He knew more than he was saying. Leaving the court after bail had been set at $50,000, he whispered to Cheryl's Aunt Marilyn: 'We've got to get her out. She's pregnant with her father's baby.'

In Selden, the case became a test of credibility.

After Cheryl's brother, apparently going back on what he'd told McCready, testified before the grand jury that he had no idea his father was having sex with Cheryl, the resolve of the prosecutor, Edward Jablonski, hardened: he would seek a murder conviction against her rather than one of manslaughter. It was the premeditation of the crime that concerned him, and the fact that, with child-abuse hot lines and plenty of counselling and police help available for dealing with child sex abuse, Cheryl had chosen murder as the way out. Many who had known Jim Pierson, including his mother, and his sister, Marilyn, refused to believe Cheryl's story.

At Newfield High School, the crime and its implications seemed to undermine all the caring and concern built into the system. The students were starting a campaign, 'Free Sean Pica', as if he were a political prisoner. 'It's scary that kids look at Sean as the way to go,' said Debra Handel, the school psychologist. 'Years ago a policeman was your friend. So were teachers.' Today's heroes, she said, wore thick gold chains and drove Porsches. 'In these kids' minds, quick is better ... My big fear is, if he gets off, kids will begin to think they can get away with murder.'

Gianelli knew that public sympathy would all be on Cheryl's side – if the physical evidence confirmed her story. 'Two weeks before my father died,' she'd told police, 'I wasn't talking to him and he kept asking me what was wrong and he knew when I was supposed to get my period. And he's like, "Did you get it? Did you get it?" for like a week straight. And I kept yelling at him, "No! Thanks to you!" and he started to get worried and started looking through the phone book for clinics and stuff so nobody would find out.

'So that's why I thought I was ... Yeah, I was really upset that this is what he was putting me through. Because I love little kids and for me to have to go through all this stuff because of him. I was really annoyed.' Eventually, she said, her father told her he had found a suitable abortion clinic.

Rob? The first time she had sex with him was after her father's death, she insisted.

Her father, said Cheryl, had had sex with her the night before his murder. Gianelli made sure the bedding and clothing was sent away for semen tests. Now he waited for the genetic evidence that would confirm Cheryl's claim that she was carrying her father's baby.

An abortion was scheduled, but before it could take place, Cheryl, by then out on bail and taking beauty classes, was rushed to hospital where she had a miscarriage. The foetus was sent to a specialized laboratory for DNA analysis. It was the first application of DNA testing of a foetus for legal purposes. The tests, like those for semen on the bedding and clothing, came back negative. Rob Cuccio and not Jim Pierson had been the father of the child.

For Cheryl's aunt and grandmother, both living now at Magnolia Drive, it was the last straw. Doubting from the start that Jim had done what Cheryl claimed he had, they were now certain he hadn't. The rows at home became constant; Cheryl moved next door with the Kossers. Friends and neighbours began wondering if there wasn't more to the murder than Cheryl was saying. Had she had her father killed because she couldn't face telling him about a baby she was having with Rob? Was there a conspiracy with Jim Junior so they could inherit their father's million-dollar estate?

And then, with the trial finally about to begin in March 1987, more than a year after the murder, it suddenly seemed that none of the questions would be answered. Because Cheryl and Sean, in a plea-bargaining arrangement, agreed to plead guilty to manslaughter. (A conviction had been registered against Rob for his part in the conspiracy, but in return for his agreement to testify against Cheryl, he would serve no jail time.)

Cheryl, now seventeen, a little dumpier after a year away from cheerleading, listened as Justice Harvey W. Sherman explained to her that he was ordering a probation report and that, as a youthful offender, she could not be sentenced to more than six years in prison. At the mention of prison, she burst into tears.

Why, asked prosecutor Jablonski, establishing the basic facts of the case, had she asked Sean Pica to kill her father?

The words simply would not come. Her breath came in gasps, the tears fell again, and she shook: 'He . . . was . . . sexually abusing me.'

242

Now it was Sean Pica's turn. Yes, he admitted, he had told Cheryl he would shoot her father for a thousand dollars. Did he tell her the night before that he planned to do it? Jablonski asked.

'I did not,' said Sean.

Cheryl had claimed that when Sean called her the night before to tell her of his intention, she had told him to forget it.

Not quite the good Scout everyone had thought him, Sean had admitted to police that he had engaged in a series of burglaries with the friend whose gun he had used. Nevertheless, Stephen Honor, a psychologist who interviewed Sean in prison, found him 'forthright and honest'. He was, just as the school psychologist had said, concerned more with results than with morality or correctness. Sean, Honor reported, 'is not really upset about the fact that he killed a man; he is upset because he has been imprisoned for the offence.'

That didn't mean he had entered cold-bloodedly into the agreement. It had been more like a game to him. 'His primary focus was on the notion that this girl needed help and that he, as a "friend" and as a "man", was "duty-bound" to help her.' Loyalty, wrote Honor, was the main force that drove Sean to kill. 'A Robin Hood complex' was how another psychologist described Sean's state of mind. He was 'someone searching for a cause, a test of his manhood'. Honor's theory was that, as Sean waited behind the tree for half an hour, filling himself with anger for a man he had never met, he was really preparing himself to kill his father and stepfather who had both, he would have felt, abandoned him and his mother.

As his lawyer, Martin Efman, put it when Sean appeared before Judge Sherman for sentencing, 'Sean

243

wouldn't be here were it not for Cheryl Pierson.' His sentence: twenty-four years in jail with a proviso that he serve a minimum of eight.

For Cheryl there would be a pre-sentence hearing in September, seven months away. In the interim, for the purposes of the probation report, she finally got to tell her story to the social-work professionals she should have talked to before deciding on her fatal course. After listening to her story, after hearing that she had first had intercourse with her father standing on a ladder as they installed insulation in the attic, after hearing that he'd tell her, 'pretend it's Rob', the probation department professionals delivered a harsh verdict.

'Although it seems likely that the defendant was abused, it cannot be substantiated,' they reported. They described her as 'unremorseful, totally dispassionate, self-centred and immature'.

Perhaps even more damaging was a remarkable letter sent to the judge by the one person no one had questioned: Cheryl's sister, JoAnn:

'The reason I am writing you,' it began, 'is to let you know how I feel and so you know the truth and not lies. I was living at the house at the time and I really didn't see anything. Sometimes we would watch TV in my father's room. Sometimes we would fall asleep in my father's bed and he would go and lay on the couch. My sister often said, "My father was always laying all over me." But she is wrong because I saw my sister always laying over my father and sometimes she would say, "Oh, Dad, I love you," and start hugging him and start fooling around with my father.

'But I'll tell you right now she is a liar because I lived with her and my father always caught my sister in lies and she was a sneak. She would always lie to my father and my father didn't like liars or sneaks. And my sister was both. But of course my father can't speak for himself. THANKS TO MY SISTER. Sometimes my sister would get me in trouble when I didn't do anything.'

Then JoAnn answered the question that would occur to anyone reading the letter: 'If you're wondering if anybody is making me say this, you're wrong. Because I am sitting on my lawn all by myself and writing how I feel.'

Paul Gianelli, short, and bland-looking until his emotions took hold and his hands started flying, knew that, if his client was not to spend serious time in jail, he would have to shoot down that devastating probation report. The only answer: to turn the pre-sentencing hearing into the trial that had been avoided by the guilty plea. Judge Sherman would express impatience at the number of witnesses Gianelli called, but counsel ploughed on.

Alberta Kosser, Cathleen's friend, had been in and out of the Pierson house for years. 'Cheryl was always in the bedroom with her father, watching TV,' she testified. One night in the Kosser house JoAnn out of the blue said, 'Cheryl slept with Daddy last night.' Did she suspect there was sexual contact between Cheryl and her father? 'Yes,' replied Alberta. Why hadn't she notified the authorities? 'I was afraid of Jimmy . . . He got to me.'

A negative picture began to emerge of genial Jim, the neighbourhood philanthropist. 'I thought he was very crude,' Alberta's husband, Michael, said. 'He was always smacking the children, pulling their hair, punching them.' Did he ever speak to Pierson about it? 'Yes, I did, and he told me it was none of my fucking business.'

One day, he said, John Fleckenstein, Cathleen's stepfather, came to see him. 'He looked upset. He said, "I hope I'm wrong. I think Jimmy and Cheryl – something is going on." He said he had walked in on them. Cheryl was under the covers, lying on top of her father. I made a point of watching after that.'

'What did you see?' asked Gianelli.

'He was always pinching, pulling her hair, fondling her, making remarks like, "Doesn't she have a nice pair of tits?" He was rubbing her bottom.'

Another friend of Cathleen's, Judy Ozarowski, recalled a Fourth of July party at which she heard Pierson say to Cheryl, 'You! You little cunt, get over here.' She formed the conviction that Cheryl was being sexually abused. Like nearly everyone else, she did nothing about it.

Grace Sargeant, whose daughter was Cheryl's best friend, remembered seeing Cheryl with a black eye. Her father had hit her for sending a boy a Valentine card. Another time her daughter had come home from the Pierson house because Jim Pierson wanted to take a nap with Cheryl. 'I feel bad I never did anything,' she said.

Another friend testified to black and blue marks on Cathleen. For her last Christmas, Pierson had given his wife a doll's pram for her Cabbage Patch doll. To Cheryl he gave a diamond bracelet.

Friends described Jimmy's terrible fits of temper when he would knock Cheryl into a wall, and the way he would paw women. And then the one person who'd tried to get help for Cheryl took the stand. Her school friend, Diana Erbentraut, said that when she asked Cheryl one day if something was going on between her and her father, Cheryl gave her a look. 'To me she looked scared. It was kind of like, help.' Diana went to the school guidance counsellor who told her to come back another time. She went, told the counsellor of her suspicions, and was told, 'Cheryl will have to come and tell me about it herself.'

Listening to the evidence, Jimmy's sister, Marilyn, found it hard to contain herself. 'My brother is on trial here!' she exploded at one point. 'Cheryl ain't right in the mind. She should get more than Pica. This child acted so lovey-dovey with this father. You tell me this is a sexually abused child!' It was true – there was no one to defend Jim Pierson and describe his acts of generosity. Apart from descriptions of his abusive behaviour, the real person was curiously absent from the proceedings. Until Gianelli introduced a big blown-up photograph of Pierson, lying bare-chested on the couch with Cheryl on his stomach. Never mind what they were or weren't doing; what stuck in the memory were the freckles, the short hair and the beefy bully's face.

Jim Junior confirmed that impression when, fair hair down past his shoulders, he was asked by Gianelli what his physical relationship had been with his father. 'He hit me and I got hit,' he replied. 'No matter what I did, it wasn't enough.'

'How about your mother? Could you please her?'

'Yes. By not upsetting my father.'

It ran in the family. Jim Senior's father had been a martinet who enforced total silence and culinary discipline at the dinner table. His son had continued the tradition. They weren't allowed to speak at table, said Jim Junior, had to eat a little of everything in turn, and couldn't drink until they'd finished eating. Slaps were frequent.

It was around the time his mother became seriously ill and Cheryl would watch TV in her father's bedroom, said Jim, that the motion-sensitive security system was installed.

It could have been that Pierson was concerned about burglars; equally, it allowed him to see from the bedroom if anyone was moving anywhere in the house, a useful safeguard if he didn't want to be taken by surprise.

A final snapshot of Jim Pierson: a relative of Cathleen's, Jay Fleckenstein, driving with her to the doctor's one day, asked her why she was having so many problems following a kidney transplant. 'She said [her kidneys] had deteriorated because of the beatings James Pierson had given her.' Why? 'She went on to say that Jimmy was screwing around with Cheryl, and she confronted him about it. She made me promise that I would not say anything to anyone. I felt she feared for Cheryl's, her and my safety.'

When Cheryl finally took the witness stand, Gianelli walked her quietly through happier early memories of her father teaching her how to ride a mini-bike, then on to the cuddling and stroking that she welcomed at first as signs of affection. After a while, rather than see him pick a fight with her mother, she would 'let him do what he wanted me to do'.

'How did you deal with the situation?' asked Gianelli gently.

'Just lay there.' And then she was sobbing. 'He'd breathe in my face. He'd look at me. I'd put a pillow over my face. I'd block it out until it was over.' When her mother died they had sex less frequently because there were often people in the house. 'But when the company left,' she testified, 'it was a couple of times a day. I was afraid to go into the shower by myself.'

Asked about the homeroom conversation with Sean Pica, she said, 'It didn't seem serious. It was more like a game.' Even when she found her father's body, it didn't seem real. 'Did you know he had been shot?' asked Jablonski.

'No.'

'Did it dawn on you that it might have been Sean Pica?'

'No.'

Did she think he'd been shot dead? 'No, I was worrying about getting him help.'

'You did not want him dead?'

'Not at that moment, no.'

When Jablonski turned to the pregnancy, Cheryl's answers were even more confusing. 'At the time when you first felt you were pregnant, had you been sexually intimate with Rob Cuccio?'

'Not until I thought I was pregnant,' she replied. 'I was two weeks late.'

'Have you been told it was Rob Cuccio's baby?'

She had not been told, but she had read it in the newspaper, she said.

Cheryl Pierson had lied frequently, had, according to some, been her father's seducer rather than the seduced, and had chosen to kill when thousands of other abused youngsters either keep silent or report to the proper authorities. The contradictions obviously worried Judge Sherman. 'A number of witnesses,' he said, seeking help from Dr Jean Goodwin, a Medical College of Wisconsin expert on child sex abuse, 'have testified that the father was a loud, boisterous, gross, vulgar, and intimidating man who exercised a lot of discipline. But my one concern is, was that not the explanation [for the killing] without the sexual context?'

It was a question no one could really answer. But Dr Goodwin, a psychiatrist, and Kathleen Oitzinger, a psychologist who had been seeing Cheryl for a year, both

249

testified that the contradictions in Cheryl's character were entirely consistent with her being a victim of incest. Like many abused youngsters, said Oitzinger, Cheryl had developed the ability to distance herself from reality, to blot it out.

It was common, Dr Goodwin explained, for victims to have revenge fantasies. Her conversation with Sean Pica was part of that fantasy life, something that 'made her feel better'. If she had not found a willing accomplice in Sean, probably nothing would have happened.

Jablonski pointed out that Cheryl was certainly not fantasizing when she and Rob had taken Sean to her house and showed him her father's arsenal of guns and when, as her father's body was being carried to the ambulance, she was seen with Rob Cuccio, 'hugging, kissing and laughing'.

In the end, Judge Sherman made up his mind: circumstantial evidence as well as the direct testimony of the defendant, he wrote in his decision, 'leads this court to conclude that Cheryl Pierson was ... the object of frequent, repeated acts of sexual intercourse by her father.' The judge told a fainting Cheryl Pierson that she must serve six months in the county jail and would be on probation for five years.

Three and a half months later, with time off for good behaviour, Cheryl Pierson emerged from prison one snowy January morning. Rob Cuccio had a stretch white limousine containing a bar and television waiting for her. It was prom time, Sweet Sixteen time again, the teenage dream. Giggling and joking she, Rob, Jimmy and a friend climbed in, then pulled open the sun roof so that they could stand up while Cheryl held up her fist in triumph – just the way she used to when the Newfield team won.

That afternoon Rob asked her to marry him, and in October 1988, a hundred guests were present when they were wed at St Louis de Montfort Roman Catholic Church. Rob's mother tells me they are still together and now have a child.

ONE OF
MY CHILDREN

The week I had lunch with Eileen Pollard, a retired head teacher living in Devon, she had been to see one of her former pupils – in prison.

It's a quite extraordinary story. Every month for the last thirteen years, Eileen and her husband, Bob, have driven, often hundreds of miles, to visit Peter Luckhurst in whichever of Her Majesty's prisons he happens to be residing. There is nothing, so far as I know, in teachers' contracts that calls for such dedication.

But it goes further than that: Peter, whom everybody still thinks of as a boy, although he has grown to manhood behind prison walls, has attracted the support of a surprisingly disparate group of people who believe he is innocent of the crime for which he was locked up. They range from a campaigning newspaperman to the lady of the manor in his village, from a social worker to a private detective, and include even the niece of the woman Peter, as a teenager, was found guilty of murdering.

From the moment he was suspected, in fact, Peter seems to have had only one real enemy: himself. Those who know him best believe his troubles all go back to his highly unusual character – a confusing mixture of stubbornness and naivety that made it all too easy for the police to nail him for the murder. Or could it be that he applied a natural wiliness to creating doubt where no doubt should exist?

Eileen met Peter in January 1974 when she was appointed head teacher at the Church of England primary school in Pluckley, a village outside Ashford, in Kent. He was eleven years old, small and underdeveloped, with pixie features, and a mop of black hair falling into his eyes. He came to school poorly dressed and unkempt, and was fiercely protective of his sister, Tracey, less than a year younger than him, who was in the same class. 'Peter comes from gypsy stock, and he is very proud of it,' said Eileen.

While smart enough, Peter had missed out on a lot in his upbringing. He was one of those half-wild boys, children of the hedgerow, that you can still find in the villages of Kent and Sussex. Fascinated by activities like shooting, ferreting and snaring rabbits, they seem like children out of another, pre-television age.

Peter got along well enough with the other children, although he had no particular friend. Soon he began staying after school to help Eileen tidy up. That was when he talked about his mother, Joyce. She had tuberculosis, he told the teacher. He was very worried about her.

After only two terms, Peter left reluctantly to attend Ashford North Boys' School. That autumn, looking out of the window, Eileen saw him standing forlornly outside her school. 'When I questioned him, he gave various excuses for not being at school,' she said. 'He said he had a cold, or he had got up too late.'

It was all pretty transparent: Peter felt he simply didn't fit in at the secondary school. He hankered for the primary school where he had found his own level.

Then, when he was thirteen, Peter's mother died. The funeral was at the church across from Eileen's school. On the day of the funeral she saw Peter outside, looking his usual untidy self. She brought him in, brushed him down and combed his hair. His mother's death, she said, 'devastated him'.

In 1978, Eileen left the Pluckley school. Her life now would be in Canterbury, where her husband, Bob, lectured at teachers' college. Peter was not on her mind – until, watching an ITV news broadcast one night in 1980, she learned that he had been charged with murder. 'I dropped the cup of coffee I was holding,' she said.

Pluckley is a piece of storybook England with thatched cottages, Norman church, the lot. Its travel-poster image, though, overlies the social reality: the toffs live at the top of Forge Hill in their substantial houses, sipping sherry at the Black Horse, while the proles live at the bottom in a 1950s council estate, Thorne Estate, taking their noisier pleasures at the Spectre Inn. Peter lived in one of the council houses with his father, Dennis, who was mostly out of work, and his sister. Anyone could have pointed the house out to you – because after Peter's mother died, some say, conditions at the Luckhurst home were 'appalling'.

At the Ashford school, other boys gave Peter a wide berth. He slept in the clothes he wore to school, and it was obvious that he didn't change his underwear. The taunts finally drove him to drop out of school. Concerned social services people, with his father's agreement, put him into a foster home. But family ties were strong: he was always walking home to see his dad and his sister, and soon he moved back with them.

He wasn't without ability. He had considerable artistic talent, Eileen Pollard said, although he would be embarrassed if you told him so. And the couple who ran Country Pine, a furniture firm where he worked for six months, found him intelligent and personable.

But he had no idea how to look out for his own best interests. He would steal small items – and get caught every time. And worse – he would admit to anything. At the Ashford school, he had taken the rap when several other boys had broken into the metalwork shop – even though he wasn't involved. When a car was damaged, Peter owned up right away to the police – even though everyone knew he hadn't done it. Petty crime detection became a simple matter in Pluckley – you simply asked Peter. He'd own up every time.

His involvement in petty crime didn't mean he didn't have friends. He was liked, in fact, by people in every strata of Pluckley society, from some of the dubious characters who kept him around as a handy scapegoat, to Lady Spens, who hired him to muck out the stables when he needed money, and who was prepared to take an indulgent view of his petty thievery.

But his special friend was Miss Gwendoline Marshall, a sweet seventy-nine-year-old woman who had lived at Enfield Lodge, halfway up Forge Hill, for forty-five years and yet who was still something of a mystery woman in the village. Miss Marshall – we would hesitate to call her Gwendoline – kept to herself in the English way. She was perfectly content most of the time to remain with her King

Charles spaniel, Sophie, within the six-acre grounds of the 1930s house she had inherited from her parents. Once a month she made a trip to London, which mystified villagers, but which was in fact to collect rent from flats she leased in Bloomsbury to art students.

She had worked for a publisher originally, but occupied her time now with painting, playing the piano and gardening. A tiny figure, only four foot ten and weighing slightly under seven stone, Miss Marshall may have been private, but she was not antisocial. Her kindness was widely noted, and when her postman retired, she left a present on his doorstep.

She had got to know Peter through his mother, who used to clean at Enfield Lodge. Like others in Peter's life, she was soon taking an almost motherly interest in the undersized boy who always said, 'When there's any trouble in the village, and I am nearby, the dirty end of the stick goes in my hand.'

'Master Luckhurst', as Miss Marshall called him, would gather firewood for her Rayburn stove and pick up windfall apples from the orchard in return for pocket money. But Peter's real payoff was the friendly ear Miss Marshall gave him as he unburdened himself about his latest scrape, or his differences with his father. She always had sympathy and suggestions.

Like the afternoon of 7 October 1980, when Peter cycled up the hill to Enfield Lodge, leaving his bicycle as usual in the driveway in order to find Miss Marshall in the garden. 'Good afternoon, Master Luckhurst,' she said, in her quaintly formal way. 'What can I do for you today?'

'I got to go to Smarden tomorrow,' he said, naming a nearby village. 'To get my shotgun permit. I expect they'll ask me where I'm going to be shooting.'

'I know, I know,' she said, smiling. 'And you want to know if you can tell them I let you shoot here. Is that right?'

He blushed. 'Yeah, that's it.'

'Of course you can.' Peter, in fact, was the only one she allowed to shoot on her property. 'Now you'll have to do something for me,' she said, as they walked back towards the house. 'I need some cookers from the orchard. The basket is in the usual place.'

When he returned from the orchard, they sat chatting on the doorstep for a while as she peeled the apples. 'And don't forget about your haircut,' she told him when he left. 'Tomorrow you and I are going to the barber's. We can't have you looking like a haystack.'

'Very good, Miss Marshall.'

The haircut would wait. The following afternoon, around three o'clock, Lucy Wilson, who lived across the road from Enfield Lodge, was working in her garden when a girl pushing a pram rushed up her driveway. 'There's something wrong at Miss Marshall's,' she said. 'Please come.'

At the lodge Mrs Wilson found the girl's husband, Alan Dryland, and his parents-in-law. Miss Marshall had invited them up to pick apples, said Dryland. But when they arrived she was nowhere to be found and the side door had been left open.

Mrs Wilson stepped gingerly into the kitchen, calling Miss Marshall's name. The first thing she noticed was a pool of fresh blood on the floor. There were more bloodstains on the kitchen cabinets, as if someone had brushed against them. When she glanced into the living room, a large red stain on the carpet caught her eye.

Fearing now what she'd find, she fetched Dryland.

The odd thing was that, apart from the blood, everything seemed in order. There was a bunch of freshly pulled carrots on the draining board, the *Daily Telegraph* lay on the table, and a pair of spectacles rested on the arm of a chair beside the grand piano in the living room. Only an open handbag in the dining room, from which protruded Miss Marshall's cheque book, gave any suggestion of an intruder.

Upstairs it was the same story: blood on the sink in the bathroom and in each of the three bedrooms, including a room which Miss Marshall used as a studio, but no sign of disorder. And no sign of a body.

Police from Ashford, who were soon swarming over the house, were as mystified as Lucy Wilson had been. It was only at 5.55 p.m., nearly three hours after the alarm had been raised, that police used a pair of garden shears to force open the padlocked door of a garden shed. It was, Detective Superintendent Earl Spencer would say, 'a dreadful murder'.

Miss Marshall lay like a broken doll between a wheelbarrow and a stack of *Telegraph* magazines. Her legs, in her gardening Wellingtons, were twisted grotesquely, her bloodied hands tied behind her back. Her face and upper body were slashed and battered and showed puncture marks from a garden fork found leaning outside the shed. In a final touch of horror, her body was pinned to the ground with a hayfork plunged through her neck.

The doctor who examined the body at the scene predicted that her murderer would be found covered with blood.

The Kent police faced a daunting situation. Miss Marshall had not been violated, so sex did not seem a motive. But neither had there been any systematic attempt to ransack and rob the house. The crime appeared motiveless. They could not have imagined how quickly the murder would be 'solved'.

Sergeant Eric Peacock, the officer who had first noticed two spots of blood on the padlocked door of the shed, was walking up Forge Hill that evening when he met Nikki Mannouch, a youth who had been in trouble with the police in the past. 'Where were you today?' the sergeant asked. He'd been to Ashford, returning to Pluckley on the 2.23 p.m. train, replied Nikki. He'd spent the rest of the day with his friend, Peter Luckhurst. The policeman might want to talk to Peter, said Nikki. Peter had told him he'd seen Miss Marshall's dog running loose and put it back over the gate. At that moment, Peter himself came riding up the hill. Yes, he confirmed, he'd found Sophie in the road and put her back in the garden.

The talk at the Spectre Inn that night, of course, was all of the murder. Peter, sipping his customary pint of light and mild and playing a game of darts, seemed his usual self. Only later, watching the news on television with friends, did he make a revealing comment. 'Christ,' he said, when the item about Miss Marshall came on, 'I expect I'll get blamed for that as usual. What would I get? Twenty-five years? I'd be an old man when I came out.'

The police, faced with a complete puzzle, had to work with what little they had. So it wasn't surprising that, the following afternoon, Peter and Nikki, two lads who'd been in trouble before, were picked up for questioning. Standard police practice.

It was standard police practice too when Peter was told to strip and was given only a blanket to wear as several officers, some behind him where he couldn't see them, fired questions at him. In the past Peter always knew that, if he 'owned up' to whatever it was they were accusing him of, he was allowed to go home. Perhaps that was why, after the grilling had gone on for some time without really getting anywhere, Peter, right out of the blue, admitted that he was the one who had killed Miss Marshall. He had been denying all along that he had been at Enfield Lodge on the day of the murder. 'It's obvious to me,' said one of the officers, 'that you went in there on your own and, for some reason, something happened whether you intended it or not. What happened?'

Peter was silent for a moment. 'I hit her with a log,' he said quietly. 'I wanted some money. I'd had too much to drink.'

He'd hit her a second time, he said. 'She fell down and I just left her.'

But who had hit her with the fork? 'It was me. I had funny feelings. I don't want my dad told.'

Did Peter want a solicitor? No, he replied, 'because I'd have to pay'. Asked if he wanted to make a formal statement, Peter insisted on writing it himself. It is quite brief – and curiously without emotion:

'I had known Miss Marshall a long time but only through my mother. I left the Spectre Inn around two o'clock. From there I went into my house, got my bike and went to [Enfield Lodge] where I left my bike and entered the house. On entering I saw Miss Marshall and I grabbed a log and hit her. I asked have you got any money. She replied no, so I hit her again on the head in trying to knock her out but failing this I got angry and forced her around upstairs and downstairs of the house but I could find no money at all except a cheque book which was no use so I left it. I hit her again and this time knocking out the lady. While unconscious I got her to the shed and tied her hands and pushed her on the floor and kicked her and I went all weird and started hitting her with a fork. On recovering from the funny turn [I] locked the door and ran like hell. I got on my bike and went home and into my shed. From my shed I saw Nick Mannouch walking past. I asked him where he was going. He said up to the village so I went with him to get his bike which he'd left there and we then went back to my house where I ate my tea and then left for Smarden.'

Oddly, although the statement is in Peter's handwriting, some of the phrasing, like 'on entering', sounds more like the stuff of police reports than the words of a village lad.

In the questioning that followed, Peter gave a quite accurate account of the situation police had found at the house. He mentioned, for example, that in dragging Miss Marshall upstairs, he'd had to step over the board at the foot of the stairs used to keep the dog from going up.

It was what he did not mention that was especially interesting. He was not aware that there was a downstairs toilet in the house – even though blood had been found on its walls. He did not mention cutting Miss Marshall's throat, a fact the police themselves were not aware of until the autopsy was completed later.

As Dudley Stephens, a journalist working for the *Kentish Express* and who later championed Peter's cause, put it to me: 'What the police knew, Peter knew. What the police didn't know, Peter didn't know.'

In any investigation there are always small anomalies. But the police believed that once the forensic tests were done – revealing, no doubt, that Peter's clothes were smothered in blood – his involvement would be confirmed once and for all.

That was the strange thing, though. No blood was visible on the clothes. 'Are these all your clothes?' a detective sergeant asked.

'Yes, why?' said Peter.

'There was a lot of blood about, but I don't see a lot on your clothes,' said the officer.

In fact, tiny specks of blood, invisible to the naked eye, were found on his boots and the sleeve of his jacket. They were so minute they could not even be matched. (For a boy whose great pleasure was hunting, it would have been unusual, indeed, if blood had not been found on him.)

He had not changed his clothes on the day of the murder, and the policeman who had issued his shotgun permit at Smarden confirmed that his hands and finger-nails were filthy as usual. Fingernail clippings, though, revealed no traces of blood.

It was only later, armed now with the knowledge that Miss Marshall's throat had been cut, that the police searched the Luckhurst home and made a very surprising discovery. In a cutlery drawer they found a kitchen knife, the five-inch blade of which was smeared with blood. The blood type matched Miss Marshall's. Whoever put it there hadn't even bothered to wipe it.

Was it Peter? If so, how did he get it there? His pockets showed no sign of blood, and he would hardly have carried a bloody knife in his hand through the village.

The story of the knife doesn't end there. Peter had spoken only of attacking Miss Marshall with a log and with the fork. Dr Bernard Charnley, a consultant path-ologist, says it was a serious wound in her index finger that resulted in most of the bleeding in the house. It was the sort of wound, he says, that a person would get fending off a knife attack. Her assailant, in other words, attacked her with the knife from the very start.

She had, apparently, been struck with a log, but only a minute amount of blood had been found on it. If the log had been the main weapon used, says Dr Charnley, he would expect to find it heavily bloodstained and with hair stuck to it.

The confession raised other questions. In support of his story of having had too much to drink, Peter said he had gone into the Spectre with £12 after cashing a social assistance cheque, and had come out with little or no cash. After numerous pints of light and mild, he had felt 'light-headed', and switched to Coke. But friends there that day say he drank very little.

As to his story of wanting to rob Miss Marshall, his social worker, Ann Colwell, says, 'He did not need money, and he was not a materialistic person anyway.' After making the confession, Colwell says, Peter fully expected he would be allowed to go home. Instead he found himself locked up.

Eileen Pollard, after learning of Peter's arrest, went to visit him immediately. She had not seen him for several years. He was by then seventeen years old. But the tiny bedraggled figure who came into the room, wearing boots several sizes too large for him, looked no more than thirteen, she told me. Peter, in turn, couldn't believe his eyes, seeing his one-time teacher in these surroundings. 'I couldn't understand how you cared,' he has told her since.

In the months leading up to the trial, she visited him regularly (hoping that her students at the nearby teachers' college where she lectured would not see her in the queue outside the prison and wonder what she was doing there).

'Peter was quite adamant that he did not want me present at the trial,' she said. 'I didn't go. I was wrong. I should have gone.'

By the time the trial opened at Maidstone in June 1981, Peter had retracted his confession. But what he had to say in the witness box certainly didn't help.

He said he called at Enfield Lodge on the day of the murder to see if Miss Marshall wanted anything. The side door was open. When Miss Marshall did not answer his calls, he went in, his knife in his hand in case of trouble.

'I saw some blood on the floor,' he testified. 'I picked up a log and noticed there was some blood on it. I dropped it.' Following the trail of blood through the house, he found Miss Marshall's glasses on the floor. He picked them up with the point of his knife, he said.

He called her name again in the garden, and eventually found his way to the garden shed, which was open. 'Miss Marshall was lying flat on her face inside. She was bloody. I knelt down almost next to her.

'I prodded her in the back a couple of times with the knife to see if she would move. She did not move. A hayfork was stuck in her neck. I pulled it out. When I first saw her I thought she could have been alive, but I could not hear her breathing and thought she was dead.' At that point he stuck the hayfork back in her, locked the shed and ran off.

Even if they believed Peter's second story – and it sounded pretty implausible – what were the jury to think of a boy who, finding the body of a woman who had befriended him, poked it with a knife and then, apparently, replaced the tine of the pitchfork in her neck? His counsel, Michael Morland QC, asked the question on everyone's minds: why had he not gone to the police?

265

His answer damned him: 'I would not give them assistance for nothing!' he said fiercely. 'I would not do it if my old man was dead!'

Suspicion and hostility towards the police were part of his gypsy heritage. And, he explained, he had been hounded by the police in the past and accused of things he hadn't done. But, remembering the gentle spinster who had met such a horrifying death, the jury could hardly feel anything but repugnance at his attitude.

So why, asked his lawyer, had he confessed to the murder?

'There was only one way of making them shut up,' he replied. 'They kept on.'

How had he known the details he'd worked into his confession? He had pieced it all together from finding the body, he said. 'I'm a bloody good detective,' he would say on another occasion.

Did he really mean, the prosecutor, Colin Nicholls QC, exclaimed, that he had been willing to face twenty years in prison rather than tell the police he had stumbled on the body? He would kill himself rather than stay in prison, was Peter's reply.

He also said, in response to Nicholls' questions, that he did feel some anger towards Miss Marshall's murderer. 'Do you hope that he might be caught?'

'I could not give two hoots,' said Peter.

'Do you feel the person who did it must be punished?'

'I think I would say good luck to them if they did not get caught. Having it on his mind would be worse than being in prison.'

They are the answers you might expect from a boy living just on the shady side of the law. But he seemed simply blind to the effect his thoughtless words had on others. As when he had told the police: 'That old lady was like a mother to me. I would not even slap her around the face.'

Peter's supporters from Pluckley, including Lady Spens, crowded the public gallery on each of the five days of the trial. None of them believed Peter capable of violence. They all thought originally that it was just a terrible misunderstanding that would be cleared up at the trial. By the end they were feeling a lot less sure of the outcome. In fact, it took the jury only two hours to return a unanimous verdict: guilty.

The evidence, said Mr Justice Stocker, had been 'overwhelming. You have been totally lacking in any compassion or pity, nor have you shown any remorse for what you have done.' He sentenced Peter to be detained at Her Majesty's pleasure – an indefinite sentence.

Journalist Dudley Stephens was in court that day. 'I think Peter had only made that confession to confuse the police,' he told me when I met him in Cardiff, where he now works for a South Wales newspaper. It's his belief that Peter was convinced that the real murderer would be exposed at the trial – just the way they are in Perry Mason mysteries on television. 'I think it was only after he was sentenced and was being led downstairs that he realized it wasn't going to happen. Because he said just two words: "Oh, shit!"'

There was one woman in the court each day during the trial who had not known Peter before and who had every reason to loathe him. She was Juliette Marshall, Miss Marshall's niece by marriage, and she is a magistrate. From the start, she would say, the police attitude had surprised her. 'We've got him!' they'd told her without any hesitation, quite early in the investigation. After listening to all the evidence at the trial, she declared: 'I think it's unlikely, on the evidence, that he did it on his own – if he did it at all. I think there was insufficient evidence to convict him.'

Juliette Marshall raised the tricky question that Peter's supporters have had to contend with ever since his conviction: it's possible that he put together his confession from what he'd seen at the house and from what the police had told him. It's more plausible that he was present when she was murdered, perhaps running off in a panic before Miss Marshall's throat was cut. Villagers even say that, after Peter was charged, police officers were still looking for a second assailant. Has Peter been protecting someone all these years?

'Come on, Peter, who do you think it was?' Bob Pollard asked him during a visit last year.

'I just don't know,' he replied. 'Do you think I would stay in this horrible place if I knew?'

There may be another explanation why Peter, if he didn't murder Miss Marshall, made no great effort to avoid being blamed for the crime. Eileen remembers questioning him closely in 1984 about who the culprit might be. He became agitated, shook his head, and said he felt responsible for her death. If he had arrived earlier at the house, she would still be alive.

'Miss Marshall would not wish you to atone for her murder,' Eileen said.

He clasped her hands, and tears filled his eyes. 'But it helps,' he replied.

The Peter Luckhurst Defence Committee worked for several years with a private detective, a former London policeman named Brian Ford. He believed that the bizarre nature of the crime, the lack of a motive and the use of the hayfork, suggested a black magic cult killing. Ford was quite certain that, even if Peter had the strength to remove the hayfork in the first place, to have replaced it exactly in the same holes was impossible. But Ford's investigations eventually led nowhere.

Stephens wrote an article in the *Kentish Express* under the headline, 'The Unanswered Questions of the Pluckley Murder'. But his editor, after lunching with Superintendent Spencer, decided that there were no unanswered questions, and what had been intended as the first shot in a newspaper campaign was the last.

If Peter Luckhurst didn't murder Gwendoline Marshall, then who did? Nikki Mannouch was widely suspected, and children would shout 'Murderer!' after him on the street. One woman claimed to have seen him arrive back in Pluckley on an earlier train that day. He fainted while giving evidence at the Luckhurst trial, and was not questioned further. After holding him for two days, the police were satisfied that his alibi was watertight, and that he was not in Pluckley at the time the woman was murdered. While denying his own involvement, Mannouch is equally adamant that Peter is not the guilty one. Peter, he says, probably knows who the killer is. 'It must have been someone Peter was ruddy scared of, I can tell you,' Mannouch told an investigative team from *The Observer*.

Dudley Stephens has a different idea. He talks of another local man who was seen burning something in his garden on the day of the murder when no one had ever seen him with a bonfire before. The man, he says, paid a coal bill in advance that day for the first time in memory. Had he come into some money? Was he setting up an alibi? Could this fellow have met Peter at the Spectre Inn that lunchtime after already killing Miss Marshall, and told him he was going back to look for more money? 'Peter,' says Stephens, 'has never been forthcoming. He won't answer these questions clearly enough.'

In 1988, Justice, the British section of the International Commission of Jurists, was asked by Peter's supporters to examine the case. But, after reviewing the facts and having a legal assistant, Michael Aspinall, interview Peter, the group declined to intervene on his behalf. For an appeal to be successful after so many years, said Aspinall, new evidence would have to be produced to show that Peter could not possibly have committed the crime, or that someone else was the culprit. Since Peter had admitted being at the scene that day, he could not definitely be ruled out as the killer; and there was no conclusive evidence linking any of the other suspects to the crime.

Aspinall, though, went right to the emotional heart of the case when he asked Peter about his claim that he had replaced the hayfork in Miss Marshall's neck. How could someone who felt she was like a mother to him do such a thing? Peter's answer was that he had been confused when he had given that testimony in court. In fact, he said, he hadn't removed the fork from her neck in the first place. That made three different versions he'd given of the facts. It didn't sound very convincing.

At the time I met Eileen and Bob, the Kent police were completing a review of the case which would be forwarded to the Home Office. A senior officer had been to see them, but Peter himself did not want to be interviewed by the police again. 'He is still very frightened of the police,' said Eileen. The Pollards were not hopeful of the outcome of the inquiry.

270

Peter might by now have been out on parole. Except that he refuses to sign the required document expressing remorse for what he is supposed to have done. 'How can I feel remorse for it when I didn't do it?' he says.

Over the years, his father and his sister, who is now married with children, have moved away from Pluckley. His sister writes and a former employer visits occasionally, but the monthly visits from the Pollards are his only real continuing contact with the outside world. He has passed exams in maths and English in prison, and reads widely. But the rural interest is still there – some of his favourite reading is about the countryside.

Peter has enjoyed the few contacts he has had with children, and the Pollards take him pictures of their grandchildren. He made the couple a large hearth rug for their new house when they moved in, and they look forward to the time when he can walk into their living room a free man and see it.

People still ask Eileen Pollard why she bothers. 'What has it got to do with you?' they say. They just don't understand. 'A village school is a very tight-knit community,' she says. 'The teachers care about the children.' She responded from the start to Peter Luckhurst, 'because I knew he would need help. The whole point is, he was one of my children.'

LADY
STARDUST

Driving north on Route 101 from the Golden Gate Bridge into Marin County I am consumed by flowers: brilliant orange nasturtiums cascading from the decks of hillside houses, gardens ablaze with poppies, the road lined with banks of daisies. There is probably no place on earth more beautiful than Marin County, with its eucalyptus trees, its lush semi-tropical greenery and its rugged seascapes. No wonder it became in the 1960s a byword for the hedonistic lifestyle as hippies and professional people flowed north from San Francisco to taste forbidden pleasures in this Shangri-La.

By the 1970s, though, the bills were coming due. Nancy Boggs, transferring from Watts, the notorious black Los Angeles neighbourhood where she had been a juvenile officer for nine years, to idyllic Marin, would say that the well-to-do families here were far more disturbed than those in the ghetto. And the case which more than any other exposed the dangerous pressures under which many in the third richest county in the United States lived was that of Marlene Olive.

Marlene knew this road well. The first time she saw it was from a rental car in the spring of 1973 when she was fourteen. Her father, Jim Olive, who could have understudied Willie Loman, the failed hero of *Death of a Salesman*, was bringing his wife, Naomi, and Marlene to Marin where, at the age of fifty-six, he was starting a new business career, his enthusiasm undimmed after being fired for the umpteenth time.

Two years later Marlene drove the by now familiar route with her boyfriend, Chuck Riley, to attend a rock concert at San Francisco's Cow Palace where, high on acid, her mind full of images of blood spatters and charred bones, she intoned over and over again her own mantra: 'I killed my parents! I killed my parents!'

The following night she and Chuck drove into San Francisco again, this time winding up at the Garden of Ecstasy for a show called *The Naked Dance of Love*. Aroused by the performance, Marlene, as they drove home across the Golden Gate Bridge, perched astride the car's gear lever, thrilling herself with the engine's vibrations. 'Hey, get off!' Chuck yelled, unable to change down as the car slowed on the long climb away from the city. It would not be true to say he was shocked at Marlene's behaviour, because he was fully convinced she was a witch.

Terra Linda, a suburb eighteen miles north of the bridge, where Jim Olive took his family to live, is not the Marin of hot tubs and psychiatrists' hideaways; rather it's a middle-class area of almost identical homes, their most distinctive feature being the high back-yard fences, not at all usual in America, with which the residents, many of them middle-management types commuting to San Francisco, secure their privacy.

Terra Linda means 'beautiful earth', but at that time,

when the development was comparatively new, there was little of the fabled Marin greenery, and the bungalow at 353 Hibiscus Way that the Olives eventually bought was especially dreary. One small window looked out on the street, while the view to the rear was confined to the fence and a concrete patio. When jury members in Chuck Riley's trial eventually visited the house, they were all struck by the smallness and meanness of the place, and Naomi Olive, who had lived nearly all her married life as a pampered ex-patriate wife in South and Central America with plenty of servants, was not fooled one bit by her husband's talk of a brighter future. Terra Linda for Naomi was the end of the line in every sense.

For Marlene, a chubby girl with striking green eyes, Marin was the most frightening thing that had ever happened to her. As the only daughter of an oil company executive, she'd attended private school at Quito in Ecuador. She dressed conservatively, spoke more Spanish than English, liked the bubblegum music favoured by pre-teens and was completely naive about drugs. To the kids at Vallecito Junior High School in their jeans and tee shirts, the new girl in her prissy skirt, sweater and blouse might have come from another planet. It didn't help when the kids inevitably tagged her 'Olive Oyl'.

No one would have predicted that within two years the demure Marlene would be accused of crimes considered shocking even in a county that had seen just about everything. Unless, of course, they knew some of the secrets hiding behind the prison-like façade of 353 Hibiscus Way.

Because Marlene was part of a profoundly disturbed family. And things had been going that way since long before she was born.

Jim Olive's story would have made a grand rags-to-riches epic – except he never made it much past the rags stage. He started out at the age of nine selling newspapers on the streets of Panama City, where his father had in 1925 become business manager of an English-language newspaper. From then on Jim's career ricocheted from one disaster to another – a lab blown up at Pennsylvania State College, prompting him to switch from science to business studies, a family real-estate venture in Panama that didn't produce a single lot sale, followed (after a wartime stint censoring soldiers' letters home) by a string of jobs in the oil industry, and the bankruptcy of an oil and gas firm he had started. That he always bounced back can only be attributed to the man's natural ebullience: his much-circulated resumé was headed 'Jim Olive, Marketeer', and made him sound like the ultimate go-getter.

Unlucky in business, he was even unluckier in love. During the war his mother sent him a picture of a quite ravishing nineteen-year-old named Naomi Wagner, the foster child of an old friend in his home town of Cuba, in New York State. In 1944, after they had known each other for less than a month, Major James Olive and Naomi Wagner were married in Cuba, NY. There is no hint in the happy wedding photographs of the dread that would follow Naomi: her mother had died when she was eight years old after spending six years in a mental asylum, and Naomi was always haunted by the fear that the same fate awaited her.

For Naomi, timid and unsure of herself, Jim's oil industry jobs, involving postings to far-off, hot, mosquito-ridden climes, his frequent absences on business trips, plus the constant entertaining expected of her, turned her into a nervous wreck. The answer, which occurred to her in 1955 when, for a time, they were living in Virginia, was to adopt a child. Marlene, the result of a liaison between the teenage daughter of a prominent family from Norfolk, Virginia, and a Scandinavian sailor, was one day old when the Olives brought her home.

Jim, who hadn't seemed that keen on the idea of a child, immediately became the doting father; Naomi, on the other hand, was the complete neurotic parent, wearing a gauze mask any time she came near the baby, and staying home because she was afraid to leave Marlene with a babysitter, One time when she did go out to dinner with friends, she insisted on taking the baby, shut herself in a bedroom with Marlene and, when Jim brought her a plate of food, flung it at him.

During Naomi's unhappy years in Ecuador, a time when she became increasingly suspicious that people were trying to cheat her and was drinking more and more heavily, she used Marlene as a barrier against the world, keeping her from playing with other children, insisting she spend her time with her mother. As Marlene grew to resent this confinement, the one bright spot in her life was her relationship with her father, her special pal who was always ready to indulge her.

And then Marlene's world exploded. Snooping in her father's study one day when she was ten, she came across a legal paper headed 'In the matter of the Adoption of an Unnamed Girl Child'. Her parents had always meant to tell Marlene she was adopted. At dinner that night Jim tried lamely to explain that she was specially loved because they had chosen her. Sitting in juvenile detention one day, Marlene would tell a writer named Richard M. Levine, 'I was angry, so angry because I thought I had been bought... Then I started thinking about who my real mother was.'

When Jim, tall and still retaining his military trimness, moved the family to Marin County – to start a small business management and tax consultancy – Naomi initially made the effort to be sociable, even accompanying him on his sales calls. But soon black despondency took over. Obsessively, she filled every closet in the house with towels, and much of the time retreated to her room to drink, to talk to herself and, her one interest, to care for her 'fishies' – the aquariums she had set up.

Marlene, feeling lost and out of her depth at school, had her own problems. Her father was working so desperately hard starting the business, he had little time for her. When she wasn't having screaming arguments with her mother – if a friend came to the house she'd tell them, 'Don't pay her any attention, she's drunk' – she too was in her room, watching horror movies and improving her English by writing poetry that mirrored her depression:

> I sit in a cold dark room
> listening intently
> for something that's not here.

A couple of months after the Olives arrived in Terra Linda, Marlene was diagnosed with a duodenal ulcer and put on a baby-food diet. It was the tranquillizers prescribed for her at this time that suddenly made life more bearable for Marlene. At Terra Linda High School, which she entered that autumn, she was known as a downer freak who sleepwalked her way through the day feeling no pain at all.

By her second summer she was hanging out with the bad kids at school, was smoking marijuana regularly and, after a new boyfriend lent her some black magic books, developing an interest in demonology and witchcraft. Her early experiments drawing magic circles in the back yard came to nothing. But Marlene soon discovered – or at least believed – that by staring fixedly at people with her unusual green eyes she could exert power over them. Soon she was wearing glitter clothes like her hero, David Bowie, and calling herself Lady Stardust after her favourite Bowie song.

For most teenagers these relatively innocent symptoms of rebellion would have been enough to carry them through the stormy years. But for Marlene, home was becoming more and more a war zone. 'Whore! Tramp! Guttersnipe!' Naomi screamed at her after waking up from her usual stupor and catching her in bed with her boyfriend. 'You're not even my mother!' Marlene would yell. 'She was probably a whore!' would be the response ringing in Marlene's ears as she slammed the door. Jim would plead with her to have patience with her mother.

Then, on a sunny autumn day in 1974, she met Chuck Riley, a grossly overweight, eighteen-stone kid with a fixation on guns and fast cars. 'Met' is hardly the word. Chuck, eighteen, was making his customary mid-morning visit to Terra Linda High School, selling pot and cocaine to kids in the school yard when, among the spaced-out teenagers on the lawn, he spotted the most beautiful girl he'd ever seen. Marlene did not notice him, didn't even respond when he spoke to her. She was sitting crying as other kids taunted her. A few minutes later a girlfriend took her into the toilets. Marlene was having her first unhappy trip on LSD.

279

Chuck, had never even had sex with a girl and he was no social catch. Naomi, meeting Chuck's mother for the first time, made it quite clear where she stood: 'I understand you're a nurse's aid and live in a lower income area,' she said. 'I can't imagine why Marlene would want to see Chuck when she knows so many boys from influential families.' But Chuck's special calling card was his access to drugs.

They began a casual affair, with all the ardour on Chuck's side. She kept him on a string, even went off with other guys, but always came back to Chuck because she knew he could never refuse to give her the free pills and joints she demanded. Rejected at times, Chuck would twice try to commit suicide by overdosing. And while Marlene's other friends would preserve a certain scepticism about her occult powers, Chuck would say: 'I began to believe, without really believing it, that Marlene was a witch.'

The pieces of the tragedy were in place. Now the players whirled faster and faster towards the inevitable climax.

'I wish my parents were dead! I wish someone would kill them,' Marlene told Chuck and some friends one day. Not an uncommon sentiment with teenagers. But she kept on about it. 'It's either me or that bitch,' she told Chuck on the phone. 'Either I'm going to do her in or myself. You must know someone who'd help.' Again Marlene was being true to teenage form: killing a parent is one way of killing yourself. She wouldn't be the first or last youngster who had difficulty deciding whose life to take.

Chuck, now dieting furiously to give himself a more presentable image, was in a dilemma. Killing wasn't his thing, yet going along with Marlene's screwball plans was the price for being her beau. So he said he knew a guy who'd do it, strung her along for a few weeks.

Naomi was still Marlene's real target. 'Bitch, crazy lady! They're going to cart you off in a straitjacket one of these days,' the girl screamed during a row over, of all things, how to slice celery. Then, biting her own arm until it was black, she threw the paring knife at her mother. 'I could lace her soup with fifty tabs of acid and watch her space to death,' she told a friend. Indeed, several times she slipped pills into her mother's food and drink. Naomi always turned up her nose: 'Too bitter.'

But there was a second enemy now: her father. As Marlene's behaviour became more outrageous early in 1975 – she was arrested in March with Chuck for a string of shoplifting offences – Jim started siding with Naomi. Marlene's school marks were a disaster. She and Chuck were arrested again, he for possessing a sawn-off shotgun, she for drug possession. The sixteen-year-old would have to spend the summer locked up in juvenile hall, the detention centre, and in September, said her father, he was sending her away to boarding school. 'No way, Father dear, I'd rather die,' she told him. It was the final betrayal.

Wistfully she wrote:

> I wish you could have stayed here
> Beside me Father to keep
> Things straight.
> Who knows these days what might happen?
> I might just break.

More urgently she told Chuck: 'They're sending me

away. You better do something fast or we're finished.'
After killing her parents, they would collect the insurance
money and go to South America, she assured him. Coke
was available for practically nothing there. She looked
into his eyes that special way.

'If it has to be done, I'll do it,' Chuck told a friend who
asked him if he really would kill for Marlene. 'I'd die for
Marlene.'

The warning signs had been there for a long time.
Social workers had urged the Olives to go for family
counselling time and again, but Naomi had a pathological
fear of psychiatry and refused. Even Jim, who, in his neat
business suits and ties, looked completely out of place
in the laid-back Marin business climate, reprimanded
Marlene for 'washing our dirty linen in public' after she
talked to a school guidance counsellor about her problems. Nancy Boggs, the juvenile worker assigned to
Marlene after her first arrest, asked to be taken off the
case. She had too many crazy families to cope with, she
claimed. But she warned her successor: 'It's a classic
blow-up situation.'

The image that will always stay with Chuck, the moment
that wakes him gasping and sobbing in the middle of the
night, is the claw hammer stuck in Naomi Olive's
forehead. One of the blows was so savage that the
hammer has lodged and won't come free. 'I had to touch
her to take the hammer out,' he will say. Then the
hammer comes loose and the blood spurts out – over his
yellow shirt, his hand. 'I'm flinging it off my hand like you
do with a paint brush when you're cleaning it. I can't
stand it. Then I see the hem of her dress and I pick it up
and wipe my hands on it.'

It had happened so quickly. How long ago was it that he had been hiding outside in the azalea bushes? A minute? An hour? A lifetime? 'Get the gun!' Marlene had told him on the phone. And then: 'What if we use a hammer to kill her? How hard do I hit her?' she had asked. 'How hard? But get the gun,' she'd added.

And like her willing slave, his brain mildly spaced-out on acid, he'd gone off to reclaim his .22 pistol from the friend he'd given it to as surety for a loan. 'Tell him,' Marlene had instructed, 'that you have a buyer for the gun so you'll be able to pay him back.' Worked like a charm.

'I'm going to meet Marlene,' he'd told his friends, Bill and Megan, a few minutes later. 'We'll be over soon. Then we can go to the beach.'

But when he reaches Hibiscus Way her father's Vega station wagon is still in the driveway. Marlene, at the kitchen window, waves him away. Oh God, he mustn't be seen. Jim Olive told him he'd kill him if he came around the house again. 'I'm going to get the paper,' Marlene calls to her father.

'We'll be going out in a few minutes,' she hisses to Chuck. 'Then you can go in.' So he hides in the bushes around the corner until he sees the green Vega go by. Marlene and her father are on their way to the shopping plaza to meet a girl whom Marlene has cheated out of forty dollars on a drug deal. Her dad is going to make good with a cheque.

Chuck rounds the corner then stops. Shit. Two mailmen have pulled up in front of the house. Talking. Get the hell out! Then the street is empty. Chuck slips through the front door which Marlene has left unlocked for him. It is the silence that strikes him first. He glances at himself in

283

the full-length hall mirror. A slimmer, handsomer Chuck than he can ever remember. Touches instinctively the infinity-sign bracelet Marlene has given him and through which, she's told him – and he believes – she can communicate with him. Then he moves cautiously to the hallway leading to the four small bedrooms. The only door closed is the one to what had been Marlene's bedroom last time he was here. Now officially it's the sewing room, but it's where Naomi dozes her days away. He turns the knob slowly.

As the Vega turns into Hibiscus Way panic grips Marlene. They are back too soon. 'Don't go in there,' she tells her father. 'You might get killed.' He looks at her quizzically and laughs. Another of Marlene's odd jokes. At the door Marlene pretends the strap on her shoe needs fixing, and hangs back.

Inside, Chuck, horrified, hears the car pull into the driveway. He runs down the hallway, looking blindly for a way out. 'I'm trapped!' All he can do is crouch behind a dresser in the hall as Jim Olive comes towards him. He turns into Naomi's room. And screams. 'Oh, my God, Naomi. Oh, my God!'

Now Mr Olive is coming out of the bedroom holding a knife he's picked up from the bedside table. He sees Chuck crouching behind the dresser. 'I'm going to kill you, you bastard,' he cries, advancing with the knife. Chuck will say he didn't even realize he had the gun. It's still inside the paper bag he used to carry it. But he's reaching inside and shooting from inside the bag. Four shots. And Mr Olive falls in the doorway. Chuck stands over him, staring in disbelief. 'I'm sorry,' he says, foolishly, then brings the gun up towards his head. Marlene rushes forward and knocks away his arm. 'No,

Chuck, no.' He fires the last two bullets harmlessly into the floor.

No teenage murderer ever seems to think about what happens next. To kill is enough. The body is a bit of a puzzle – like an uninvited guest. Some teenagers simply leave it there, as if, by ignoring it, it will go away. For a while that's what Marlene and Chuck did. The bodies – they could deal with them later. The first need, Marlene saw, was to calm and reassure Chuck.

He had slumped on the sofa in the living room and was staring into the fireplace. He had a technique for coping with the unthinkable. He would close his eyes and imagine he was driving fast along the winding cliff roads beside the Pacific. He could hear the throaty song of the engine, feel the pull on the bends.

'It's gonna be okay, Chuck,' said Marlene, nestling against his shoulder. 'It's gonna be okay. They can't interfere now.'

She brought him a can of beer from the refrigerator and handed him two Valium tablets which he swallowed without noticing. 'Baby, I love you. You know that. It had to be done.' Her voice was soft, lulling, stilling the images that were beginning to crowd into his mind. 'We can even get married if you want to.'

She left him with a lingering glance and went into her bedroom. He followed a few moments later. Curiously she seemed to be playing with a collection of lettered beads, turning them this way and that to make different combinations. 'What's that?' he asked.

'They came from my baby bracelet when I was born,' replied Marlene. 'It's my real mum's name. My dad said he'd tell me the name when I'm twenty-one.' She could

285

have been crying, he wasn't sure. 'I guess I'll never know now.' And then she undid her blouse, unzipped her jeans and let them drop to the floor. It was worth it, wasn't it? she whispered in his ear as she thrust herself down on him. Now she was his. Do it, Chuck. You can do it now. No one to stop us. Worth it? Oh, yes, God, worth it. Yes. Yes.

Smoking a cigarette afterwards he looked around at the clutter of her room, the mess of prescription drug bottles, magazines and glittery clothing that used to drive her mother right around the bend. 'Where's my damn robe?' said Marlene. One of the two cats, Rascal, was sleeping on it. 'Oh, my God, the cats!' she exclaimed. 'We can't let them get in there.'

For a minute it hadn't been real. As if the horrors in the room across the hall would go away if you didn't think about them. But as Chuck emerged from Marlene's room, Mr Olive's legs were still blocking the hallway. He lifted him by the shoulders and dragged him back into the sewing room.

'We got to get the fucking wallet and the keys and stuff,' she told him. Scared that Mr Olive might open his eyes any minute, Chuck rifled through the man's pockets, handing their contents to Marlene. His diary, she noted, had no appointments in it except for a dental check-up the following week. 'Can't find his wallet.'

'Try the inside pocket.'

Chuck rolled the body over on its side and put his hand inside the safari jacket. He noticed four splashes of blood in neat formation. 'They were a tight pattern,' he would say, not without a touch of conceit about his marksmanship.

While Marlene emptied the wallet and the contents of

286

her mother's handbag, Chuck pulled off Jim Olive's wedding ring and his Penn State Class of '37 ring. Because her fingers had grown thick and arthritic, Naomi's rings did not come off as easily. Marlene tugged until one came away, sending her sprawling.

'We got to get this place cleaned up,' she said, surveying the blood spatters all over the walls. 'Come and help me.' She washed the claw hammer, leaving it in the sink, then, being careful not to touch or even look at the two objects in the sewing room, they carried most of the furniture into the hallway. Only when she discovered blood on her father's favourite portrait of her, a doe-eyed painting done by an artist in Ecuador, did Marlene speak. 'Curse that bitch,' she said between clenched teeth. 'Getting blood all over my picture.'

Then, with buckets and cloths, they discovered the first rule of the murderer's trade: that blood is the very devil. The walls were still smeared pink when Chuck finished rubbing them, and the shag rug was a mess. Even when he helped Marlene to start a fire in the fireplace to burn his bloodstained shirt and the rags they'd used, it wouldn't start properly.

This was a drag, thought Chuck. There seemed no end to this cleaning-up. Sensing his impatience, knowing now that she needed him for what was to come, Marlene quickly agreed to his suggestion that they walk over to see Bill and Megan. 'Wait a minute. I better feed the cats,' she said. And before they left they used a blanket to cover Naomi's crushed face with the gaping hole in the forehead, the glasses broken and askew like a Francis Bacon portrait.

Then they were out in the Saturday afternoon sun, walking past people cutting grass or washing their cars, two kids just taking the breeze. Their friends had left for the beach, so they ambled over to Northgate, the huge regional shopping centre that dwarfs and overwhelms Terra Linda, to call on Chuck's brother, Kerry, who was working the weekend in a menswear store. Chuck, Kerry would remember, was as white as a sheet and bug-eyed, and Marlene didn't say a word.

At Chuck's home, his dad, who delivered cakes from a truck for the Dolly Madison company, was doing his books, and too busy to hassle Chuck about his late hours, his brushes with the law, his speeding tickets that had seen him lose the use of his '67 Buick Skylark. His mother, more forgiving, asked them to stay to dinner. No thanks, Mum. Bill and Megan had called. They'd be picking up Marlene and Chuck. Just time for him to get some marijuana and cocaine from his stash.

And really none of this was happening for Chuck; it was all in some other country of the mind. Even when they returned later to Hibiscus Way they didn't go near the bedroom. Only the jangling phone disturbed him. It was Jim's business partner, another ex-military type, Colonel Phil Royce, wondering why he hadn't turned up for a meeting they were supposed to have. 'Don't answer it!' Chuck told Marlene. He was forgetting all about it, until they went to a drive-in and the movie, a piece of crap called *Death Race 2000*, started. It was about a cross-country car race in which killing pedestrians was the aim. Every time bodies thumped and blood gushed, Chuck could see Naomi's face again, and feel the hammer in his hand.

He left the thinking to Marlene. Earlier she'd phoned home in front of her friends, pretending to speak to her mother. Now, after considering whether to try to fake a robbery attempt (too late – they'd cleaned up the house), or push the car off a cliff with the bodies inside (Marlene didn't want to lose the car), she asked him if he had any petrol at home. Yeah, there's a couple of cans in the garage. Then their problem is solved.

On the way home from picking up the petrol, she told him that the plan was to wrap up the bodies and burn them. Where? 'Out by China Camp.'

Talking to the police later, Chuck would remember the chill he felt when she said that: 'Right then and there, I knew it was going to involve her witchcraft.'

It was, after all, the summer solstice, a night when witches are abroad. And China Camp, a piece of scrubland near the neighbouring town of San Rafael, where kids went to picnic or to make love, had once been an Indian burial ground.

If *Death Race 2000* had reminded Chuck of the gore, the scene back at Hibiscus Way was purest Hitchcock. He pulled the Vega up as close as possible to the door leading into the house from the crowded garage. 'We got to take our clothes off so we don't get blood on them,' said Marlene. Naked, Chuck opened the door to the sewing room, then staggered back, retching. 'Christ, the stench.' They emptied two aerosols of Lysol disinfectant spray into the room, and it still stank.

And then they learned rule two of the murder game: dead bodies weigh a ton. 'Lift! Lift! I can't get the blanket under.'

Chuck: 'I am lifting, dammit.'

'Then we'll have to put the blanket on the floor and roll her on to it.' Dead; they didn't know the meaning of the word until they heard that body thump on the floor.

289

'His arm, I can't bend it,' Chuck said. 'It's stiffened already.'

'Then stand him up.'

'I can't. He keeps collapsing.'

Finally they used a quilt as a skid to drag the two bodies across the living room, heaving and panting as they stuffed them in the back of the station wagon. The last thing that caught Marlene's eye was the bloodstained mattress. They'd take that too, she said. It would help to cover the bodies if they were stopped.

They weren't, though. A cop they passed was too busy eating his lunch in his cruiser to pay them any attention.

China Camp, where Chinese coolies building the Southern Pacific Railway had once lived, had been Chuck's teenage playground. He'd dirt-biked here, practised target-shooting, and smoked, inhaled and shot up every imaginable illegal substance. The only thing he hadn't had here during those unhappy fat-boy years was sex.

So why, knowing the terrain so well, would he stupidly strand the Vega, its wheels spinning helplessly, on the rutted road leading to the concrete firepit? He made Marlene sit on the tail to put extra weight on the rear, he rocked the car back and forth, he shoved dirt and sticks under the rear wheels and he got Marlene to gun the engine while he shoved. The dirt shot out as if from a cannon, covering him in muck. 'Motherfucker!' he screamed.

There was only one thing for it. To get at the car jack, they yanked the mattress out then hid the bodies in long grass nearby. After jacking up one corner of the car, Chuck shoved the mattress under the wheel which was hanging in the air. Marlene stepped on the gas; the wheel chewed into the mattress, flinging the stuffing all over the place – and the car stayed stubbornly stuck.

Should they just burn the car right there with the bodies? They'd try one last thing, said Chuck. He pulled out what was left of the mattress and shoved in the spare tyre in its place. Then he floored it. With a screech of rubber, a lurch and a horrible thump, the Vega shot forward.

Into the back went the bodies again, then out again when they got to the firepit, a disused concrete water cistern. This time they couldn't lift Naomi's body over the lip of the firepit, so they set both bodies side by side against a log, poured on petrol and heaped wood over them.

Leaving a lit cigarette inside a box of matches to give them time to escape, they jumped into the car, and bounced back towards the road, stopping only to set fire to the mattress that still lay beside the track. Worried that the fire had not caught, they circled back past China Camp once. Thank God. A plume of smoke was rising above the trees.

Chuck was still shaky. No sense going back to the house. He needed to drive. He turned on to Route 101. In twenty minutes the Golden Gate Bridge rose like a phantom out of the morning sea mist ahead of them.

It was 4 a.m. when they coasted back into the driveway of 353 Hibiscus Way. Marlene would say that she had always had a fantasy that she would one day have sex in her parents' bed. But Chuck was just not up to it. Two hours later they were awakened by the radio alarm – a reminder of Jim Olive's early-to-rise business habits. 'You better get out there to make sure they burned,' said Marlene.

He stopped at a petrol station on the way to refill one of the petrol cans ('Making an early start cutting the grass?' asked the attendant). This time it was light and he didn't get stuck. Thin wisps of smoke still rose from the embers. Nothing was to be seen of Naomi's body except a few bones and a blackened skull. But, oh my God, the upper part of Jim's body was blackened but still plain to see, one stiffened arm still raised accusingly above his head. Working with precision this time, Chuck built a pyre of wood for the remains, poured on the petrol and watched the flames shoot high in the air.

A little too high perhaps. Because shortly afterwards an early morning dirt-biker noticed the fire and reported it to the local fire department. Brush fires during the dry season, which had just started, can be a real danger. Chuck, back home having breakfast at his parents' house with Marlene, would have quailed if he'd known a truck with siren wailing was heading at that moment for the firepit.

Vince Turrini, the fireman who answered the call along with a summer helper, found the fire still smoking. The two soaked it with a hose then shovelled the ashes into the firepit. 'Darned fools, why couldn't they make their fires inside the pit?' Then he found some bone remains. Back at the station he put in his report: 'Carcass (probably deer).' Naw, his colleagues joshed him. More likely a body.

Colonel Royce, Jim's friend and business partner, was surprised not to see him in church as usual that Sunday morning. Throughout the following week he continued to phone the Olive number, getting only a busy signal. On the Friday and again on Saturday, he called at the house and peered through the window. 'There's dirty dishes in the sink, and clothes scattered all over,' he told his wife. 'You should call the police,' she said.

Royce accompanied the officer who, shortly afterwards, kicked in the back door to the garage. The first thing they noticed was the absence of the car and the presence in the garage of the family luggage, suggesting the couple had not gone on holiday. Jim Olive's driver's licence, credit cards and other personal papers were sitting on the dining room table. The living room was stacked with bags and boxes, items that Marlene and Chuck had bought using the Olives' credit cards and cheque books, and hadn't even bothered to unpack. There were no signs of a burglary, though the policeman was puzzled that the bedding had been stripped in the master bedroom. There was little to see in the sewing room: Marlene had engaged Chuck's help in moving furniture around to turn it into a second sitting room. 'I'll leave a note for Marlene,' said Royce. 'This is very odd.'

He had only been home a short time when Marlene rang. She couldn't make out where her parents had gone, she told him. She'd been away on a camping trip to Lake Tahoe and come back four days earlier to find the house empty. That evening Marlene was at home smoking hash with a couple of friends when she saw the policeman pull up outside. Would she accompany him to the station to answer some questions?

'I want my daddy,' she would cry during the hours of interrogation. Detective Bart Stinson, called in after midnight to take charge of the case, knew immediately that Marlene's Lake Tahoe story was a lie. What was the weather like at Tahoe? 'Pretty good,' she replied, 'although it got cold at night.' Stinson's married daughter, who lived at Tahoe, had only that day been telling him about the freak rain and snow storm they'd had the previous weekend. And when Stinson produced some of the sales slips from the spending spree dated the previous weekend, there was no point in her trying to keep up the bluff.

Then she told him of a vision she'd had, of seeing her father standing over her mother and a pool of blood and crying, 'Nomi, Nomi, Nomi!' She'd found blood on the rug in the sewing room. Stinson ordered Marlene taken to the Marin General Hospital for psychiatric assessment, and arranged to meet two juvenile officers at 353 Hibiscus Way.

Dawn was breaking as the officers walked from room to room. The first thing Stinson noticed was that the sewing room had a scrubbed appearance and was the only clean room in the house. He immediately noticed discoloration on the rug underneath the ironing board. Running his fingernails through the rug pile he came up with dark, crusted particles. Probably blood, he thought.

To Scott Nelson, a juvenile officer, Marlene later that morning told a whole set of different stories – that her father had killed her mother, that her mother had killed her father, that bikers had killed them both. The one thing she knew for sure was that they were dead. How did she know?

'I saw their bodies.'

'Where?'

'In a room.'

'Where are they now?'

'China Camp. Firepits.'

Then she switched back to storyland. Her parents had been arguing, had driven out to China Camp, then left for a holiday together. The blood on the floor? Naomi had slipped carrying one of the fish tanks and cut her foot . . .

Stinson wasn't buying it. Marlene had mentioned that her friend, Deanna Krieger, had helped to clean up the blood. 'Find her,' he instructed. That was when the story really became unbelievable.

Yes, said Deanna after consulting a lawyer, she had helped in the clean-up. Marlene had told her all about the murders. Deanna had even had sex with Marlene and Chuck in the Olives' bed. She knew that Marlene had been looking for a hired gun to kill her parents for some time. And maybe that was not so surprising. Marlene had weird eyes and called herself a high priestess. Chuck had been her slave. Once she'd seen Marlene carve her initials with a knife on his back. Other times she ordered him to go to shops and steal expensive items for her. Sometimes, even in company, she'd order him to perform cunnilingus on her – although Deanna didn't call it that. She knew Marlene hated her mother; she just couldn't understand why she and Chuck hadn't run away. Why it had had to end in murder. Where were the bodies? Marlene had told her that too. At China Camp. 'Crispy fried.'

When the police, after recovering a few pounds of bone fragments from the firepit, went to pick up Chuck Riley from his home, he wasn't there. But his mother handed them a letter that had arrived for him from Marlene who was being detained in juvenile hall. In it she told him the story she'd told the police, urged him to get in touch with Deanna to square the story with her and, most damagingly, had written, 'I have no guilt feelings at all about my folks. NONE. NEITHER SHOULD YOU! Relax.'

Chuck, arrested at the water-bed factory where he now worked, was, Stinson would say, surprisingly calm and friendly. He seemed genuinely amazed when told he was being arrested for the murder of the Olives: 'You got to be kidding! What do you know about that?' He listened for a few minutes to Deanna's taped description of how Marlene had 'croaked off' her parents, then buried his face in his hands. 'I did it, I did it!' he sobbed. 'I didn't want to do it. Marlene made me do it. She kept asking me and asking me and begging me for months. Telling me to do it or she wouldn't love me any more.'

In the coming weeks Marlene would do her best to keep her love hook in Chuck, telling him in letters, 'I love you more than the world,' and warning him not to confess to those stupid charges. 'Your slave and lover,' Chuck would sign his passionate replies. But it was too late for denial: Chuck had already confessed to both murders, saying that he had picked up the claw hammer by the front door, where Marlene had left it, before going about his bloody business in the sewing room.

In the end his confession did Marlene no harm. In juvenile court she insisted that she'd played no part in plotting her parents' murders. The judge decided otherwise, but his hands were tied: all he could do was order that Marlene, who had just turned seventeen, be detained until she was twenty-one.

And now we come to the strangest twist in the story, a matter about which readers will have to make up their own minds. Under California law at that time, Chuck Riley, if found guilty of killing two or more people, would face an automatic death sentence. He had confessed to two murders, and his able lawyer, William O. Weissich, saw no possibility of convincing a jury that Chuck was either insane, bombed out of his mind on drugs, or hopelessly under the influence of a witch. But Dr Charles

Cress, a defence psychiatrist who spent seventeen hours with Chuck, was unimpressed by parts of the confession. Chuck's words seemed 'soap-opera-ish' – as if part of a script. And when he said on several occasions, 'Everything's so confused in my mind, I wonder what really happened,' it seemed to Dr Cress that Chuck was approaching the truth.

One night Chuck had a nightmare in which he was entering the Olive house again, only this time when he went into the sewing room, the hammer was already buried in Naomi's forehead. That, he came to believe, was what had happened. A lie-detector test supported his new version, but it would still make a thin case in court, Weissich believed.

And there it stood until a man named Loyal Davis heard about the situation. Davis is very, very Marin County, a burly figure with a silvery-blond mane of hair, a building contractor turned hypnotist. What was there to lose? Weissich invited Davis to put his client in a trance.

When I spoke to him recently, Davis told me that Chuck was one of the most suggestible subjects he had ever hypnotized. 'Hypnotism is done before you start,' Davis explained. 'The explanation is the most important part. They know what they are going to do, what they are going to feel. The more they look for it, the more they drift off.'

Chuck hardly needed the cues. Davis took him back to the moment when he was standing in front of the sewing room door. 'I opened it, and there was Mrs Olive on the bed, and she was dead. There's a hammer in her head.'

Sobbing now: 'Yeah, coming out of her forehead. Do you know what it's like to see a hammer in somebody?' It hurt him to see her, he said. But he had to touch her in

297

order to pull out the hammer. 'It was really hard. Blood. Blood. No. No.'

Hypnotized two weeks later by Dr Gerald Hill, a psychiatrist, Chuck this time assumed the role of Marlene and described sneaking back into the house as her father waited in the car and striking her sleeping mother with the hammer.

It must be said that the jury in Chuck's trial simply didn't buy the second version, even though halfway through the trial Weissich had Chuck hypnotized a third time by another psychiatrist, Dr David Spiegel, with the same results. Ultimately Dr Spiegel, after studying the facts of the case, would conclude that in psychological terms, only Marlene could have killed her mother. The jury, after a six-week trial, found Chuck guilty on both counts, and he was sentenced to death. In December 1977, California's mandatory death sentence was ruled unconstitutional, and Chuck's sentence was commuted to one of life imprisonment.

At the request of Richard M. Levine, whose seven-year study of the case produced *Bad Blood*, a remarkable study of this fatally flawed family, Chuck allowed Davis to hypnotize him in San Quentin prison on six occasions. Twice he recreated the murder scene, sticking once again to his claim that Naomi Olive was dead when he found her.

'It would be almost impossible for him not to be telling the truth,' Davis told me. 'I totally believe one hundred per cent that she was in a state of dying when he came in there.' And Chuck? 'He was a big, dumb kid who was controlled by this young girl who convinced him she was a witch.'

Naomi Olive's real murderer? 'There were only two

people there,' said Davis. 'The father and the daughter, and I don't think it was the father.'

When last heard from, Marlene had chosen a life of prostitution and drugs. She visited Chuck once in prison, but they had little to say to each other. After checking with the hospital where she was born in Virginia, she had finally learned her real mother's name: Jeanette Ellen Etherbridge. With only a little more detective work she might have tracked her down. But she didn't. Perhaps by then she didn't see the point.

GRAN'S
BEST BUDDY

A nice kid, Darren Huenemann. His teachers at Mount Douglas Secondary School thought highly of the studious-looking boy with the red hair and gold-rimmed glasses. Polite, keen, his clothes always clean and on the conservative side, he just didn't give any trouble. And he could have been a real brat. Everyone knew his grandmother was worth millions. You only had to look at the brand-new Honda Accord she'd bought him for his sixteenth birthday to know he would never want for anything. It could have been a recipe for ruin for a lot of youngsters – drugs, wild parties, girls. Not Darren.

Like the summer of 1990. When most kids would have been happy just goofing around, going to the beach, Darren was scouting for a play the school could put on in the following winter. It was his stepfather, Ralph Huenemann, a professor at the University of Victoria, who suggested *Caligula*, by Albert Camus, the French existentialist writer. When school resumed in September Darren put forward his proposal, even offering to contribute a couple of thousand dollars of his own money to make it a quality production. It went without saying that Darren would play the lead.

The amazing thing was how easily Darren seemed to slip into the part of the bloodthirsty Roman emperor. The role seemed made for him, even if it did seem at such odds with the Darren the staff knew. 'Since money is the only thing that counts,' declares Caligula early on in the play, 'people should set no value on their lives or anyone else's.'

It's a portrayal of ultimate evil, although it would be hard to imagine a less likely setting for Caligula's dastardly deeds than Victoria, on Canada's West Coast. With its benign climate and British traditions, the British Columbia capital is the happy hunting ground of the retired and the laid-back.

Darren, who seemed such a typical product of this genteel environment, was nevertheless completely convincing as Caligula, his delivery cold and menacing as he recited, after sentencing a friend to death in the drama: 'A man needn't have done anything for him to die.' It was so unlike the Darren his teachers knew; everyone said it just went to show what a good actor he was.

His mother, Sharon, had plenty of reasons to be proud of him. She didn't know how many times she'd heard people describe him as 'a perfect little gentleman'. And to the matriarch of the family, Doris Leatherbarrow, he was always 'Gran's best buddy'.

There was no doubt that Darren aimed to please. From his early teens he had flattered the women of the family shamelessly, complimenting his aunts on their 'great hair' or 'that terrific dress', while his stepfather, Ralph, director of the university's Centre for Asia-Pacific Initiatives, could only feel gratified when Darren talked about his plans to go to university to get his history and drama teaching credits.

He seemed so mature for his years that his grandmother found it easy to talk to him about business affairs involving her chain of ladies' clothing shops. She sometimes embarrassed relatives by talking openly about the fact that he would one day be a very rich young man.

There was another side to Darren though – a side his mother and grandmother would not have recognized. It would emerge at Friday night sessions of Dungeons and Dragons, the computer fantasy game, when he would tell his friends of his plans to 'snap Granny's neck'.

That other Darren was a braggart, a big talker who wanted his friends to call him 'Lord Darren', who had cards printed styling himself 'His Celestial Transcendency, Viscount Darren Charles Huenemann', and who, by the autumn of 1989, was telling them how, by murdering his grandmother, he would inherit her fortune of about four million dollars. The plans got more grandiose as time went on. By the spring of 1990 he was telling friends at school that he'd have to kill not only his grandmother, but his mother. And maybe his stepfather too because he was executor of his grandmother's will. It was all talk, of course. He was just showing off, trying to grab attention. Knock it off, Darren, they'd tell him.

Yes, all talk. But during the exceptionally hot and languid summer of 1990, while lolling in a canoe in the Pacific rollers off Chatham Island, a few miles from home, eighteen-year-old Darren explained the details of his murder plan to two friends, David Muir, a fifteen-year-old piccolo player in the school band, and Derik Lord, sixteen and something of a misfit at school. Several days later they went to a firm called Capital Iron and bought two crowbars and two pairs of long, black rubber gloves for a total cost of twenty dollars.

The most disturbing feature of the Darren Huenemann murders is that, unlike many of the other cases described in this book, there was no provocation. There was no history of physical or sexual abuse. Muir and Lord were a fairly average pair of teenagers with quite normal strengths and insecurities. The worst you could say of Darren was that his emotions may have been warped by an over-controlling mother, but probably no more so than those of the children of thousands of other well-meaning but anxious parents.

In the absence of any logical explanation for the crimes, some have blamed his grandmother who may, unthinkingly, have spoken too frankly to her grandson about his financial prospects on her death. But then, as Annie Ward, Doris' sister reminded me, if Doris had been a man no one would have criticized her for her behaviour. It's standard form for any rich man to put a paternal arm around his heir's shoulder and declare, 'Some day, son, all this will be yours.' And no one ever accuses them of inviting their own deaths.

Any understanding, though, of this West Coast tragedy must begin with the epic story of Doris Leatherbarrow. Her sister led me first to a picture hanging on the wall of her Toronto apartment. It was a photograph of the prairie log cabin where Doris and her three brothers and three sisters were born. Their mother, Nellie, was only sixteen when she married Onofry Kryciak, a poor immigrant Ukrainian farmer in Saskatchewan. Doris, robust, round-faced as she would always be, was born to them two years later, in December 1920. As her mother coped with the endless feeding, cleaning, nappy-washing and cooking,

Doris became like a second mother. Annie, the third child, remembered Doris, while she was still at school, hitching up the horse to the sleigh long before daylight on bitterly cold winter mornings to carry her brothers and sisters to the little school in Calder.

Annie put in my hand a silver medal that Doris had won in a speech contest and read me a letter from a school friend of Doris' in which she recalled how her friend had always excelled at her studies. But at the age of fifteen Doris left school, and within a year, while Annie and her friends cried and pleaded with her not to, had married a local farmer's son, George Artemko. It's not hard to understand why: she clearly loved George, but, with his nice car and his plans to take her to the softer climate of British Columbia, he also offered her a chance to escape from a harsh life of drudgery. Doris, like her brothers and sisters, had absorbed a lesson for life: however much hard work it took, they would never be poor again.

She managed a restaurant while George found a job in a shipyard, and soon, encouraged by Doris' glowing descriptions of British Columbia, the rest of the family moved to Vancouver from Saskatchewan. In the spring of 1943 Doris and George's only child, Sharon, was born; three months later George was killed in an accident at the shipyard.

If prairie poverty had been Doris' first lesson, George's death was her second. The resolve hardened within her to be financially independent. She took advantage of a sympathy offer to work cutting steel plates for ships in the shipyards. In the late 1940s, around the time she met Rene Leatherbarrow, whom she would marry in 1953, Doris conceived the idea of owning her own dress shop. Typically it took ten years before they opened Rene's

Ladies Apparel in a shopping strip in Surrey, a suburb of Vancouver – ten years of saving and scheming during which Doris never let go of the idea of being a businesswoman.

The timing was right, the formula a winning one. The shop prospered, and they would soon open another and then another. But almost from the start there was discord. Rene couldn't understand why, now that money was no problem, they couldn't live it up. He wanted to quit his job with the telephone company and devote all his time to the shops: Doris still liked the security of his pay cheque coming in, and, according to Rene, wanted to treat him as the shop handyman rather than an equal partner. After she found him 'stepping out' with one of her employees, Doris divorced him in 1969.

While her mother spent her days driving around her chain of shops and enjoying cut-and-thrust business dealings with mainly Jewish wholesalers, Sharon grew up in the shadows. According to Lisa Hobbs Birnie, author of *Such a Good Boy*, she was usually cared for by babysitters and, as she grew older, made extravagant demands on her mother as if to compensate for the attention she felt she was lacking. At nineteen and against Doris' wishes, Sharon married Brent Weinberger, a Jewish medical student from Los Angeles whom she had met on a bus tour of California. The marriage lasted only six months,

Sharon returned from California with a tan and a new Ford Mustang, and went to work for her mother. Pretty and impeccably groomed, the young woman did not stay single long. Romance sprang up with a policeman, Charles (Chuck) Gowan, who had given the attractive young woman in the blue convertible a speeding ticket.

With Doris forking out over twenty thousand dollars towards the cost of a new house not far from her own Japanese-style bungalow, the couple were married, and on 19 September 1972 Sharon gave birth to a baby boy. They named him Darren Charles, and from the start he was his grandmother's darling.

Chuck did not remain on the scene for long. Hired into the business, he quickly got on the wrong side of Doris, and was fired. Sharon made a scene, and denied Doris access to Darren for a while – the cruellest blow she could possibly have struck. Maybe it was the money that finally brought mother and daughter together; Chuck, to his shocked amazement, found himself served with divorce papers when his son, on whom he doted, was two. Sharon sold the house and moved into an apartment in the home of Jean Symonds, a Scottish woman who, caring for Darren while Sharon was at work, spoiled him while taking much abuse from the tantrum-prone toddler.

Once he was beyond the tantrum stage, though, Sharon set to work creating her idea of the perfect child. Darren must always be nicely dressed and polite, must never play with the wrong children and, it went without saying, must always secure the best marks at school. To do less would be to disappoint his mother.

When Darren was three, Sharon met husband number three – Ralph Huenemann. A mild academic, handy around the house, passionate about choral and chamber music, Ralph, a widower with two older children, seems to have been content during the fifteen years of their marriage to offer no challenge to the powerful, some would say overbearing, mother-and-daughter team. He wisely had nothing to do with the business.

'He was a friendly, talkative little tot,' Ralph would

307

recall of Darren. 'He always called me "Mr Huenemann". One day, after the marriage, he asked me with great solemnity if he could call me "Dad". We really were one big, happy family.'

It certainly looked that way. Growing up for Darren meant long summer days around Grandma's swimming pool, happy Thanksgiving turkey feasts, and lavish Christmas mornings when the presents seemed to go on and on. People who knew him then describe a normal, inquisitive little boy. His only unusual characteristic: whenever his mother or grandmother appeared, he became especially polite, some would say rather over-doing it. 'The other kids would be jumping in the pool and Darren would be complimenting me on my outfit,' recalled one great-aunt.

In 1987, when Darren was sixteen, Ralph went to work at the University of Victoria, and, to be handy for his work, he and Sharon bought a new three-bedroom French provincial split-level house in the posh Ten Mile Point district of Saanich, on Vancouver Island. It meant that Sharon was now separated from her mother by the twenty-four-mile-wide Strait of Georgia. Doris lived on a quiet street of expensive homes in Delta, part of Tsawwassen, not far from the mainland ferry terminal, and family visits back and forth were frequent. In addition, every other week Sharon would stay at her mother's from Wednesday to Friday, helping her with the business. This arrangement would be central to the murder scheme.

On Wednesday, 3 October 1990, Sharon parked her car as usual at the Swartz Bay terminal before boarding the ferry. Doris, who would be seventy in December, met her at the Tsawwassen end in her white Cadillac El Dorado.

She had cut back her chain of dress shops from eight to four, and talked of buying a condominium apartment and retiring. But her energy still seemed unbounded. Especially that week, as she kept up a hectic pace to ensure that everything would be in order when she left the following Tuesday for a holiday trip to Paris and Venice with her sister, Annie. On Friday, after a busy day in her Surrey warehouse, handling orders, writing cheques and attending to countless details, she and Sharon stopped work just after 5 p.m. and headed home for supper. It would have to be a quick meal because Sharon was catching the seven o'clock ferry back to Vancouver Island.

On the way home, they probably talked of Sharon's appointment the following morning with an estate agent to see a turn-of-the-century house that was for sale. In the three years since they'd moved from the mainland, Sharon had become involved in a protracted dispute with the builder of their French provincial house, and she was now determined to sell it.

As they pulled into the carport of the large bungalow at 811 Forty-ninth Street and got out, they could not have helped noticing the crisp autumn feel in the air and the smell of damp leaves. No time to linger – they bustled into the kitchen, Sharon put out the two plates and cutlery on the counter and sliced up celery and tomatoes, while Doris popped two frozen portions of her famous lasagne into the microwave and put beans and beetroots to warm on the stove. They hadn't sat down when the door chimes sounded.

Across the Strait of Georgia, in Saanich, Ralph Huenemann arrived home from practising his tennis strokes on the mechanical server at the Oak Bay

Recreational Club. Darren was in the kitchen making dinner with his girlfriend, seventeen-year-old Amanda Cousins. Ralph talked with the two teenagers, then went to his bedroom, intending to wait until Sharon arrived home at around nine before eating. At about eight thirty Darren, after getting a phone call, told his father that he and Amanda were going for a drive downtown, and Ralph went to the recreation room to watch television. Around ten o'clock Ralph heard the door open, and Darren put his head in to say that he was tired and was going to bed early. Ralph would say later that he must have fallen asleep, because when he woke it was six minutes past midnight, the TV was still on, but there was no sign of his wife.

He phoned the ferry terminal then called the police. An officer suggested he drive the route from the terminal in case Sharon had had car trouble. When he arrived at the terminal twenty minutes later, it was to find Sharon's car still standing locked in the empty parking lot. 'I knew then that something was wrong,' Ralph said later. He phoned Doris' place from the terminal. The phone rang and rang. At that point he called the Delta police, and they agreed to check the house.

Returning home, Ralph sat up for the rest of the night, impatiently phoning the police for news, but hearing nothing. It was six in the morning and just getting light when a police cruiser pulled into the driveway and Sergeant Gordy Tregear of the Saanich police got out. 'It's one of the worst jobs of all,' Tregear would tell me later. 'Breaking the news.'

'Where's my wife?' Ralph demanded. Tregear asked if he could step inside, then he explained that Sharon and Doris had been found murdered. 'Ralph didn't show the emotion you would expect,' said Tregear. Darren, yawning the sleep away, came in a moment later. When Ralph told him the news, he held on to his father and sobbed. 'After the police left,' said Ralph, 'Darren and I both sat down on the kitchen floor and cried and cried and cried.'

Peering through the windows of 811 Forty-ninth Street at about 2 a.m., two patrol officers had made out the bodies of the women lying on the tiled floor in the kitchen area. A few lights were on; all the doors were locked except for a patio door which slid open at their touch. Doris Leatherbarrow, dressed in black slacks and a matching sweater with a single flower embroidered on the front, lay on her back, ankles crossed, arm flung out as if in sleep – except for a black-handled kitchen knife protruding from her neck. Her daughter lay a few feet away, also on her back, her white sweater soaked in blood, a knife resting on her chest. The faces of both women had been covered with red and white checked dishcloths, as if they were human sacrifices in some bizarre ritual.

Beyond the frightful carnage, the first thing the police noticed was a burning smell and the insufferable heat in the house. The source was quickly found: two burners on the gas stove were still on beneath the charred remains of the beans and beetroots. Drawers in the master bedroom had been pulled out and clothing scattered as if by thieves; a key to the front door was found lying on the floor outside the bedroom. If it was a robbery, these thieves had been remarkably inept – money and jewellery was still hidden in places any experienced thief would look, and expensive electronic equipment – TVs, the video and stereo – was untouched. The women's clothing had not been tampered with, so it was easy to eliminate

311

any possibility of a sexual attack. The most significant evidence was of an obvious and domestic nature: the counter was set with two dinner places and two plates of celery and tomatoes had been put out. But two extra plates had been set on the counter, and there were four servings of lasagne in the microwave. Had the murderers arrived as the women were preparing dinner, two people known to the women who had been invited to stay for a meal?

The following afternoon Detective Bill Jackson, in charge of the investigation at the Delta end, awaited the arrival of Ralph Huenemann and his son, who had crossed on the ferry to give an account of their movements the previous day. Darren described picking up Amanda and bringing her to his house at around 6.30 p.m. After dinner he'd driven Amanda and some school friends around Victoria before dropping her at her house.

It was when Darren came to discussing his grandmother's affairs that Jackson had to hide a certain feeling of surprise. The detective knew that the boy had been devastated that morning on learning the news. Now he was almost matter-of-fact, listing the jewellery and cash in the house, estimating its worth at about a hundred thousand dollars. 'I'll inherit everything,' he told Jackson brashly. He figured, with the four dress shops, he'd be collecting something like four million dollars. When Jackson got hold of wills signed by Doris and Sharon on 25 May 1989, they confirmed Darren's claim. Doris had been determined that her fortune should stay in family hands. She had left half her money to Sharon and half to Darren. Sharon, abiding by her mother's wishes, had left only a small bequest to Ralph and the rest to her son.

Leaving the police station, Darren had a tip for

Jackson. If he wanted to know how someone might have broken into his grandmother's house, he said, he should know that she kept a front-door key in one of those plastic hide-a-key gizmos under the woodpile behind the garage. Odd that, thought Jackson: according to a neighbour, Doris for some reason had stopped hiding it in the woodpile several months before. In Saanich, when Tregear checked with Amanda Cousins, she confirmed Darren's story of his whereabouts on the night of the murders.

In the following days Darren busied himself visiting 'his' clothing shops, offering a twelve-thousand-dollar reward (matched by his stepfather) for the apprehension of the killers, and suggesting to his great-aunt Mary, who was executor of the wills, that a two-thousand-dollar joint sponsorship of the school production of *Caligula* would be a fitting tribute to his grandma. Meanwhile the police net spread wide, seeking a motive and suspects for the mysterious killings, no matter how far-fetched the link. The likeliest candidate for a while was the house-builder with whom Sharon was in legal dispute over the Saanich residence, and who felt he had been cheated by her.

So it was just a case of routine tying-up of loose ends when two detectives called on Don Neumann, the principal at Mount Douglas. What kind of kid was Darren, who were his friends? He was Mr Perfect, of course. Polite, a keen student when the subject took his interest. Friends? Not too many friends, but Derik Lord's name came up.

Two youths were on the driveway of the Lord home when the detectives pulled up in their unmarked car. One was a chunky, square-faced boy whirling around on a bike. The other, with narrow, foxy features, identified himself as Derik Lord. The sixteen-year-old middle child of Eloise, a private school teacher, and David, an electrician with the provincial electricity authority, Derik was a solitary kid who'd had run-ins with the school authorities. But he'd never been in trouble with the police, and climbing into the cruiser to answer a few questions was a new experience for him. 'Are we going anywhere?' he asked the officer. No, he replied, they just wanted to be private.

Did Derik know Mrs Huenemann? 'Yes, she was a nice lady.' Had he heard any rumours at school about the murders? He shook his head. They chatted for another ten minutes, Derik apparently relaxed, even joking. Had he ever been to Darren's grandma's house in Tsawwassen? No, but he had been over to Tsawwassen the week before the murders, he said. Why? Just to see the Tsawwassen shopping mall with David Muir. But it was dead, so they came home again on the ferry. David Muir? Yes, that was him, just riding off on the bike. The night of the murder? He and David had been downtown. Darren had picked them up then driven them home. Amanda was with them.

About the same time, following a tip from a female classmate of Darren's, Tregear was interviewing another Mount Douglas student, Toby Hicks. 'A nice kid,' Tregear would remember, 'real straight.' Had Darren ever said anything about killing his grandma? Sure, said Toby. 'He said, "If I kill Granny I'll get half the money. But if I kill my mother I'll get it all."' He'd inherit between four and four and a half million dollars, he'd estimated.

The next day Tregear was surprised to learn that Darren and his father, outraged that the police had been questioning Darren's friends, had engaged a prominent

Victoria lawyer, Chris Considine. From now on, if the police had any questions for Darren, they'd have to ask them through Considine. 'It did seem peculiar,' Tregear told me. 'We were trying to find out who had killed the wife and mother, and here was a lawyer suddenly throwing up roadblocks.'

When the police asked Considine if Darren and Ralph would take lie-detector tests, they were flatly turned down. Darren was so outraged at the police questioning his classmates that he would not co-operate. Ralph, to show solidarity, was refusing too. Doors were slamming on the cops. Darren, they discovered, had hired lawyers for Derik, David and Amanda. Students they tried to question at Mount Douglas clammed up because, the police found out later, they'd been told to by Darren. But each obstacle he threw in their way only increased their suspicions.

David Muir, who Tregear would remember as a likeable young man, well spoken and with a wide vocabulary, finally told the police in the presence of his parents that the real purpose of his trip to Tsawwassen on 21 September, two weeks before the murder, was to open a post office box just across the American border from Canada in Point Roberts. He and Derik shared an interest in knives and intended using the box number to purchase knives forbidden by Canadian law, later smuggling them across the border to sell to their schoolmates. The smuggling escapade did not interest Tregear. He was more intrigued to learn that school had finished at 2 p.m. on Friday, the day of the murder, an hour earlier than they'd been led to believe in the previous alibi stories.

Amanda Cousins, interviewed again, said that she had

315

been with Darren when he drove Derik and David to the ferry on 21 September, picking them up again a few hours later. On certain details, Amanda's story did not fit with David's.

What was the real purpose of the 21 September excursion? There were too many parts missing from the puzzle to discern the picture, but now several big pieces fell into place. A cab driver, Parmjet Bhinder, remembered driving two youths from the ferry terminal to the Tsawwassen mall on the day of the murder at 4.55 p.m. Later, shown a bunch of photographs, including two of Derik and David, Bhinder would pick out David as the guy who'd sat next to him, chatting about the weather.

Another cabbie, Paul Martin, would pick out Derik Lord as one of two youths he had picked up at the mall at 6.45 p.m. the same day. They were in one awful rush to catch the seven o'clock ferry, and when he hit a traffic jam, they threw a twenty-dollar bill on the seat and ran the rest of the way to the terminal. And then, the best stroke of luck: Daniel May, aged thirteen, who had been playing football on the street with his sixteen-year-old brother, Gregory, a few doors from Doris' house just before supper on the evening of the murder, picked out pictures of Derik and David as the two youths he'd seen hanging around suspiciously, then walking in the direction of the Leatherbarrow house.

The police had the two boys placed at the murder scene at the right time but, apart from his wild talk, there was nothing at all tying Darren to the crime. He was home free – unless he convicted himself out of his own mouth. The police applied for permission to wiretap the three boys' telephones as well as Darren's car. It only remained to set the trap.

On 22 November, six weeks after the murder, Tregear and Jackson knocked on the door of John and Vivien Muir's home and asked to see their son, David. As soon as they were seated in the living room, his parents present, they read him his rights then told him he had been identified both by a cabbie and by a witness who was on the ferry the night of the murders. They urged him to think carefully about giving a full account of what had happened, and then left.

At the first chance he got, David phoned Derik Lord. And police, eavesdropping, heard the authentic voices of the conspirators for the first time.

'House of Lords,' said Derik, picking up the phone. 'Lucifer speaking.' The anxiety was plain to hear in David's voice as he told of the police visit and the positive identification.

'They'vee got to be lying. They've said nothing to Darren,' said Derik, more to convince himself.

'We've got to change the story,' said David. 'Tell them we were there to pick up a package but went the wrong way.'

'Could you call Darren?'

'No, I'm not even supposed to be talking to you. My mum's left and I've got to do this real quick.'

As soon as he was off the line with David, Derik called Darren and told him to come over.

'Why?'

'Just come on over!'

'It's David,' said Darren intuitively. 'Is he saying something? What did they say to him?'

A few minutes later Darren called David's house, then got right back to Derik. 'He's let the police bully him into this thing,' he said bitterly. 'I'd start to sue [the police]!

317

I'd laugh in their faces. They're a bunch of idiots! They don't know!'

Derik: 'Have you talked to Dave at all?'

'No, Iron Lady [David's mother] wouldn't let me past.' A note of hysteria crept into Darren's voice: 'Dave is out of line, out of line! And you are in a puddle up to your knees. Dave is the most malleable boy I've ever met.' His voice was high, almost out of control: 'Don't panic! Don't let them push you around. And tell his mother to fuck off.' The police were hearing Caligula now, as his voice rose almost to a screech: 'Oh, I can't believe this bunch of weirdos. I love you all!'

Jackson and Tregear, listening to the tape, could only look at each other in amazement. What kind of kookie kid were they dealing with?

Kookie perhaps, but smart. Three days later, the two officers called on Derik Lord at the K-mart discount department store where he worked part time. 'It was you who killed Darren's mother and grandmother and not David,' said Jackson in an undertone. 'I wonder what Darren will say when we tell him it was you who killed his mother.'

The scare tactic worked. A few minutes later, in response to a panicky call from Derik, Darren roared into the K-mart parking lot and picked up his shaken friend. This time, though, Darren outwitted the eavesdropping officers by playing the radio extra loud so their conversation could not be overheard.

The time for games was over. On 27 November, Tregear and Jackson arrested David Muir at his home. Half an hour later Don Neumann, the Mount Douglas principal, witnessed a scene not as uncommon as it once was in North American schools, as one of his students,

Derik Lord, was summoned to his office, not for a stern talk about marks, but to be charged with two counts of first-degree murder, handcuffed and led away.

Once again the two boys took the ferry ride to Tsawwassen – this time to be locked up in the cells at the local police station. David Muir seemed to be the more vulnerable of the two. If he wanted to give them a statement, Jackson and Tregear told the chunky, sullen teenager, the Crown would consider using him as a witness against the other two (in the event, David's confession was not used in court, and he stood as a co-accused). The youth was silent for a while then, in a matter-of-fact tone, he began to talk.

He and Derik had only really become friendly with Darren during the previous Christmas holidays when they'd gone to his house to play Dungeons and Dragons. Their bonds had become closer during the spring as they talked and dreamed about exotic knives and developed plans for their smuggling scheme. It was not until June, as they drove around town in the Honda or shot the breeze at Darren's house, that he invited their ideas on how he should murder his mother, his grandmother and his stepfather. Blow them up? Stage a car accident? The difficulties of wiping out all three seemed daunting – until Darren discovered that his great-aunt, not his father, was executor of the wills. Now there were only two to deal with.

David thought Darren's murder talk was just another game. It didn't seem out of place, after all, in the context of computer-game magicians and devils. But around the time of the canoe trip to Chatham Islands the invisible line between fantasy and reality was crossed, and suddenly they were talking specifics. That was when Darren explained the plan to murder the two women when they were together at his grandmother's house. They discussed buying two crowbars to do the job, and rubber gloves so they wouldn't get blood on themselves. They'd use knives from the cutlery drawer in the house so that the weapons could not be traced back to them.

What was in it for Derik and David? Derik wasn't getting along with his parents. With his new-found wealth, Darren promised, he'd buy Derik fifty acres in the wilderness and build him a cabin where he could be by himself. There'd be new motorbikes for both of them, and fancy imported knives. For Derik the picture was irresistible: tooling up the highway on his own Kawasaki Ninja, headed for his very own pad in the mountains, and no parents to bug him! Bliss, man. For David, in addition to the motorbike, there'd be a souped-up Honda CRX car and a couple of thousand a month until Darren came into his inheritance. At that time David would get a hundred thousand dollars. It was a teenage vision of paradise. A vision devoid of parents, cops or awkward questions.

The plan was laid for Friday, 21 September. Darren drove them to catch the 1 p.m. ferry, David carrying an old black bag containing the eighteen-inch-long crowbars and the rubber gloves. At the other end, they took a taxi to the Tsawwassen mall, where David got out his map of the lower mainland and they started looking for the house. They walked this way and that. This was ridiculous. They couldn't even find the house. Some hit men they were! Finally, time simply ran out on them; they caught a cab back to the terminal to catch the 7 p.m. ferry, the same boat Sharon was taking home.

Darren had Amanda in the car when he picked them up at the terminal, so he couldn't say much. At that point she hadn't been told the reason for their trip. The hit was rescheduled for Friday, 5 October. This time there mustn't be any mistakes.

Amanda, aware now of the murder plot, had been told to say she'd followed the boys in Darren's car to Victoria's Chinatown after school – at a time when Darren was delivering them to the 3 p.m. ferry. This time David and Derik found the house first time, although the white Cadillac was not yet in the driveway. They loitered in the nearby schoolyard, removing the crowbars from the bag and hiding them inside their jackets. At 6 p.m. they checked again, and this time the car was there.

Sharon Huenemann was surprised to see her son's two friends, David in his jean jacket, Derik in a tan jacket, both wearing running shoes, standing in the twilight when she opened the door. 'Come in,' she said. 'What brings you here?' Derik mumbled that they had been visiting his dad, whose work often took him out of town.

'It's two of Darren's friends,' she told her mother, introducing the boys.

'You boys better have something to eat,' said Doris. 'It'll be late by the time you get home. Come and try some of my lasagne.' They shook their heads, but not firmly enough. No one left Doris Leatherbarrow's house with an empty stomach. She put two extra portions of lasagne in the microwave and got out two more plates.

'Would you like a ride to the ferry after?' asked Sharon. They nodded and thanked her. The two boys eyed each other, moving warily, waiting for their chance. It came as Sharon left the kitchen and walked into the living room.

Derik, following her, pulled the short, brutal crowbar out of his jacket. He swung it high and brought it down hard, fracturing Sharon's skull. He hit her repeatedly, but

321

still her throat gurgled and she made pathetic wounded-animal sounds.

Hearing the noise, Doris turned from the microwave. In that instant David Muir was standing in front of her, his crowbar raised. It took only one blow, and she sank unconscious to the floor.

Sharon, her eyes rolling wildly, had seen it. 'Why are you doing this?' she somehow managed to ask. 'Why are you doing this?'

The boys paid no attention to her. They had dropped their bloody crowbars on the counter. One searched the kitchen drawers while the other went to the bathroom in search of towels. Not finding them, they settled for dishcloths, pulled on their black rubber gloves and, with two long, vicious-looking knives selected from the cutlery drawer, got to work.

Sharon was still staring wildly. Derik began stabbing her in the throat. 'For Chrissake cover her face,' he told David. 'She's staring at me.' David pulled the dishcloth up over her eyes.

Turning to Doris, David had his own problems. Because she had fallen face down, he had to try and reach under her to cut her throat, but the knife seemed blunt. 'It's not working,' he said, and headed for the bedrooms, where he pulled out drawers to make it look like a burglary. By the time he got back, Derik, after dispatching Sharon, had turned Doris over on her back and plunged the knife so deep into her throat it had severed the spinal cord.

While Derik went upstairs to search the master bedroom, David rummaged behind the stove where, Darren had told them, his grandmother kept money and documents. He didn't search well enough – the police would find valuable jewellery there and an envelope containing $260. He had better luck in Doris' handbag – it yielded $1,580 which he stashed inside his jacket in a brown paper bag. Following their plan to the letter, they went to the woodpile in the back garden and, despite what the neighbour would say later, found the house key and threw it down in the hall, just as a burglar might have done. Before leaving, David put a dishcloth in place over Doris Leatherbarrow's face, not out of respect for the dead, but 'because I didn't want to remember her face'.

Then the two of them, David, the school band piccolo player who babysat the band leader's kids, and Derik, who wanted to be a cop when he grew up, slipped the crowbars back into the black bag, let themselves out of the patio door, thinking mistakenly they'd locked it behind them, and walked back down the road towards the Tsawwassen mall. David looked at his digital watch. It was 6.36 p.m. The boys who had been playing football on the street, they noted, must have gone in for supper.

It was a close thing catching the seven o'clock ferry. They had to abandon their cab when it hit traffic approaching the terminal. Luckily for them, the *Queen of Esquimalt* was a few minutes late leaving. They ran up the ramp and just made it. When they were well out from shore they dropped the bag containing the crowbars, the gloves and the map from the stern of the ship. It sank instantly, and they went below to phone Darren to arrange for him to pick them up at the terminal.

David's confession, Tregear told me, was all the more astonishing for the emotionless tone in which it was delivered. 'It made the hair stand up on the back of

323

my neck,' said the veteran cop. It was also pure gold. For the first time the police realized that Amanda Cousins knew all about the murders. Darren could still have been charged on the basis of David's statement, said Tregear, but Amanda's version, as one who hadn't actually participated in the killings, would be much more powerful.

In the witness box, Amanda, fair-haired, blue-eyed, her voice low and well modulated, would seem contained and almost angelic. But that was later. The sixteen-year-old whom two officers, Lyle Beaudoin and Ian Stabler, met at the home of her mother, Sara, that evening was plainly terrified. Darren had dumped her several weeks earlier, saying that it was safer that way. Alone, full of fears, she would wake from nightmares so frightening she'd think she was having a heart attack, and she took to keeping a long kitchen knife under her pillow. Perhaps the police came to her just in time; Amanda might have done herself harm.

But even with the assurance that she would be a Crown witness and not an accused, Amanda could not at first bring herself to talk. She and her divorced mother had already been told there would be a heavy price to pay: Sara, close to getting a degree in education, would have to give up her studies so that she and Amanda could be hidden away and protected until the time came for her to testify,

Beaudoin held out his hand to Amanda. 'Do you trust me?' he asked. She nodded. 'You remind me of my own daughter when she's afraid to tell the truth,' he said. The words were enough. Her sobs, held back for so long, went on and on. Her mother put her arm around her. 'Tell me the truth, Amanda,' she said.

Darren, she said, had phoned her out of the blue during the summer to talk. She only knew him from his reputation at Mount Douglas: 'weird and funny and kind of unique and eccentric', always showing off with crazy sayings and mysterious Latin quotations. Following the first call, he sent her a rose and incense and bombarded her with calls twice a day. Sexual attraction didn't seem to enter into it. 'I've watched you for a long time,' he told her. 'I wanted someone who would be a credit to me.' Because she was new to the school and lonely, because her parents had broken up and she was a bit of a rebel, and because she looked so 'sweet and innocent', he would say quite unabashedly, she was the ideal person to 'represent me'.

Most girls, after listening to this inflated poppycock, would have given him the brush-off. For Amanda, the lonely outsider, the approach had a peculiar attraction. He talked wildly of leading an invasion of Borneo at the head of toga-clad soldiers, of having a bronze statue made of himself and set on a mountaintop. So when he started talking about knocking off his mother and grandmother to inherit the fortune, it didn't seem that unusual. When he finally asked her out on a date on 22 August, it was only to drive her around town while he kept asking her if she knew anyone who was into satanic cults.

The murder talk made her uncomfortable, but she did not take it seriously. Until 2 September, when Darren showed up with a cheesecake for her seventeenth birthday. Had she told anyone about his murder plans? he asked. Of course not, she replied. Well that was just as well, he said, because if she told anyone he would have to kill them too.

Why didn't she drop him right then? Because, on one hand, she still felt it was Darren talking crazy, and on the other, she was feeling the first pangs of fear.

She was seeing him more often now. He'd got her the job of stage manager for the school production of *Caligula*. 'When I've killed Mom and Gran, I'll be able to play the part better,' he assured her one day.

He made a date with her for dinner on 21 September, the day of the first murder attempt. They'd be picking up Derik and David later when they returned on the ferry from checking out their mailbox on the mainland, he told her when he collected her from her home. But after Darren met the boys off the boat and they got into the car, he seemed angry. They hadn't found the mailbox, the two claimed. Darren's mother had been on the ferry, but hadn't seen them. What was going on? Amanda asked Darren when she finally got him on his own. 'You mean you don't know? You haven't guessed?' It was then he told her that the pair had failed in their first murder attempt. 'Morons', he called them.

'Maybe they didn't want to find the place,' she said. 'Maybe they didn't want to do it.'

Darren brushed her suggestion aside. It had to be done soon, he said, as they drove around the darkened streets. His grandmother was going to Paris soon and she'd been talking about buying a retirement condominium apartment before going. For $150,000! He made it sound as if it was his money she was spending.

Why hadn't she gone to the police at that point? Who would have believed her? She would have been the one who ended up looking like an idiot.

In the days leading up to the 5 October deadline, Darren was on the phone to her constantly. He told her of one minor change in the plan. He was so mad at Dave, whom he blamed for the 21 September fiasco, that now Dave would not get his pay-out when he'd done the murders. Instead, he'd have Derik bring him to the house one night, hiding him in the trunk of the car on some excuse, persuade him to let himself be chained up, then inject an air bubble into his veins. They'd dump David's body into the sea from the canoe. But a canoe can be tricky, especially in the dark. A few days later he came up with a better idea: Dave's body would go into a construction skip.

'What if I tell someone?' Amanda asked. If she did, he'd stuff her into a crawl space under some building, he told her with that glint that might or might not mean he was kidding. And if he didn't kill her, he explained helpfully, Derik and David, as juveniles, would receive a maximum sentence of three years for the murders, and then they'd be out looking for her.

The night of the murders, Darren picked her up from home at around 7 p.m. She was under no illusions now why he had courted her, why her presence was needed. She was the alibi for Darren, Derik and David when the police came calling.

At the Huenemann house they drank iced tea, and Darren, edgy and excitable, brought out the tarot cards. Her present, he told her after studying the cards, was full of confusion, and she possessed a secret that could get her into a lot of trouble. His fortune was more assured: after initial difficulties he would come into power and wealth.

The sound of the phone snapped the tension. It was Derik and David reporting in from on board the ferry. For once, as he and Amanda waited for the boat to arrive, Darren seemed subdued. 'There's a part of me hoping it hasn't come off,' he told her. 'She is my mom. I might feel badly for a little while.'

David looked upset as he got into the car, but Derik was chatty and excited. Darren couldn't get enough of the details. 'Hey, you shouldn't have wasted that lasagne,' he said. 'My gran makes the best lasagne you ever tasted.'

'No way we're going back for it,' said Derik.

David, more subdued, offered Amanda a packet of chocolate-covered almonds he'd bought on the ship, then counted the money they'd taken from Doris' house and divided it with Derik.

'Jeez,' Derik told Darren excitedly, 'I had to stick your mom quick. She was yelling, "Why you doing this?" Man, we didn't want the fucking neighbours to hear.'

Darren drove to Derik's house where David recovered his bicycle from the basement. The last Amanda saw of him he was furiously pedalling home like any other fifteen-year-old who'd stayed out beyond his curfew. Not pedalling fast enough, as it happens: he was supposed to be in at 9 p.m., but he was thirty-five minutes late. His parents said that as a punishment he'd have to stay in the following night. Rules are rules.

Amanda didn't finish telling her story to the officers until 3 a.m. Later that day, Tregear and Jackson were back at Mount Douglas where Darren was called out of class and, in the corridor, charged with two counts of first-degree murder and handcuffed.

David and Derik, to the discomfiture of some students and teachers at Mount Douglas, were released on bail and returned to school during months of legal manoeuvring to determine whether they should be tried as young offenders. The decision was critical: under Canadian law, as young offenders they would not, as Darren had said, receive more than three-year sentences. If convicted in adult court they would face minimum sentences of twenty-five years, with no possibility of parole.

One of the factors in deciding whether the Young Offenders Act applies is whether the accused is amenable to treatment. 'But you don't treat what is not there,' said Dr Roy O'Shaughnessy, clinical director of the Juvenile Service. Nothing in his personality would have predicted that David Muir would commit murder, and the day after he did so, he was no different, said O'Shaughnessy. Everyone seemed helpless to explain how two apparently normal boys of fifteen and sixteen could bludgeon and stab two women to death. In David's case, the experts talked of above-average abilities and a supportive family.

In Derik Lord's case, there had been some hints of trouble. He had a quick temper, and one day, reprimanded at school, he climbed up to a beam above the classroom and refused to come down. Later he threatened to blow up the staff room. Otherwise Derik came from a normal family, showed no sign of having been abused, and had a clear understanding of right and wrong. It could be that Darren Huenemann was more perceptive than the experts: the one quality he perceived in all three of the teenagers he recruited for his scheme was that they were all loners with few or no friends. They were outsiders who were at first flattered and later intimidated by the attention of the brilliant, mercurial and obviously wealthy Huenemann boy.

Derik and David would lose out in this all-or-nothing legal gamble: on 13 March 1992, three justices of the British Columbia Court of Appeal confirmed a lower-court decision to send both youths for trial in adult court.

By then Darren Huenemann's fate had been long

329

settled. His trial began on 24 June 1991 at New Westminster in the midst of another particularly hot summer. Amanda Cousins' testimony was decisive. Not even defence lawyer Chris Considine's attempt in his cross-examination to portray her as 'a teenager in turmoil' could disturb her poise in the witness box. And her obvious remorse at not having blown the whistle on the conspiracy earlier made a positive impression on the jury.

When David and Derik returned from their first futile attempt to find Doris Leatherbarrow's house, testified Amanda, 'this was the first time I realized the talk was being put into action. I was really scared. Even after this I kept saying to myself, even if they found the house, they wouldn't have done it. I think I was trying to make it not happen by believing it wouldn't.'

She was deeply frightened of Darren by then: 'I felt if I lost his trust, I'd quite possibly be killed.' When he told her that the killings were now to take place on 5 October, 'All I thought of was what could I do to stop this. I imagined myself going to the police station and telling them this story, and them looking at me and saying, "Well, are you sure he wasn't joking?"' Once the police started making inquiries, Darren would know who had squealed.

The most pathetic witness was Ralph Huenemann, still trying to believe in his stepson's innocence. In the lead-up to the trial, one of Doris' sisters, exasperated, had said, 'I don't know why Darren doesn't come out and admit it.' Ralph replied: 'You wait until the trial. It will all come out. He had nothing to do with it.'

Bookish and quiet-spoken, Ralph recalled in the witness box that the relationship between Darren and his mother had been especially strong. 'They spent a lot of time talking together. They had a very special relationship.' As for Doris, Darren was her best buddy. It was not what you'd think of as a normal grandmother-grandson relationship: 'Doris talked about business all the time.' (Although Ralph was not asked about it, the relationship was odd in other ways: Doris had complained to Sharon that several times Darren had touched her in a sexual way in the swimming pool and was certain he had tried to drown her on one occasion. This helped to explain why, for a year prior to the murders, Darren had been seeing a psychiatrist. It was at that point too that Doris, without apparently telling Darren, made a small change in her will stipulating that, on her death, he would not inherit most of his share of her fortune until he was twenty-five.)

In his final answer, Ralph did what he could to save his stepson. Was Darren the kind of person capable of committing such a crime? Considine asked.

'I've known him for fifteen years,' Ralph replied, 'and the character I know is incapable of doing it.'

Ralph would finally have his eyes opened when Stanley Dick, a small-time offender, took the stand and testified that in prison while he was awaiting trial Darren had offered him ten thousand dollars to kill Amanda so that she couldn't testify. She might be hard to get at because she was being protected by the police, he'd said. It would probably mean having to shoot her on the courtroom steps. Another inmate, approached with a similar offer, had even phoned a hit man who had, with sensible professional discretion, declined the commission. Ralph also heard testimony that Darren, while in prison, had given friends detailed accounts of the security system at the Huenemann house so that they could burgle the place on their release from prison.

It was a very shaken Ralph Huenemann who approached Tregear after hearing the testimony. 'He asked us for protection,' said Tregear.

But it was all hearts and flowers when Darren went into the box to give his version of events. His family had been a loving one, he said. His grandma? 'I loved her,' he told Considine. 'Always loved her. She's my grandma. Do you know how hard it is to look into this courtroom,' he said, swallowing a sob, 'and not see Mum and Gran sitting there!' A reporter there that day told me Darren's performance was amazing – and completely lacking in credibility. 'One minute great gasping sobs, the next he was perfectly cool.'

He put the entire blame for the murders on David and Derik who, he said, had killed the two women in the course of a robbery. He had only driven them to and from the ferry on the two occasions so that they could set up a post office box on the mainland. Why hadn't he told the police this when questioned? 'We were kids, we were just trying to prevent someone from getting grounded,' he explained. When they told him what they'd done he kept quiet because they'd threatened to implicate him in the murders, he claimed.

Why didn't he tell his father? 'Do you know how hard it would be to look into that man's eyes and tell him two people I knew did this? I loved him and didn't want to hurt him.' And then the jury met Darren the avenging angel: 'The law would give these two people who killed two people I loved – they killed my mother and my gran – twenty-five years; and twenty-five years for that is not enough!' he said indignantly. 'I wanted these people to pay – and I still do.' His voice had a manic edge to it now. 'No, not life in prison! This was a family affair. I wanted to kill them. So I agreed to go along with what they asked. It didn't give me the right to do it, but it gave me the want.'

There really didn't seem any point in the Crown cross-examining after this remarkable performance. The verdict, guilty on both counts of first-degree murder, seemed only a formality. Darren still wanted the last word. Chin quivering, he told Justice William Selbie: 'I am not guilty of the charges placed on me. I have no anger or scorn. All I find is a hurt that these members of the jury and this court could find I could do such a thing ... I will always have memories of Mum and Gran to cherish. I thank you, my lord, and this court for a speedy verdict.'

Without a word of comment, the judge imposed the automatic sentence: life imprisonment without the possibility of parole for twenty-five years. Leaving the courtroom, Darren was free to be himself again. His words came quite clearly as the door shut behind him: 'Fuck this court.'

In January 1993, he was removed to the Kent maximum security institution after he was overheard offering fellow inmates thirty thousand dollars to kill Ralph Huenemann, whom he blamed for holding back thirty-five thousand dollars that Darren needed to pay for legal costs in a pending appeal. Told a contract might be out on his life, Ralph Huenemann said wearily, 'Anything is possible. I've learned that in the last two years.'

On 11 May 1992, nearly a year after Darren's trial, Derik Lord and David Muir, grown into men in the nineteen months since the murder, were put on trial in what was essentially a rerun of the Huenemann hearing. Derik smirked through much of the evidence, while David never smiled and kept his head averted. Called to testify, Darren refused to be sworn, and was returned to prison.

How two teenagers could enter into such a diabolical plan, said Justice Thomas Fisher after guilty verdicts were recorded, 'is beyond normal understanding.' They too received life sentences although, because of a quirk in the law affecting juveniles, they will be eligible for parole after ten years. Darren Huenemann, who will never see a penny of his grandmother's fortune under the terms of a law that prevents criminals from benefiting from their crimes, was born eleven days too soon to take advantage of the ten-year parole concession. As a result, he will remain in prison fifteen years longer than his co-conspirators.

Caligula was never presented at Mount Douglas. With the arrest of its star, the school authorities cancelled the production. The audience never got to hear Darren declare, 'I live, I kill, I exercise the rapturous power of the destroyer ... the glorious isolation of a man who all his life long nurses and gloats over the ineffable joy of the unpunished murderer.'

In the end it had not turned out that way for Darren Huenemann; he would not go unpunished. He would have a lifetime in jail to ponder Caligula's final admission: 'I have chosen a wrong path, a path that leads to nothing.'

When I arrived at the door of her Toronto apartment for our appointment, Annie Ward, Doris' sister, asked to see my identification. You can't be too careful, she said. Especially with Darren taking out a contract on his stepfather. Who could feel safe?

She told me of the shock she'd had when the police showed her the black-handled knives the two boys had used. 'It floored me,' she said. 'We gave those knives to Doris for Christmas. They were German knives, Henckels. A friend told me there is nothing better in this world than those knives.' She got her own set of Henckels from the kitchen – so that we could check the spelling of the name. The knives were no doubt perfect for slicing chicken or green peppers, but with their thin, stiletto blades, it would be hard to imagine a meaner murder weapon.

As I copied down the spelling, Annie was remembering the Darren she'd known. 'He was such a nice kid,' she said. 'Always helpful, always so polite.' The first time she saw him following the murders of his mother and grandmother was at the funeral. 'I went up to him. I was crying. "I know you'll miss your mum and your gran even more than I will," I said. He put his arms around me and said, "There, there, Auntie Ann, everything will be all right."'

The apartment was silent for a moment, then she added: 'He wasn't crying. He was smiling.'

BIBLIOGRAPHY

Lisa Hobbs Birnie, *Such a Good Boy*, Macmillan Canada, 1992

Albert Camus, *Caligula*, Hamish Hamilton Ltd, 1948

Charles Patrick Ewing, *Kids who Kill*, Lexington Books, 1990

Rupert Furneaux, *Famous Criminal Cases 2*, Roy, 1955

Leonard Gribble, *The Hallmark of Horror*, John Long, 1973

Tom Gurr and H. H. Cox, *Famous Australasian Crimes*, Frederick Muller, 1957

Anthony Holden, *The St Albans Poisoner*, Hodder & Stoughton, 1974

Dena Kleiman, *A Deadly Silence: The Ordeal of Cheryl Pierson*, Atlantic Monthly Press, 1988

Isabel LeBourdais, *The Trial of Steven Truscott*, Gollancz, 1967

Richard M. Levine, *Bad Blood: A Family Murder in Marin County*, Random House, 1982

Joan Merriam, *Little Girl Lost*, Pinnacle Books, 1992

Gitta Sereny, *The Case of Mary Bell*, Eyre Methuen, 1972

Bill Trent with Steven Truscott, *Who Killed Lynne Harper?*, Optimum, 1979

Patrick Wilson, *Children Who Kill*, Joseph, 1973
Winifred Young, *Obsessive Poisoner*, Robert Hale, 1973

INDEX